Meeting the
Ethical Challenges
of LEADERSHIP

Casting

Light

or

Shadow

Craig E. Johnson

Sage Publications
International Educational and Professional Publisher
Thousand Oaks ▪ London ▪ New Delhi

For information:

Sage Publications, Inc.
2455 Teller Road
Thousand Oaks, California 91320
E-mail: order@sagepub.com

Sage Publications Ltd.
6 Bonhill Street
London EC2A 4PU
United Kingdom

Sage Publications India Pvt. Ltd.
M-32 Market
Greater Kailash I
New Delhi 110 048 India

Printed in the United States of America

Library of Congress Cataloging-in-Publication Data

Johnson, Craig E. (Craig Edward), 1952–
 Meeting the ethical challenges of leadership: Casting light or shadow
/ by Craig E. Johnson.
  p. cm.
 Includes bibliographical references and index.
 ISBN 0-7619-2397-7 (c: acid-free paper) — ISBN 0-7619-2334-9
 (p: acid-free paper)
 1. Leadership—Moral and ethical aspects.   I. Title.
HM1261 .J64 2001
303.3′4—dc21   00-012629

01 02 03 04 05 06 07 7 6 5 4 3 2

Acquiring Editor:	Marquita Flemming
Editorial Assistant:	MaryAnn Vail
Production Editor:	Diana E. Axelsen
Editorial Assistant:	Cindy Bear
Typesetter/Designer:	Tina Hill
Indexer:	Rachel Rice
Cover Designer:	Michelle Lee

Contents

Part II: Looking Inward

Meeting the
Ethical Challenges
of LEADERSHIP

To my students

Acknowledgments

Colleagues and students provided practical and emotional support during the writing of this text. My thanks go, first of all, to the Academic Affairs Office of George Fox University. Robin Baker and Mark Weinert released me from part of my teaching load so that I could begin this project. I also want to acknowledge the hard work of my research assistant, Amanda Martell, who located sources and proofed chapters, and I thank Belinda Pilcher for keeping the office running smoothly. Faculty in the Departments of Communication Arts and Writing/Literature encouraged me along the way, sharing in both the highs and lows of the writing process. They caught my excitement for this project, and for that, I am grateful. Bill Essig provided valuable insights into ethical diversity, while John Stanley of Messiah College directed me to materials on spiritual development. Students enrolled in my classes gave me valuable feedback on chapter content, exercises, and cases.

My appreciation goes to Roger Smitter of North Central College and Sara Boatman of Nebraska Wesleyan College for their comments on the manuscript. I'm particularly indebted to editor Marquita Flemming, who became an enthusiastic advocate for this project at Sage. Finally, I want to thank my wife, Mary, for understanding my need to write another book.

PART I

The Shadow Side of Leadership

Introduction

□ Of Heroes and Villains

The image of the heroic leader is alive and well in popular culture. Pick up a leadership book in the business section of your local Barnes and Noble or Borders bookstore, and chances are that you will find stories of dynamic leaders. These heroes introduce revolutionary products, rescue their companies from financial ruin, and reform their corporate cultures to make them more flexible and responsive to customer needs. A few aisles over, in the fiction section, you can immerse yourself in the lives of mystery, science fiction, western, and adventure heroes. Television series and feature films celebrate the adventures of Hercules, She-Ra, Luke Skywalker, James Bond, and other larger-than-life leaders who conquer the forces of evil.

Underlying all these inspirational stories is the assumption that leadership is a powerful, positive force. Rarely, for example, do we read about corporate villains who destroy their organizations in their attempts to transform them. Part of the attraction of reading leadership success stories is the hope that we can emerge as heroes ourselves. The typical business leadership book tells readers how to achieve success by adopting the strategies used by the captains of industry. Overlooked in most of these accounts is the recognition that the same qualities and tactics that lead to triumph can also lead to tragedy. Decisiveness can mean quick turnaround times but degenerate into authoritarianism. Effective public speaking techniques can be used by demagogues as well as by democrats. CEOs fashion corporate visions that serve themselves, rather than the public.

Fortune magazine columnist Stanley Bing believes that far too many business tycoons, Hollywood celebrities, and politicians follow the teachings of Niccolo Machiavelli.[1] Machiavelli was a political adviser in Renaissance Italy who counseled princes to do whatever it took to maintain their power. He took the position that the ends justify the means. In his tongue-in-cheek book, *What Would Machiavelli Do?*, Bing demonstrates how many modern "princes" use mean, Machiavellian tactics to achieve their goals. These strategies range from manipulation, verbal attacks, and lies to physical intimidation, hatred, fear, and control. Some examples of modern-day Machiavellians can be found in Table I.1.

The power that comes from being a leader can be used for evil as well as for good. When we assume the benefits of leadership, we also assume ethical burdens. I believe that we must make every effort to act to benefit, rather than damage, others—to cast light instead of shadow. If you're looking for a collection of positive tales of heroic leaders or another how-to book outlining the steps for expanding your power, you should look elsewhere. In the chapters to come, I'll describe leaders who make wise and (in some cases) inspirational choices. I'll supply just as many illustrations of leaders who make morally stupid and evil decisions.

You should find this book helpful if you are a leader or an aspiring leader who (a) acknowledges that there are ethical consequences associated with exercising influence over others, and (b) seeks to develop the capacity to make more informed ethical choices and to follow through on choices. There is no guarantee that after reading the following chapters you will act in a more ethical fashion in every situation. Nor can you be sure that others will reach the same conclusions as you do about what is the best answer to an ethical dilemma. Nevertheless, you can increase your ethical competence. This book is dedicated to that end.

Whatever the specific context, leaders face similar types of ethical choices. For that reason, I draw examples from a variety of settings—business, coaching, education, government, nonprofit organizations, and the military. Most are based on real-life events, but I don't hesitate to draw from fictional sources as well. Sometimes, literature and drama can teach us lessons that reality cannot. Cases play an important role in

Table I.1   The Ends Justify the Meanness

Leader	Tactic
IBM chairman Lou Gerstner	Never relax or let others enjoy life
Publisher Steve Brill	Be unpredictable; alternate between compassion and cruelty
Oprah Winfrey	Believe that you are born to greatness
Richard Nixon	Paranoia—assume everyone is against you
Film producer Scott Rudin	Make enemies, feed your anger
Media mogul Ted Turner	Fire anybody, including family members (Turner fired his son at dinner)
Miramax head Harvey Weinstein	Engage in "glorious excess" (fine food, limousines, expensive apartments, exotic vacations)
Bill Clinton	Lie when necessary; "manage" the truth
Warnaco, Inc. chair Linda Wachner	Humiliate followers whenever possible
Martha Stewart	Strive for perfection; leave nothing to chance

SOURCE: Bing, S. (2000). *What would Machiavelli do? The ends justify the meanness.* New York: HarperBusiness.

this book. Look for two case studies in every chapter—one in the body of the chapter and the other at the end. You'll also find a feature titled "Leadership Ethics at the Movies." Each of these boxes describes a film that brings important concepts to life. Analyzing these movies on your own or, better yet, in a group, will deepen your understanding of leadership ethics.

The next two chapters focus on the "dark side" of leadership in the belief that the first step in mastering the ethical challenges of leadership is to recognize their existence. Chapter 1 outlines common shadows cast by leaders: abuse of power and privilege, deception, misplaced and broken loyalties, inconsistency, and irresponsibility. Chapter 2 explores why leaders cause more harm than good and introduces the ethical capacity model. At the end of the second chapter, I'll pause to preview the remaining sections of the book, which are based on the foundation laid in Part I.

▣ Defining Terms

Because this is a book about leadership ethics, I need to clarify what both of these terms mean. Leadership is the exercise of influence in a group context.[2] Want to know who the leaders are? Look for the people having the greatest impact on the group or organization. Leaders are change agents engaged in furthering the needs, wants, and goals of leaders and followers alike. They are found wherever humans associate with one another, whether in a social movement, sports team, task force, non-profit agency, state legislature, military unit, or corporation.

No definition of leadership is complete without distinguishing between leading and following. Generally, leaders garner the most press coverage. The turnaround of the Chrysler Corporation is a case in point. Lee Iacocca gets most of the credit for saving Chrysler from bankruptcy, but the company's turnaround was the result of the labor of thousands of followers. This includes assembly line workers and their supervisors, truck drivers who delivered vehicles to showrooms, company accountants who tracked payroll and expenses, warehouse workers who kept the production floor stocked with parts, and salespeople who convinced consumers to buy Chrysler products. In truth, leaders and followers function collaboratively, working together toward shared objectives. They are relational partners who play complementary roles.[3] Leaders exert a greater degree of influence and take more responsibility for the overall direction of the group; followers are more involved in implementing plans and doing the work. Important leader functions include establishing direction, organizing, coordinating activities and resources, motivating, and managing conflicts. Important follower functions include carrying out group and organizational tasks (engineering, social work, teaching, accounting), generating new ideas about how to get jobs done, engaging in teamwork, and providing feedback.[4] During the course of a day or week, we typically shift between leader and follower roles, heading up a project team at work, for example, while taking the position of follower as a student in a night class.

Viewing leadership as a role should put to rest the notion that leaders are born, not made. That the vast majority of us will function as leaders if we haven't already done so means that leadership is not limited to those with the proper genetic background, income level, or education. Consider the case of Erin Brockovich, the inspiration for the film of the same name. A destitute, twice-divorced mother of three, she talks her way into a job with the legal firm that failed to win her personal injury lawsuit. In the film (and apparently in real life), Brockovich dresses like a street-walker, alienates her coworkers, and sasses her employer. Yet when she discovers that Pacific Gas and Electric Company (PG&E) has been poisoning the residents of Hinkley, California, she emerges as a leader. Brockovich talks her boss into taking the case and convinces hundreds of townspeople to join the suit. PG&E eventually pays out more than $300 million in restitution. Brockovich proves that nearly anyone can take a leadership role, even without the benefit of a stylish wardrobe, a decent car, tact, a stable family life, or good child care!

Leadership should not be confused with position, although leaders often occupy positions of authority. Those designated as leaders, such as a disillusioned manager nearing retirement, don't always exert much influence. On the other hand, those without the benefit of a title on the organizational chart can have a significant impact. Lech Walesa was an electrician in a Polish plant. Nonetheless, he went on to lead a revolution that led to the overthrow of the nation's communist government.

Human leadership differs in important ways from the patterns of dominance and submission that characterize animal societies. The dominant female hyena or male chimpanzee establishes its rule over the pack or troop through pure physical strength. Each maintains authority until some stronger rival (often seeking mates) comes along. Unlike animals, which seem to be driven largely by instinct, humans consciously choose how they want to influence others. We can use persuasion, rewards, punishments, emotional appeals, rules, and a host of other means to get our way. Freedom of choice makes ethical considerations—judgments about whether human behavior is right or wrong—an important part of any discussion of leadership. We may be repulsed by the idea that a male lion will kill the offspring of the previous dominant male when he takes control of the pride. Yet we cannot label his actions as unethical because he is driven by a genetic drive to start his own bloodline. We can and do condemn the actions of leaders who decide to lie, belittle followers, and enrich themselves at the expense of the less fortunate.

One final note before moving on to examine the shadow side of leadership: Some philosophers distinguish between *ethics*, which they define as the systematic study of the principles of right or wrong behavior, and *morals*, which they describe as specific standards of right and wrong

("Thou shall not steal"; "Do unto others as you would have others do unto you"). Just as many scholars appear to use these terms interchangeably. I will follow the latter course.

Notes

1. Bing, S. (2000). *What would Machiavelli do? The ends justify the meanness.* New York: HarperBusiness.

2. Bass, B. M. (1990). *Bass and Stogdill's handbook of leadership* (3rd ed.). New York: Free Press.

3. Kelley, R. (1992). *The power of followership: How to create leaders people want to follow and followers who lead themselves.* New York: Doubleday/Currency, p. 41; Hollander, E. P. (1992, April). The essential interdependence of leadership and followership. *Current Directions in Psychological Science, 1*(2), 71-75.

4. Johnson, C. E., & Hackman, M. Z. (1997, November). *Rediscovering the power of followership in the leadership communication text.* Paper presented at the National Communication Association convention, Chicago.

1

The Leader's Light or Shadow

We are not angels, but we may at times be better versions of ourselves.

—Historian Erwin Hargrove

▣ What's Ahead

This chapter introduces the metaphor of light and shadow to highlight the ethical challenges of leadership. Leaders have the power to illuminate the lives of followers or to cover them in darkness. They cast shadows when they (a) abuse power, (b) hoard privileges, (c) engage in deceit, (d) act inconsistently, (e) misplace or betray loyalties, and (f) fail to assume responsibilities.

▣ A Dramatic Difference

In "Leading From Within," educational writer and consultant Parker Palmer introduces a powerful metaphor to dramatize the distinction between ethical and unethical leadership. According to Palmer, the

9

difference between moral and immoral leaders is as sharp as the contrast between light and darkness, between heaven and hell.

> A leader is a person who has an unusual degree of power to create the conditions under which other people must live and move and have their being, conditions that can either be as illuminating as heaven or as shadowy as hell. A leader must take special responsibility for what's going on inside his or her own self, inside his or her consciousness, lest the act of leadership create more harm than good.[1]

Psychotherapist Carl Jung was the first social scientist to identify the shadow side of the personality. He used the term to refer to the subconscious, which could include both negative (greed, fear, hatred) and positive (creativity, desire for achievement) elements.[2] Unlike Jung and other researchers who use the shadow label to refer to the hidden part of the personality, both good and bad, Palmer equates shadow with destruction. Palmer and Jungian psychologists agree on one point, however: *If we want to manage or master the dark forces inside us, we must first acknowledge that they exist.* For this reason, Palmer urges us to pay more attention to the shadow side of leadership. Political figures, classroom teachers, parents, clergy, and business executives have the potential to cast as much shadow as they do light. Refusing to face the dark side of leadership makes abuse more likely. All too often, leaders "do not even know they are making a choice, let alone how to reflect on the process of choosing."[3]

When we function as leaders, we take on a unique set of ethical challenges in addition to a set of expectations and tasks. These dilemmas involve issues of power, privilege, deceit, consistency, loyalty, and responsibility. How we handle the challenges of leadership will determine if we cause more harm then good. Unless we're careful, we're likely to cast one or more of the shadows described in the next section.

▣ The Leader's Shadows

The Shadow of Power

Power is the foundation for influence attempts. The more power we have, the more likely others will comply with our wishes. Power comes from a variety of sources. The most popular power classification system identifies five power bases.[4] *Coercive power* is based on penalties or punishments such as physical force, salary reductions, student suspensions, or embargoes against national enemies. *Reward power* depends on being able to deliver something of value to others, whether tangible (bonuses, health insurance, grades) or intangible (praise, trust, cooperation). *Legitimate power* resides in the position, not the person. Supervisors, judges, police officers, instructors, and parents have the right to control our behavior within certain limits. A boss can require us to carry out certain tasks at work, for example, but in most cases, a boss has no say in what we do in our free time. In contrast to legitimate power, *expert power* is based on the characteristics of the individual regardless of his or her official position. Knowledge, skills, education, and certification all build expert power. *Referent (role model) power* rests on the admiration that one individual has for another. We're more likely to do favors for a supervisor we admire or to buy a product promoted by our favorite sports hero.

Leaders typically draw on more than one power source. The manager who is appointed to lead a task force is granted legitimate power that enables her to reward or punish. Yet to be successful, she'll have to demonstrate her knowledge of the topic, skillfully direct the group process, and earn the respect of task force members through hard work and commitment to the group.

There are advantages and disadvantages of using each power type. Coercion, for instance, usually gets quick results but invites retaliation and becomes less effective through time. Researchers report that U.S. workers are more satisfied and productive when their leaders rely on forms of power that are tied to the person (expert and referent), rather than on forms of power that are linked to the position (coercive, reward, legitimate).[5] Leaders, then, have important decisions to make about the types of power they use and when. (See Case Study 1.1, which highlights the uses and possible abuses of one form of legitimate power.)

That leadership cannot exist without power makes some Americans uncomfortable. Harvard business professor Rosabeth Kanter even declares that power is "America's last dirty word."[6] She believes that for many of us, talking about money and sex is easier than discussing power. We admire powerful leaders who act decisively but can be reluctant to admit that we have and use power. Our refusal to face up to the reality of power can make us more vulnerable to the shadow side of leadership. Cult leader Jim Jones presided over the suicide of 800 followers in

CASE STUDY 1.1

The Executive Order: An Abuse of Power?

The last part of the Clinton presidency saw a flurry of executive orders that set aside millions of acres as national monuments. Clinton, driven by the desire to leave an environmental legacy for his administration, used the 1906 Antiquities Act to create the Grand Staircase-Escalante National Monument in Utah, preserve rocks and reefs off the California coast, and double the amount of Grand Canyon desert in federal hands. The Antiquities Act allows the president to protect federal lands with historical, scientific, or archaeological significance.

Executive orders are an implied power taken from the U.S. Constitution, which states that presidents must "take care that the laws be faithfully executed." They have the force of law, however, and stand until another president or the House and Senate overturns them. Theodore Roosevelt was the first chief executive to make heavy use of executive orders, issuing more than 1,000, largely to protect the environment. Since that time, presidents from both parties have employed executive orders to achieve a variety of political objectives. Franklin Roosevelt issued 3,522 executive orders to further the New Deal and the war effort. Harry Truman ended segregation in the military with one, and John F. Kennedy created the Equal Employment Opportunity Commission with another. Although Clinton issued more than 300 executive orders during his 8 years in office, he used fewer than did two-term Republicans Ronald Reagan (402) and Richard Nixon (355).

---

the jungles of Guyana. Perhaps this tragedy could have been avoided if cult members and outside observers had challenged Jones's abuse of power.[7] Conversely, ignoring the topic of power prevents the attainment of worthy objectives, leaving followers in darkness. Consider the case of the community activist who wants to build a new shelter for homeless families. He can't help these families unless he skillfully wields power to enlist the support of local groups, overcome resistance of opponents, raise funds, and secure building permits.

I suspect that we treat power as a dirty word because we recognize that power has a corrosive effect on those who possess it. We've seen how Richard Nixon used the power of his office to order illegal acts against his enemies and how special prosecutor Kenneth Starr wielded his authority to coerce witnesses into testifying against Bill Clinton. Even highly moral individuals can be seduced by power. Former Sena-

---

CASE STUDY I.I (Continued)

Are executive orders an abuse of presidential power? Polls showed that most Americans backed Clinton's efforts to save environmentally sensitive areas. These tracts of land couldn't have been set aside any other way because of the deadlock created by Republican control of Congress and Democratic control of the White House. Yet many citizens living near the newly protected lands and their representatives saw the issue differently, calling them "land grabs" that overrode local autonomy. Some observers are concerned about the precedent that executive orders set regardless of whether a Democrat or Republican uses them. Executive orders have become one of a president's favorite tools. Chief executives are tempted to use this strategy instead of negotiating with the legislative branch. As a result, the nature of politics in the United States is changing, shifting from the art of compromise to government by executive decree.

Discussion Probes

1. Brainstorm a list of the advantages and disadvantages of executive orders for the president, Congress, and the nation as a whole.
2. On the basis of your list, how would you answer the question of whether executive orders are an abuse of presidential power?
3. What limits, if any, would you put on the use of presidential decrees? What ethical issues or concerns would you take into consideration when setting these limits?
4. Can you think of a justification for stripping the office of president of the power to issue executive orders?

SOURCE: Eisinger, R. K. (2000, January 20). Penning in open spaces. *The Oregonian*, pp. D1, D2.

---

tor Mark Hatfield is widely admired for being the only senator to oppose the Gulf of Tonkin resolution that authorized the war in Vietnam. Yet the Senate later reprimanded him for using his office to secure jobs for his wife.

The greater a leader's power, the greater the potential for abuse. This prompted Britain's Lord Acton to observe that "power corrupts, and absolute power corrupts absolutely." The long shadow cast by absolute power can be seen in the torture, death, starvation, and imprisonment of millions at the hands of Hitler, Idi Amin, Pol Pot, Stalin, and other despots. Large differences in the relative power of leaders and followers also contribute to abuse. The greater the power differential between a supervisor and a subordinate, the higher is the probability that the manager will make demands or threats when friendly, reasonable requests would work just as well and create a more positive emotional climate.[8]

Power deprivation exerts its own brand of corruptive influence. Followers with little power become fixated on what minimal influence they have, becoming cautious, defensive, and critical of others and new ideas. In extreme cases, they may engage in sabotage, such as when one group of fast-food employees took out their frustrations by spitting and urinating into the drinks they served customers.

To wield power wisely, leaders have to wrestle with all the issues outlined above. They have to consider what types of power they should use and when and for what purposes. They also have to determine how much power to keep and how much to give away. Finally, leaders must recognize the dangers posed by possessing too much power while making sure that followers aren't corrupted by having too little.

The Shadow of Privilege

Leaders almost always enjoy greater privileges than followers do. The greater the power of leaders, generally the greater are the rewards they receive. Consider the perks enjoyed by corporate CEOs, for example. Top business executives in the United States are the highest paid in the world, averaging approximately $871,000 a year.[9] They also eat in private dining rooms, travel in chauffeured limousines, and are showered with public accolades.

The link between power and privilege means that abuse of one generally leads to the abuse of the other. Leaders who hoard power are likely to hoard wealth and status as well. Focused on their own desires, they neglect the needs of followers. Some of the same CEOs who wouldn't hesitate to spend thousands on themselves make sure that their employees have to account for every penny. Former CBS executive Lawrence Tisch once insisted that a company photographer finish every exposure on a roll of film before taking it out of his camera. Ted Turner returned letters without postmarks to the company mail room and made the clerks cut off and reuse the stamps.[10]

Leader excess is not a new phenomenon. Ancient Chinese philosophers criticized rulers who lived in splendor while their subjects lived in poverty. Old Testament prophets railed against the political and social elites of the nations of Israel and Judah, condemning them for hoarding wealth, feasting while the poor went hungry, and using the courts to drive the lower classes from their land.

The passage of time hasn't lessened the problem but has made it worse. According to the United Nations, the richest 225 people in the world have a net worth that is equal to the annual income of the poorest 2.5 *billion* people. The poorest of the poor literally live in a hell on earth, deprived of such basic necessities as food, shelter, clean water, and health care. For evidence of this fact, we need look no further than the African country of Rwanda. Of that nation's citizens, 70% live below the poverty line, at least 11% of the population is HIV positive, 10% of its children suffer from malnutrition, and the average woman lives to be only 43 years old (in part because one in every nine mothers dies during childbirth).[11]

Most of us agree that (a) leaders deserve more rewards because they assume greater risks and responsibilities, and (b) some leaders get more than they deserve. Beyond this point, however, our opinions are likely to diverge. Americans are divided over such questions as these: How many additional privileges should leaders have? What should be the relative difference in pay and benefits between workers and top management? How do we close the large gap between the world's haves and have-nots? We'll never reach complete agreement on these issues, but the fact remains—privilege is a significant ethical burden associated with leadership. Leaders must give questions of privilege the same careful consideration as questions of power. The shadow cast by the abuse of privilege can be as long and dark as that cast by the misuse of power.

The Shadow of Deceit

Leaders have more access to information than do others in an organization. They are more likely to participate in the decision-making processes, network with managers in other units, have access to personnel files, and formulate long-term plans. Knowledge is a mixed blessing. Leaders must be in the information loop to carry out their tasks, but possessing knowledge makes life more complicated. Do they reveal that they are "in the know"? When should they release information and to whom? How much do they tell? Is it ever right for them to lie?

Figure 1.1. Shredded

SOURCE: Cartoon by Gary Markstein at the *Milwaukee Journal Sentinel*, Wisconsin, 2000. Reprinted by permission of Copley News Service and Gary Markstein.

No wonder leaders are tempted to think ignorance is bliss! If all these challenges weren't enough, leaders face the very real temptation to lie or hide the truth to protect themselves. Tobacco executives, for instance, swore before Congress that smoking was safe although they had sponsored research that said otherwise. Firestone hid evidence of tire defects from the public and federal regulators. Bill Clinton tried to salvage his image and his presidency by proclaiming, "I did not have sexual relations with that woman" [Monica Lewinsky].

The issues surrounding access to information are broader than deciding whether to lie or to tell the truth. In *Lying: Moral Choice in Public and Private Life*, ethicist Sissela Bok defines lies as messages designed to make other people believe what we ourselves don't believe.[12] Although leaders often decide between lying and truth telling, they are just as likely to be faced with the questions related to the release of information. Take the case of a middle manager who has learned about an upcoming merger that will mean layoffs. Her superiors have asked her to keep this information to herself for a couple of weeks until the deal is completed. In the interim, employees may make financial commitments (home and car purchases) that they would postpone if they knew that major changes were in the works. Should she voluntarily share information about the merger despite her orders? What happens when a member of her department asks her to confirm or deny the rumor that the company is about to merge?

Privacy issues raise additional ethical concerns. Customers of U.S. Bank were outraged to find out that the firm had sold their personal financial information to other companies. E-commerce firms routinely track the activity of Internet surfers, collecting and selling information that will allow marketers to better target their advertisements. In sum, leaders cast shadows not only when they lie but also when they engage in deceptive practices. Deceitful leaders

- Deny having knowledge that is in their possession
- Withhold information that followers need
- Use information solely for personal benefit
- Violate the privacy rights of followers
- Release information to the wrong people
- Put followers in ethical binds by preventing them from releasing information that others have a legitimate right to know

Patterns of deception, whether they take the form of outright lies or hiding or distorting information, destroy the trust that binds leaders and followers together. Consider the popularity of conspiracy theories, for example. Many citizens are convinced that the Air Force is hiding evidence of alien landings in Roswell, New Mexico. They also believe that law enforcement officials are deliberately ignoring evidence that John F. Kennedy and the Reverend Martin Luther King Jr. were the victims of elaborate assassination plots. These theories may seem illogical, but they flourish, in part, because government leaders have created a shadow atmosphere through deceit. The FBI, for example, initially denied that its agents used incendiary devices at the Branch Davidian compound in Waco, Texas, but was later forced to change its story. Not until after the

Gulf War did we learn that our "smart bombs" weren't really so smart and missed their targets.

The Shadow of Inconsistency

Leaders deal with a variety of constituencies, each with its own set of abilities, needs, and interests. In addition, they like some followers better than others. The leader-member exchange theory (LMX) is based on the notion that leaders develop closer relationships with one group of followers.[13] Members of the in-group become advisers, assistants, and lieutenants. High levels of trust, mutual influence, and support characterize their exchanges with the leader. Members of the out-group are expected to carry out the basic requirements of their jobs. Their communication with the leader is not as trusting and supportive. Not surprisingly, members of the in-group are more satisfied and productive than are members of out-groups. Situational variables also complicate leader-follower interactions. Guidelines that work in ordinary times may break down under stressful conditions. A professor may state in her syllabus that five absences will result in flunking a class, for example. She may have to loosen her standard, however, if a flu epidemic strikes the campus.

Diverse followers, varying levels of relationships, and elements of the situation make consistency an ethical burden of leadership. Should all followers be treated equally even if some are more skilled and committed or closer to us than others? When should we bend the rules and for whom? Shadows arise when leaders appear to act arbitrarily and unfairly when faced with questions such as these, as in the case of a resident assistant who enforces dormitory rules for some students but ignores infractions committed by friends. Of course, determining whether a leader is casting light or shadow may depend on where you stand as a follower. When Michael Jordan played for the Chicago Bulls, Coach Phil Jackson allowed him more freedom than other players. Jordan was comfortable with this arrangement, but his teammates weren't as enthusiastic. Developing in-groups and out-groups may be inevitable, but leaders should strive to be as equitable as possible.

Issues of inconsistency can also arise in a leader's relationships with those outside the immediate group or organization. Misgivings about the current system of financing political elections stem from the ability of large donors to "buy" elected officials and influence their votes. Laws often favor those who have contributed the most, as in the case of the nation's scrap metal dealers. They contributed $300,000 to political candidates and committees from both parties and were rewarded with a provision that exempted them from millions of dollars of hazardous waste cleanup costs. According to *Time* magazine, those who give ("first-class citizens") can expect to be bailed out when they make bad business decisions, get more time to pay their debts, and kill legislation they don't like. The rest of us ("second-class citizens") get stuck with a disproportionate share of the tax bill and, because of legislation that protects producers and manufacturers, pay higher prices for goods ranging from farm products to prescription medications.[14]

The Shadow of Misplaced and Broken Loyalties

Leaders must weigh a host of loyalties or duties when making choices. In addition to their duties to employees and stockholders, they must consider their obligations to their families, local communities, professions, the larger society, and the environment. Noteworthy leaders put the needs of the larger community above selfish interests. Ben & Jerry's corporation, for example, has received praise for its "capitalism with a conscience." The firm has supported Vermont dairy farmers, promoted peace, and helped the homeless, among other causes. In contrast, those who appear to put their interests first are worthy of condemnation. Doctors at the Ohio State University Medical Center were harshly criticized for putting the needs of their hospital and the medical profession ahead of the public in the case of Michael Swango. Swango, a doctor, stands accused of killing 60 patients. This may make him the most prolific serial killer in U.S. history. Nurses accused Swango of poisoning patients when he was an internist at the Ohio State University Medical Center. Yet faculty put their loyalty to their young colleague and the hospital above the needs of the sick. They believed Swango instead of the nurses (who were of lower status) and protected the image of the hospital by undermining any criminal investigation. Administrators appeared more interested in fending off potential lawsuits than in finding out the truth. As a result of these misplaced loyalties, Swango received his medical license and allegedly continued his career as a killer.[15]

Loyalties can be broken as well as misplaced. If anything, we heap more scorn on those who betray our trust than on those who misplace their loyalties. Many of history's villains are traitors—Judas Iscariot, Benedict Arnold, and Vidkun Quisling (he sold out his fellow Norwegians to the Nazis). Leaders cast shadows when they violate the loyalty of followers and the community. Mergers and acquisitions, for example, are a common form of corporate betrayal. Executives of the new conglomerate typically ensure consumers that they will benefit from the merger. Quality and service, they claim, will improve, not suffer. Employees are told that the best elements of their current companies will be maintained. Sadly, these promises are broken more often than not. Quality and service decline as the new firm cuts costs to pay for its expansion. Important corporate values such as family support and social responsibility are lost, and benefits are slashed.

That I've placed the loyalty shadow after such concerns as power and privilege should not diminish its importance. Philosopher George Fletcher argues that we define ourselves through our loyalties to families, sports franchises, companies, and other groups and organizations.[16] Political strategist James Carville points out that the significance of loyalty is reflected in the central role it plays in drama. "Take apart any great story," he claims, "and there's loyalty at its heart."[17] As evidence of this fact, he points to Shakespeare's *Romeo and Juliet*, the *Godfather* trilogy, the HBO series *The Sopranos*, and even episodes of *The Andy Griffith Show* (Carville doesn't claim to have excellent taste).

You may think that Carville overstates his case, but loyalty is a significant burden placed on leaders. (To learn about Carville's laws of loyalty, turn to Case Study 1.2 at the end of this chapter.) Well-placed loyalty can make a significant moral statement. Such was the case with Pee Wee Reese. The Brooklyn Dodger never wavered in his loyalty to Jackie Robinson, the first black player in the major leagues. In front of one especially hostile crowd in Cincinnati, Reese put his arm around Robinson's shoulders in a display of support.[18]

Pay particular attention to the shadow of loyalty as you analyze the feature films highlighted in each chapter. In most of these movies, leaders struggle with where to place their loyalties and how to honor the trust that others have placed in them. Loyalty plays an important role in *Saving Private Ryan*, the film described in Box 1.1.

BOX 1.1 Leadership Ethics at the Movies: *Saving Private Ryan*

Key cast members: Tom Hanks, Matt Damon, Tom Sizemore,
                    Edward Burns, Jeremy Davies

Synopsis:

After landing on the beaches of Normandy, an army captain (Tom
Hanks) is asked to lead seven men on a mission to find and return a
private who parachuted behind German lines. All three of the private's
brothers have been killed in battle, and Army Chief of Staff George
Marshall wants to spare the private's mother any additional grief. The
company loses two of its members while locating Private Ryan (Matt
Damon), who does not want to be rescued. The rescue party and the
remnants of Ryan's paratroop unit then combine forces to hold a strategic bridge. This film is likely to increase your appreciation for those
who fought in World War II.

Rating: R, for some of the most intense, graphic war sequences ever
filmed and for profanity

Themes: Conflicting duties, loyalty, sacrifice, obedience, the horrors of
war, courage under fire, morality on the battlefield

The Shadow of Irresponsibility

Earlier, I noted that the breadth of responsibility is one of the factors
distinguishing between the leader and follower roles. Followers are
largely responsible for their own actions or, in the case of a self-directed
work team, for their peers. This is not the case for leaders. They are held
accountable for the performance of their entire department or unit.
Determining the extent of a leader's responsibility, however, is far from
easy. Can we blame a college coach for the misdeeds of team members
during the off-season or for the excesses of the university's athletic
booster club? Are Nike executives responsible for the actions of their
overseas contractors who force workers to work in sweatshops? Do
employers "owe" followers a minimum wage level, a certain degree
of job security, and safe working conditions? If military officers are

punished for "following orders," should their supervisors receive the same or harsher penalties? Rabbis and pastors encourage members of their congregations to build strong marriages. Should they lose their jobs when they have affairs?

Leaders act irresponsibly when they (a) fail to take reasonable efforts to prevent followers' misdeeds, (b) ignore or deny ethical problems, (c) don't shoulder responsibility for the consequences of their directives, (d) deny their duties to followers, and (e) hold followers to higher standards than themselves. We don't hold coaches responsible for everything their players do. Nonetheless, we want them to encourage their athletes to obey the law and to punish any misbehavior. Most of us expect Nike to make every effort to treat its overseas labor force fairly, believing that the company owes its workers (even the ones employed by subcontractors) decent wages and working conditions. Generally, we believe that officers giving orders are as culpable as those carrying them out and have little tolerance for religious figures who violate their own ethical standards.

These, then, are some the common shadows cast by leaders faced with the ethical challenges of leadership. Identifying these shadows raises an important question: *When faced with the same ethical challenges, why do some leaders cast light and others cast shadow?* The next chapter explores the forces that contribute to the shadow side of leadership.

▣ Implications and Applications

- The contrast between ethical and unethical leadership is as dramatic as the contrast between light and darkness. Take care lest you cast more shadow than light.

- Certain ethical challenges or dilemmas are inherent in the leadership role. If you choose to become a leader, recognize that you accept ethical burdens along with new tasks, expectations, and rewards.

- Power may not be a dirty word, but it can have a corrosive effect on your values and behavior. You must determine how much power to accumulate, what forms of power to use, and how much power to give to followers.

- Abuse of privilege is the evil twin of power. If you abuse power, you'll generally overlook the needs of followers as you take advantage of the perks that come with your position.

- Access to information will complicate your life. In addition to deciding whether to tell the truth, you'll have to determine when to reveal what you know and to whom, how to gather and use information, and so on.

- A certain degree of inconsistency is probably inevitable in leadership roles, but you'll cast shadows if you are seen as acting arbitrarily and unfairly.

- As a leader, you'll have to balance your needs and the needs of your small group or organization with loyalties or duties to broader communities. Expect condemnation if you put narrow, selfish concerns ahead of society as a whole.

- Leadership brings a broader range of responsibility, but determining the limits of your accountability may be difficult. You'll cast a shadow if you fail to make a reasonable attempt to prevent abuse or to shoulder the blame, deny that you have a duty to followers, or hold others to a higher ethical standard than you are willing to follow.

◻ For Further Exploration, Challenge, and Self-Assessment

1. Create an ethics journal. In it, describe the ethical dilemmas you encounter as a leader and follower, how you resolved them, how you felt about the outcomes, and what you learned that will transfer to future ethical decisions. You may also want to include your observations about the moral choices made by public figures. Make periodic entries as you continue to read this text.

2. Rosabeth Kanter argues that "organizational powerlessness can (with apologies to Lord Acton) corrupt."[19] Do you agree? What are some of the symptoms of powerlessness?

3. Which shadow are you most likely to cast as a leader? Why? What can you do to cast light instead? Can you think of any other ethical shadows cast by leaders?

4. Look for examples of unethical leadership behavior in the news and classify them according to the six shadows. What patterns do you note?

CASE STUDY 1.2

Chapter End Case:
Making a Case for Loyalty

Democratic political consultant James Carville was the most visible defender of Bill Clinton during the Monica Lewinsky scandal, attacking special prosecutor Ken Starr and congressional Republicans on a series of television talk shows. For his efforts, in the press Carville was called a "hatchet man," "buffoon," "Clinton's button man," and "political rottweiler." Ordinary citizens weren't so critical, however, often complimenting him for "stickin'" with the president even if they didn't agree with Carville's decision to do so. Inspired by these statements of support, Carville highlights the importance of loyalty in a book titled *Stickin': The Case for Loyalty.*

Carville believes that the changing economy has broken the loyalties that created communities. Migration, downsizing, chain stores, and e-mail have destroyed a sense of belonging. "Stickin'" with friends and communities is one way to reconnect society. Nonetheless, loyalty should be based on careful reflection, not on blind obedience or habit. Carville didn't think that sexual infidelity was grounds for denouncing Clinton, a man who befriended him when he was a little-known political consultant. He was much more tempted to abandon the president when Clinton supported legislation restricting immigrant rights.

After surveying the role of loyalty in everything from friendship and family to religion and the arts, Carville concludes that there are no absolutes when it comes to determining the limits of loyalty. Instead, he develops the following 10 guideposts that will help us "navigate through some of the treacheries of life and come up with a way to land on the ground somewhere between a backstabber and a sycophant" (p. 210).

1. Be careful about loyalty to yourself because self-loyalty generally excuses selfish behavior.
2. Too much loyalty is just as bad as not enough loyalty.

Notes

1. Palmer, P. (1996). Leading from within. In L. C. Spears (Ed.), *Insights on leadership: Service, stewardship, spirit, and servant-leadership* (pp. 197-208). New York: John Wiley, p. 200.

2. Jung, C. B. (1933). *Modern man in search of a soul.* New York: Harcourt.

3. Palmer (1996), "Leading from within," p. 200.

CASE STUDY 1.2 (Continued)

3. Loyalty is instinctive. In most cases, go with your "gut instinct" when deciding where your loyalties lie.

4. Most of our decisions about loyalty will involve people, not causes. For example, how loyal should I be to fellow soldiers, family, and friends?

5. Loyalty is demonstrated through testing. It's easy to be loyal when someone has done something right; it's much harder to stick with someone who has made a mistake.

6. Loyalty is an investment through time that is usually repaid by the other party.

7. Money—but not a friend—can be replaced. The pain of a lost friendship lasts much longer than a financial setback, so put friendship first.

8. The better someone treats you, the more loyal you are likely to be to that person.

9. A nasty opponent inspires loyalty to your side.

10. Stick with your friends while "stickin'" it to your enemies. Any enemy of a friend is an enemy of yours.

Discussion Probes

1. Do you agree with Carville's decision to stick with President Clinton? Even if you disagree with his choice, do you admire him for his loyalty?

2. Is the loss of loyalty a major problem for society as Carville claims?

3. How do you determine where your loyalties should be?

4. Evaluate Carville's loyalty guideposts. Which do you like? Dislike? Why? Do the guideposts apply equally to both leaders and followers?

5. How much of the impeachment crisis was motivated by misplaced loyalties on both sides?

6. Carville is married to a leading Republican strategist. Does this fact influence your evaluation of him and his loyalty guideposts? Do you respect him more or less?

SOURCE: Carville, J. (2000). *Stickin': The case for loyalty.* New York: Simon & Schuster.

4. French, R. P., & Raven, B. (1959). The bases of social power. In D. Cartwright (Ed.), *Studies in social power* (pp. 150-167). Ann Arbor: University of Michigan, Institute for Social Research.

5. Hackman, M. Z., & Johnson, C. E. (2000). *Leadership: A communication perspective* (3rd ed.). Prospect Heights, IL: Waveland, Ch. 5.

6. Kanter, R. M. (1979, July-August). Power failure in management circuits. *Harvard Business Review, 57*(4), 65-75, p. 65.

7. Pfeffer, J. (1992, Winter). Understanding power in organizations. *California Management Review, 34*(2), 29-50.

8. Kipnis, D., Schmidt, S., Swafflin-Smith, C., & Wilkinson, I. (1984, Winter). Patterns of managerial influence: Shotgun managers, tacticians, and bystanders. *Organizational Dynamics*, 58-67.

9. Neuborne, E. (1996, October 7). USA leads the world in CEO pay. *USA Today*, p. 2B.

10. Bing, S. (2000). *What would Machiavelli do? The ends justify the meanness.* New York: HarperBusiness.

11. Income disparity statistic were taken from *Money* (2000, March), p. 30. Data about Rwanda were reported in Greenfield, K. T. (2000, April 17). Rwandan sorrow. *Time, 155,* 63-67.

12. Bok, S. (1979). *Lying: Moral choice in public and private life.* New York: Vintage.

13. For more information on LMX theory, see

Graen, G. B., & Cashman, J. F. (1975). A role-making model of leadership in formal organizations. In J. G. Hunt & L. L. Larson (Eds.), *Leadership frontiers* (pp. 143-165). Kent, OH: Kent State University Press.

Graen, G. B., & Scandura, T. (1987). Toward a psychology of dyadic organizing. *Research in Organizational Behavior, 9,* 175-208.

Vecchio, R. P. (1982). A further test of leadership effects due to between-group variation and in-group variation. *Journal of Applied Psychology, 67,* 200-208.

14. Barlett, D. L., & Steele, J. B. (2000, February 7). How the little guy gets crunched. *Time, 155,* 38-41.

15. The terrifying story of Dr. Swango is told in Stewart, J. B. (1999). *Blind eye: How the medical establishment let a doctor get away with murder.* New York: Simon & Schuster.

16. Fletcher, G. (1993). *Loyalty: An essay on the morality of relationships.* New York: Oxford University Press.

17. Carville, J. (2000). *Stickin': The case for loyalty.* New York: Simon & Schuster, p. 183.

18. Rampersad, A. (1997). *Jackie Robinson.* New York: Knopf.

19. Kanter (1979), "Power," p. 66.

2

Shadow Casters

In the deeps are the violence and terror of which psychology has warned us. But if you ride these monsters down, if you drop with them farther over the world's rim, you find what our sciences can not locate or name, the substrate, the ocean or matrix or ether which buoys the rest, which gives goodness its power for good, and evil its power for evil, the unified field: our complex and inexplicable caring for each other, and for our life together here.

—Writer Annie Dillard

☐ What's Ahead

This chapter examines why leaders cast shadow instead of light. Shadow casters include (a) inner motivations or "monsters"; (b) faulty decision making caused by errors in thinking, groupthink, organizational pressures to violate personal moral codes, and cultural variables; (c) ethical ignorance; and (d) ethical flabbiness that comes from a lack of moral exercise. To address these shadow casters, we need to engage in leadership development aimed at expanding our ethical capacity as leaders. Effective leadership development programs incorporate assessment, challenge, and support and broaden our knowledge, skills, perspectives, and motivation.

▣ Shadow Casters

Only humans seem to be troubled by the question "why?" Unlike other creatures, we analyze past events (particularly the painful ones) to determine their causes. Coming up with an explanation provides a measure of comfort and control. If we can understand *why* something bad has happened (broken relationships, cruelty, betrayal), we may be able to put it behind us and move on. We are also better equipped to prevent something similar from happening again. Such is the case with shadows. Identifying the reasons for our ethical failures (what I'll call "shadow casters") is the first step to stepping out of the darkness they create.

As you read about the shadow casters, keep in mind that human behavior is seldom the product of just one factor. I identify several reasons that leaders cast shadows. As Case Study 2.2 on Salomon Inc. at the end of the chapter illustrates, however, these elements typically combine to produce unethical behavior. Leaders struggling with insecurities, for example, are particularly vulnerable to external pressures. Faulty decision making and inexperience often go hand in hand; we're more prone to make poor moral choices because we haven't had much practice.

The Monsters Within

Parker Palmer believes that leaders project shadows from their inner darkness. That's why he urges leaders to pay special attention to their motivations lest "the act of leadership create more harm than good." Palmer identifies five internal enemies or "monsters" (a term he borrows from the quote at the beginning of the chapter) living within leaders that produce unethical behavior.[1] I'll include one additional monster to round out the list.

> *Monster 1: Insecurity.* Leaders are frequently deeply insecure people who mask their inner doubts through extroversion and by tying their identity to their roles as leaders. Who they are is inextricably bound to what they do. Leaders project their insecurities on others when they use followers to serve their selfish needs.

Monster 2: Battleground mentality. Leaders frequently use military images when carrying out their tasks, speaking of "wins" and "losses," "allies" and "enemies," and "doing battle" with the competition. For example, IBM chief Lou Gerstner inspired hatred of Microsoft by projecting a picture of Bill Gates on a large screen and telling his managers, "This man wakes up hating you."[2] Acting competitively becomes a self-fulfilling prophecy; competition begets competitive responses in response. This militaristic approach can be counterproductive. More often than not, cooperation is more productive than competition. Instead of pitting departments against each other, for instance, a growing number of companies use cross-functional project teams and task forces to boost productivity.

Monster 3: Functional atheism. Functional atheism refers to a leader's belief that she or he has the ultimate responsibility for everything that happens in a group or organization. "It is the unconscious, unexamined conviction within us that if anything decent is going to happen here, I am the one who needs to make it happen."[3] This shadow destroys both leaders and followers. Symptoms include high stress, broken relationships and families, workaholism, burnout, and mindless activity.

Monster 4: Fear. Fear of chaos drives many leaders to stifle dissent and innovation. They emphasize rules and procedures instead of creativity and consolidate their power instead of sharing it with followers.

Monster 5: Denying death. Our culture as a whole denies the reality of death. Leaders, in particular, don't want to face the idea that projects and programs should die if they're no longer useful. Leaders also deny death through their fear of negative evaluation and public failure. Those who fail should be given an opportunity to learn from their mistakes, not be punished. Only a few executives display the wisdom of IBM founder Thomas Watson. A young executive entered his office after making a $10-million blunder and began the conversation by saying, "I guess you want my resignation." Watson answered, "You can't be serious. We've just spent $10 million educating you!"[4]

Monster 6: Evil. Many other demons lurk in leaders and followers alike—greed, jealousy, envy, rage—but I single out evil for special consideration. Palmer doesn't specifically mention evil as an internal monster, but it is hard to ignore that some individuals seem driven by a force more powerful than insecurity or fear. Teenage insecurities and a desire to vanquish their enemies sparked the murderous rampage of Dylan Klebold and Eric Harris at Columbine High. These factors, however, don't totally explain how these privileged suburban children became heartless killers. Evil may help us answer the question "why?" when we're confronted with monstrous shadows such as those cast by the Columbine shooters or Oklahoma City bomber Timothy McVeigh.

Faulty Decision Making

Identifying inner monsters is a good first step in explaining the shadow side of leadership. Yet well-meaning, well-adjusted leaders can also cast shadows, as in the decision to launch the *Challenger* space shuttle despite safety concerns. Engineers warned that gaskets called O-rings might malfunction in low temperatures, leaking fuel that could cause an explosion. NASA executives dismissed their warnings, and all seven aboard the spacecraft died.

Blame for many ethical miscues can be placed on the way in which ethical decisions are made. Moral reasoning, while focused on issues of right and wrong, shares much in common with other forms of decision making. Making a wise ethical choice involves many of the same steps as making other important decisions—identifying the issue, gathering information, deciding on criteria, weighing options, and so on. A breakdown anywhere along the way can derail the process.

Decision-making experts David Messick and Max Bazerman speculate that many unethical business decisions aren't the product of greed or callousness but stem instead from widespread weaknesses in how people process information and make decisions. In particular, executives have faulty theories (a) about how the world operates, (b) about other people, and (c) about themselves.[5]

Theories About How the World Operates

These assumptions have to do with determining the consequences of choices, judging risk, and identifying causes. Executives generally fail to take into account all the implications of their decisions (see Table 2.1). They overlook low-probability events, fail to consider all the affected parties, think that they can hide their unethical behavior from the public, and downplay long-range consequences. In determining risk, decision makers generally fail to acknowledge that many events happen by chance or are beyond their control. America's involvement in Vietnam, for example, was predicated on the mistaken assumption that the United States could successfully impose its will in the region. Other times, leaders and followers misframe risks, thus minimizing the dangers. For

Table 2.1   Decision-Making Biases

Theories of the World

Ignoring low probability events even when they could have serious consequences later

Limiting the search for stakeholders and thus overlooking the needs of important groups

Ignoring the possibility that the public will find out about an action

Discounting the future by putting immediate needs ahead of long-term goals

Underestimating the impact of a decision on a collective group—industry, city, profession, etc.

Acting as if the world is certain instead of unpredictable

Failure to acknowledge and confront risk

Framing risk differently than followers

Blaming people when larger systems are at fault

Excusing those who fail to act when they should

Theories About Other People

Believing that our group is normal and ordinary (good) while others are strange and inferior (bad)

Giving special consideration and aid to members of the "in group"

Judging and evaluating according to group membership (stereotyping)

Theories About Ourselves

Rating ourselves more highly than other people

Underestimating the likelihood that negative things will happen to us like divorce, illness, accidents, and addictions

Believing that we can control random events

Overestimating our contributions and the contributions of departments and organizations

Overconfidence which prevents us from learning more about a situation

Concluding that the normal rules and obligations don't apply to us

SOURCES: Hackman, M. Z., & Johnson, C. E. (2000). *Leadership: A communication perspective* (3rd ed.). Prospect Heights, IL: Waveland Press, p. 249. Reprinted by permission.
Messick, D. M., & Bazerman, M. H. (1996, Winter). Ethical leadership and the psychology of decision making. *Sloan Management Review, 37*(2), 9-23. See also Bazerman, M. H. (1986). *Management in managerial decision making*. New York: John Wiley.

instance, a new drug seems more desirable when it is described as working half the time, rather than as failing half the time.

The perception of causes is the most important of all our theories about the world because determining responsibility is the first step in assigning blame or praise. In the United States, we're quick to criticize the person when larger systems are at fault. Consider the Sears automotive repair scandal, for example. Investigators discovered that Sears automotive technicians, who were paid commissions based on the number and cost of the repairs they ordered, charged customers for unnecessary work. Although the mechanics should be held accountable for their actions, the commission system also was at fault. Executives should be blamed for creating a program that rewarded dishonesty. Messick and Bazerman also point out that we're more likely to blame someone else for acting immorally than for failing to act. We condemn the executive who steals. We are less critical, however, of the executive who doesn't disclose the incompetence of another manager.

Theories About Other People

These theories are "our organized beliefs about how 'we' differ from 'they'" (competitors, suppliers, managers, employees, ethnic groups).[6] Such beliefs, which we may not be aware of, influence how we treat other people. Ethnocentrism and stereotyping are particularly damaging. *Ethnocentrism* is the tendency to think that we are better than they are, that our way of doing things is superior to theirs. We then seek out (socialize with, hire) others who look and act like us. Military leaders often fall into the trap of ethnocentrism when they underestimate the ability of the enemy to resist hardships. For example, commanders have no trouble believing that their own citizens can survive repeated bombings but don't think that civilian populations in other nations can do the same. Such was the case in World War II. The British thought that bombing Berlin would break the spirit of the Germans, forgetting that earlier German air raids on London had failed to drive Britain out of the war. *Stereotypes,* our beliefs about other groups of people, are closely related to ethnocentrism. These theories (women are weaker than men, Asians have technical but not managerial skills, the mentally challenged can't do productive work) can produce a host of unethical outcomes, including sexual and racial discrimination.

Theories About Ourselves

The last group of theories concerns self-perceptions. Leaders need to have a degree of confidence to make tough decisions, but their self-images are often seriously distorted. Executives tend to think that they (and their organizations) are superior, are immune to disasters, and can control events. No matter how fair they want to be, leaders tend to favor themselves when making decisions. Top-level managers argue that they deserve larger offices, more money, or stock options because their divisions contribute more to the success of the organization. Overconfidence is also a problem for decision makers because it seduces them into thinking that they have all the information they need, so they fail to learn more. Even when they do seek additional data, they're likely to interpret new information according to their existing biases.

Messick and Bazerman emphasize that unrealistic self-perceptions of all types put leaders at ethical risk. Executives may claim that they have a "right" to steal company property because they are vital to the success of the corporation. Through time, they may come to believe that they aren't subject to the same rules as everyone else or that they'll never get caught.

Contextual Pressures

Faulty individual beliefs aren't the only factors contributing to breakdowns in the ethical decision-making process. Group, organizational, and cultural forces are at work as well. Conformity is a problem for many small groups. Members put a higher priority on cohesion then on coming up with a well-reasoned choice. They pressure dissenters, shield themselves from negative feedback, keep silent when they disagree, and so on.[7] Members of shadowy groups engage in unhealthy communication patterns that generate negative emotions while undermining the reasoning process. Some organizations are also shadow lands. Car dealerships, for instance, are known for their deceptive practices, and computer retailers are rapidly earning the same reputation. Obviously, working in such environments makes moral behavior much more difficult, but no organization is immune from ethical failure. Top managers at some organizations may fire employees who talk about ethical issues so that they can claim ignorance if followers do act unethically. This "don't ask, don't tell" atmosphere forces workers to make ethical choices on their own without the benefit of interaction. They seldom challenge the questionable decisions of others and assume that everyone supports the immoral acts.

BOX 2.1 Leadership Ethics at the Movies: *The Hurricane*

Key cast members: Denzel Washington, John Hannah, Deborah Unger,
Liev Schreiber

Synopsis:

Rubin ("Hurricane") Carter, an African American fighter from
Patterson, New Jersey, was competing for the middleweight boxing
crown when he was falsely imprisoned for murder. This film chronicles Carter's attempts to free himself, first on his own and then with
the help of three white Canadians and one black teenager transplanted
from the Bronx to Toronto. As he faces nearly two decades of disap-
pointment, Carter (played by Denzel Washington) learns to overcome
his anger and hatred toward whites and to transcend his circumstances. Ultimately, the Hurricane and his followers prevail, and the
boxer-turned-author and activist is freed.

Rating: R for language and brief nudity

Themes: Overcoming inner monsters or demons, spirituality, character,
race relations, the power of words, suffering, injustice

Organizational communication scholars Charles Conrad and
Marshall Scott Poole also identify a number of less obvious, "hidden"
organizational pressures that derail the ethical decision-making process.[8] Division of labor allows low-level employees to claim that they just
follow orders and upper-level employees to claim that they only set
broad policies and therefore can't be held accountable for the illegal acts
of their subordinates. When tasks are broken down in small segments,
workers may not even know that they are engaged in an improper activity. The secretary who shreds documents may not realize that the papers
are wanted in a civil or criminal investigation. As I noted earlier, systems
or procedures can encourage immoral behavior, as in the case of the
nationwide emphasis on student achievement tests. The mounting pressure to boost test scores encourages teachers to cheat by giving students
the answers or extra testing time.

Socialization is yet another hidden pressure that can encourage
employees to violate their personal codes. Organizations use orientation
seminars and other means to help new hires identify with the group.

Loyalty to the organization is essential. The socialization process, however, may blind members to the consequences of their actions. This may have happened at Microsoft. A federal judge ruled that the company used unfair tactics to monopolize software and Web browser markets. Many Microsoft executives and employees refused to acknowledge any wrongdoing. Instead, they claimed that the court's ruling was just the latest in a series of unfair attacks against the company.

The pressures of organizational ethical decision making create a type of "ethical segregation." Leaders and followers may have strong personal moral codes that regulate their personal lives but act much less ethically while at work.

Cultural differences, like group and organizational forces, can also encourage leaders to abandon their personal codes of conduct. A corporate manager from the United States may be personally opposed to bribery. Her company's code of conduct forbids such payments, and so does federal law. She may, nonetheless, bribe custom officials and government officials in her adopted country if such payments (a) are an integral part of the national culture and (b) appear to be the only way to achieve her company's goals.

Ethical Deficiencies

Leaders may unintentionally cast shadows because they lack the necessary knowledge, skills, and experience. Not understanding how to make ethical decisions can be an issue, as can ignorance of ethical perspectives or frameworks that can be applied to ethical dilemmas. Every year in my introductory communication class, I ask students to read and respond to the Multiply Abused Children example (Case Study 2.1). Groups of students generally reach a consensus about whether Hanson was justified in exaggerating his statistics to raise money for this most worthy cause. When I ask them about the standards they used to reach their conclusions, however, they generally give me a blank look. Some teams make their decision on the basis of personal feelings ("We don't like to be lied to no matter how good the cause"). Other groups employ a widely used ethical principle ("Lying is always wrong"; "It's okay to lie if more people are helped than hurt") in their deliberations but don't realize that they've done so.

It's possible to blunder into good ethical choices, but it's far more likely that we'll make wise decisions when we are guided by some

CASE STUDY 2.1

Multiply Abused Children

Save the Kids is a nonprofit group that pushes for tougher laws against those who sexually abuse children. Currently, Save the Kids is in its biggest lobbying effort ever in an attempt to get the state legislature to pass a law that requires convicted sex offenders to register their whereabouts with local police departments. The organization's founder, Steve Hanson, is convinced that such a law can significantly reduce the number of child abuse cases in the state. Unfortunately, contributions aren't keeping up with expenses, and Save the Kids may have to drastically reduce its lobbying efforts just as the sex offender registration bill comes before the legislature. Chance are, this law will pass only if Save the Kids keeps up its lobbying campaign. Mr. Hanson is now raising money for Save the Kids through a series of speeches. To encourage contributions, Hanson knowingly exaggerates both the number of convicted sex offenders in the state as well as the number of children who are abused every year.

Discussion Probes

1. Do you agree with Hanson's decision to exaggerate to raise money for Save the Kids? Why or why not?

2. Does the amount of exaggeration make a difference in your evaluation of Hanson's action? What if he decides to exaggerate only slightly? What if he greatly inflates the figures?

3. Do Hanson's intentional lies make a difference in how you evaluate his decision? What if he exaggerated because he didn't check his facts carefully?

4. How do you determine whether someone is justified in lying? What standards do you use to determine whether you should tell the truth?

---

widely used ethical principles and standards. These ethical theories help us define the problem, highlight important elements of the situation, force us to think systematically, encourage us to view the problem from a variety of perspectives, and strengthen our resolve to act responsibly.

Making and implementing ethical decisions takes both critical thinking and communication skills. We must be able to articulate our reasoning, convince other leaders of the wisdom of our position, and work with others to put the choice into place. Managers who want to eliminate discriminatory hiring practices, for instance, will have to listen effectively, gather information, analyze and formulate arguments, appeal to moral principles, and build relationships. Failure to develop these skills will doom their reform efforts.

In *How Good People Make Tough Choices*, ethicist Rushworth Kidder encourages readers to develop their ethical fitness by putting their ethical commitments to work in real-life settings.[9] Kidder's exhortation implies that many of us are ethically unfit or flabby. Faulty decision making, ethical ignorance, and underdeveloped skills surely contribute to this condition, but lack of practice plays a role as well. Studying ethical theories and discussing ethical cases are essential to any ethical fitness program. Reasoning and communication skills can be sharpened during class. Ultimately, however, we need the firsthand experience that comes from tackling real-life leadership dilemmas.

☐ Stepping Out of the Shadows: Expanding Our Ethical Capacity

Taking on the role of leader is a stretching experience. We must acquire additional skills to tackle broader responsibilities (see the discussion of the difference between leading and following in Chapter 1) and master a new set of ethical dilemmas. This requires continuous leadership development. Researchers at the Center for Creative Leadership (CCL) define leadership development as "the expansion of a person's capacity to be effective in leadership roles and processes."[10] Leadership development programs assume that (a) individuals can expand their leadership competence and (b) the skills and knowledge they acquire will make them more effective in a variety of leadership situations, ranging from business and professional organizations to neighborhood groups, clubs, and churches.

The CCL researchers report that individuals develop a number of capacities in leadership development programs, including heightened self-confidence, greater creativity, and a broader, systematic point of view. I believe that we can expand our ethical capacity as well. The same elements that go into developing other leadership competencies should also go into building our ethical effectiveness. The three most important components of the leadership development process, according to the CCL researchers, are assessment, challenge, and support (see Figure 2.1).

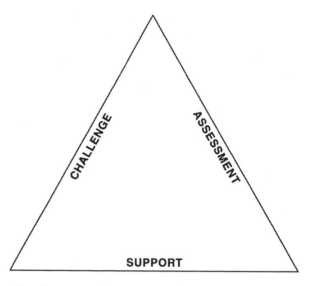

Figure 2.1. Developmental Components

Successful developmental programs provide plenty of feedback that lets participants know how they are doing and how others are responding to their leadership strategies. Assessment data provoke self-evaluation ("What am I doing well?" "How do I need to improve?") and provide information that helps answer these questions. Simply put, leaders learn to identify gaps between current performance and where they need to be. The most powerful leadership experiences also challenge people. As long as individuals don't feel the need to change, they won't. Difficult experiences force leaders outside their comfort zones and give them the opportunity to practice new skills. To make the most of feedback and challenges, leaders need support. Supportive comments ("I appreciate the effort you're making to become a better listener"; "I've got confidence that you can handle this new assignment") sustain the leader during the struggle to improve. The most common source of support is other people (family, coworkers, bosses), but developing leaders can also draw on organizational and learning resources. Supportive organizations believe in continuous learning (more on this in Chapter 9), help individuals develop growth plans, provide funds for training, reward progress, and so on. Learning resources include mentors, experts, conferences, books, Web sites, tapes, and videos.

All three elements—assessment, challenge, and support—should be part of your plan to increase your ethical capacity. You need feedback about how well you handle ethical dilemmas, how others perceive your character, and how your decisions affect followers. You need the challenges and practice that come from moving into new leadership positions. Seek out opportunities to influence others by engaging in service projects, chairing committees, teaching children, or taking on a supervisory role. You also need the support of others to maximize your development. Talk with colleagues about ethical choices at work, draw on the insights of important thinkers, and seek out groups that will support your efforts to change.

Feedback, challenge, and support are incorporated into the design of this book. To encourage assessment, I ask you to reflect on and evaluate your own experiences and to get feedback from others. To highlight challenge, I introduce a number of cases and encourage you to explore ideas further. To provide support, I gather and organize concepts from a variety of sources, identify additional resources, tell the stories of leaders, and encourage you to work with others (friends, small group members, classmates) to increase your ethical competence. Make this text one part of a larger, continuing program to develop your ethical capacity and other leadership abilities.

The remaining chapters are based on the foundation laid in these first two. Now that I have identified the leader's shadows and their causes, we're ready to expand our ethical capacity to better master them. Ethical capacity, according to the CCL, consists of knowledge, skills, perspectives, and motivations. You need to increase your understanding, sharpen your skills, broaden your worldview, and strengthen your motivation to become more ethically competent. (A model of this process is found in Figure 2.2.) Expect to learn new terminology along with key principles, decision-making formats, and important elements of the ethical context. This information will be drawn from a number of fields of study—philosophy, communication, theology, psychology, political science, organizational behavior—because we need insights from many disciplines to step out of the shadows. You can anticipate reading about and then practicing a variety of skills, ranging from information gathering to listening and conflict management. Some material will encourage you to challenge your assumptions and to develop new perspectives on ethical problems. You'll also find that motivation is a central concern of this book. I'll touch on the "why" of ethics when discussing

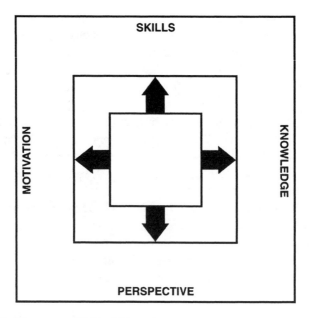

Figure 2.2. Elements of Ethical Capacity

such topics as character, altruism, communitarianism, and servant leadership.

Part II, Looking Inward, focuses on the inner dimension of leadership. Chapter 3 examines the role of character development in overcoming internal enemies, whereas Chapter 4 explores the nature of evil, forgiveness, and spirituality. Part III, Ethical Standards and Strategies, addresses our ethical deficiencies by describing ethical theories and techniques that can be applied to ethical problem solving. Chapters 5 and 6 survey a wide range of perspectives, both general and leader focused, that can help us set moral priorities. Chapter 7 then describes systems or formats that we can use to make better ethical choices. Part IV, Shaping Ethical Contexts, looks at ways that leaders can shed light in a variety of situations. Chapter 8 examines ethical group decision making, Chapter 9 describes the creation of ethical organizational climates, and Chapter 10 highlights the challenges of ethical diversity.

The ultimate goal of developing ethical capacity is to cast light, rather than shadow. Measuring your progress toward this goal is more difficult than, say, determining whether you are mastering the principles of accounting or learning computer skills. There is no one widely accepted ethics exam to tell you how you stack up against other leaders. Further, ethical development, like other aspects of leadership development, never ends. We never reach a point that we can say that we have reached full ethical capacity, that we have "arrived" as moral leaders. We can always develop further.

Marking our progress may be difficult for the reasons described above, but it is not impossible. You'll know that you are becoming more ethically competent if you note the following milestones.

- *Greater self-awareness.* Feedback and personal reflection (particularly on the inner dimension of leadership) will deepen your self-understanding. You'll become more aware of your strengths, weaknesses, and motivations. You should develop a clearer grasp of your mission and your values.

- *Greater self-confidence.* Participants in leadership development programs often rate self-confidence as the most important outcome of their experiences. They become more self-assured as they master new, difficult situations and are more willing to take on greater leadership challenges. Expect the same benefit from mastering ethical dilemmas. As you resolve moral problems, you should gain the confidence you need to shoulder the heavier ethical burdens that come with greater responsibilities.

- *Stronger character.* Character consists of displaying admirable qualities in a variety of settings (more on this in the next chapter). You can mark your progress by noting if you consistently demonstrate positive traits no matter what context you find yourself in.

- *Heightened ethical sensitivity.* Expanding your ethical capacity will make you aware of a wider array of ethical problems. You'll become more sensitive to the presence of ethical dilemmas and issues.

- *Sounder ethical reasoning.* Rejecting faulty assumptions, building arguments, gathering information, and taking a systematic approach to problem solving are all part of reasoned ethical decision making. You should be able to offer a well-reasoned, thorough defense of the conclusions you reach.

- *Greater resistance to outside pressures.* Resisting group, organizational, and cultural pressures to set aside your personal convictions is an important sign of growth.

- *Better follow-through.* There is a gap between believing and doing. Holding the right values and making reasoned choices are not enough; you must

ETHICAL CAPACITY DEVELOPMENT MODEL

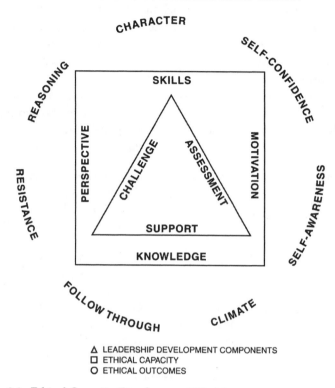

Figure 2.3. Ethical Capacity Development Model

follow through by implementing your choices. Acting on what you think and believe is a significant indication that you're making ethical progress.

- *Healthier ethical climate.* Progress comes from reshaping the ethical environment in addition to resisting external pressures. Expanding ethical capacity means working to change the climate of your small group, organization, and community.

Now that I've identified the key components of a successful leadership development program, defined ethical capacity, and identified some visible outcomes of ethical growth, I'm ready to end the chapter by putting these elements together in the comprehensive model of ethical development found in Figure 2.3.

▣ Implications and Applications

- Unethical/immoral behavior is the product of a number of factors, both internal and external. All these elements must be addressed if you want to cast light, rather than shadow.

- "Good" leaders can and do make bad ethical decisions. Honorable intentions alone won't save you from casting shadows.

- Beware of faulty assumptions about how the world operates, other people, and yourself. These can lead to underestimating risks and overestimating your abilities and value to your organization.

- Never put cohesion first when making important group decisions.

- Your organization, no matter how high-minded, may undermine your personal moral code.

- When it comes to ethics, ignorance is dangerous. Learning about ethical standards and principles will likely help you make wiser ethical choices.

- Experience is vital. Put what you're learning to use in solving real-life ethical dilemmas.

- Leadership development (expansion of your capacity to be effective in leadership roles and processes) provides a useful framework for understanding ethical growth. You develop your ethical capacity (composed of knowledge, skills, perspectives, and motivations) in the same way that you develop your other leadership capacities—through assessment, challenge, and support.

- Ethical development is a lifelong process. You're making progress if you demonstrate one or more of the following: (a) greater self-awareness and self-confidence; (b) strong, consistent character; (c) heightened ethical sensitivity; (d) sound ethical reasoning; (e) resistance to pressures to compromise personal standards; (f) better follow through on choices; and (g) creation of a healthier ethical climate.

▣ For Further Exploration, Challenge, and Self-Assessment

1. What monsters would you add to the list provided in the chapter?
2. Analyze a time when you cast a shadow as a leader or as a follower. Which of the shadow casters led to your unethical behavior?
3. Does your employer pressure you to abandon your personal moral code of ethics? If so, how? What can you do to resist the pressure?

(text continued on p. 46)

CASE STUDY 2.2

Chapter End Case:
Casting Shadows at Salomon Inc.

In the 1980s, John Gutfreund, CEO of Salomon Inc., a giant brokerage house, was considered one of the movers and shakers of the financial world. *Business Week* magazine proclaimed him "The King of Wall Street." In just a few short years, however, Gutfreund had been ousted from his "throne," and his financial empire was in ruins. The story of Gutfreund's fall from power is a vivid demonstration of the high cost of poor moral choices.

Salomon's ethical troubles began in the firm's government securities division. When the U.S. government issues treasury bonds to finance the national debt, it relies on a select group of dealers, including Salomon, to acquire and then resell the bonds to other dealers and private individuals. This arrangement worked well for many years until Salomon's government securities trader, Paul Mozer, began to corner a large share of the market. Concerned that Salomon's growing influence would reduce income from bond sales, the Treasury Department passed a regulation (called the Mozer law) preventing any one brokerage and its customers from bidding on more than 35% of the total bonds available at a given auction.

Mozer protested this "rash decision" by the Treasury Department and, in February 1991, circumvented the new rule. He exceeded the 35% regulation by entering a bid from Salomon and one in the name of a customer (without that firm's knowledge or consent). Mozer later confessed to his boss, John Meriwether, but claimed that this was his first and only offense. Gutfreund and other company executives took no action against Mozer. On May 22, he once again submitted an illegal bid in the name of a customer. The firm investigated and found that Mozer had made a series of illegal bids, not just one, dating to the previous December. On August 8, some 3 months after first learning of hearing of Mozer's criminal behavior, Gutfreund finally revealed this information to the Treasury Department, which then threatened to suspend Salomon's trading privileges. Soon Gutfreund resigned, and investor Warren Buffet assumed his role on a temporary basis. Buffet appointed himself chief legal compliance officer, ordered all Salomon officers to report every legal and moral violation (except parking tickets) directly to him, and spent hours answering the questions of federal investigators and the press.

Warren Buffet's single-minded devotion to restoring the firm's ethical image kept it from collapse, but the fallout, nevertheless, was severe. In addition to paying millions of

CASE STUDY 2.2 (Continued)

dollars in fines, the company lost three quarters of its stock underwriting business, was prevented from making $4 billion in bond trades, and saw its stock value plummet. Trader Mozer spent 4 months in jail, Gutfreund lost his pension and stock options, and several executives received limited or lifetime bans from the securities market.

Greed and jealousy motivated Mozer. He was paid on the basis of his performance and was jealous of competing traders at other firms who received bigger bonuses. It is harder to explain the inaction of Mozer's superiors, however, in particular, CEO Gutfreund. Why did he fail to punish the rogue trader (who had antagonized government officials), and why did he wait 3 months before reporting to the Treasury Department? The executive's style may account for part of his hesitation. Gutfreund admitted that he was an "indecisive" manager. He depended heavily on the firm's "stars" (like Mozer) to produce profits. When the stars violated the rules, he was reluctant to rein them in.

Corporate culture also played a role in the scandal. Stock and bond trading is a high-stakes/high-risk business. Gutfreund sanctioned this "bet the company" atmosphere. His formula for success was to wake up every day "ready to bite the ass off a bear." Gutfreund once challenged Meriwether to a million-dollar game of Liar's Poker. Meriwether responded by raising the stakes to $10 million. In Liar's Poker, two or more players hold a dollar bill against their chests. They make statements, some true and some false, about the serial numbers on the bills. The winner is the person who correctly challenges the false claims of the other players. Gutfreund and Meriwether never played their winner-take-all game. Their reckless example, however, helped create a go-for-broke atmosphere that was to cost the company dearly.

Discussion Probes

1. What shadow casters contributed to the downfall of Salomon Inc.? Was any factor more important than the others? Why?

2. Who is most at fault for what happened? Defend your choice.

3. How can corporate image be restored after scandals such as this one?

4. What steps can firms, particularly ones in high-pressure/high-stakes environments, take to prevent ethical abuses?

5. What leadership lessons do you draw from this case?

PRIMARY SOURCE: Useem, M. (1998). *The leadership moment.* New York: Times Business, Ch. 7.
SECONDARY SOURCE: Lewis, M. (1989). *Liar's poker.* New York: Norton.

4. Can you think of any other signs of ethical progress beyond those named in the chapter?
5. Create a plan for expanding your ethical capacity that incorporates assessment, challenge, and support.

Notes

1. Palmer, P. (1996). Leading from within. In L. C. Spears (Ed.), *Insights on leadership: Service, stewardship, spirit and servant-leadership* (pp. 197-208). New York: John Wiley, p. 200.
2. Bing, S. (2000). *What would Machiavelli do? The ends justify the meanness.* New York: HarperBusiness.
3. Palmer (1996), "Leading from within," p. 205.
4. Garvin, D. A. (1993, July-August). Building a learning organization. *Harvard Business Review, 71*(4), 78-91.
5. Messick, D. M., & Bazerman, M. H. (1996, Winter). Ethical leadership and the psychology of decision making. *Sloan Management Review, 37*(2), 9-23.
6. Messick & Bazerman (1996), "Ethical leadership," p. 9.
7. Janis, I. (1971, November). Groupthink: The problems of conformity. *Psychology Today,* 271-279; Janis, I. (1982). *Groupthink* (2nd ed.). Boston: Houghton Mifflin; Janis, I. (1989). *Crucial decisions: Leadership in policymaking and crisis management.* New York: Free Press; Janis, I., & Mann, L. (1977). *Decision making.* New York: Free Press.
8. Conrad, C., & Poole, M. S. (1998). *Strategic organizational communication: Into the twenty-first century* (4th ed.). Fort Worth, TX: Harcourt Brace, Ch. N12.
9. Kidder, R. M. (1995). *How good people make tough choices: Resolving the dilemmas of ethical living.* New York: Fireside.
10. McCauley, C. D., Moxley, R. S., & Van Velsor, E. (Eds.). *The Center for Creative Leadership handbook of leadership development.* San Francisco: Jossey-Bass, p. 4.

PART II

Looking Inward

3

 The Leader's Character

Leadership always comes down to a question of character.

—Management expert Warren Bennis

What's Ahead

This chapter addresses the inner dimension of leadership ethics. To shed light rather than shadow, we need to develop strong, ethical character made up of positive traits or virtues. We promote character development through understanding the components of moral action, paying attention to role models, learning from hardship, establishing effective habits, determining a clear sense of direction, and examining our values.

Elements of Character

In football, the best defense is often a good offense. When faced with high-scoring opponents, coaches often design offensive game plans that run as much time as possible off the clock. If they're successful, they can rest their defensive players while keeping their opponent's offensive unit on the sidelines. Building strong, ethical character takes a similar proactive approach to dealing with our inner monsters or demons. To keep from projecting our fears on others, we need to go on the offensive, replacing or managing our insecurities through the development of positive leadership traits or qualities called virtues. Interest in virtue ethics dates at least to Plato, Aristotle, and Confucius. The premise of virtue ethics is simple: Good people (those of high moral character) make good moral choices. Despite its longevity, this approach has not always been popular among scholars. Only recently have modern philosophers turned back to it in significant numbers.[1]

Proponents of virtue ethics start with the end in mind. They develop a description or portrait of the ideal person (in this case, a leader) and identify the admirable qualities or tendencies that make up the character of this ethical role model. They then suggest ways that others can acquire these virtues.

There seems to be widespread agreement about the qualities of model leaders. To determine if this is the case, divide a blank sheet of paper into two columns. In the first column, list the qualities or characteristics you associate with a model political leader. In the second column, list the traits of an ideal business leader. Now compare your two lists. There may be minor variations between them, but chances are the similarities far outweigh the differences. Americans tell researchers that they want elected officials to act with integrity, restrain their impulses, respect others, rally followers, exercise good judgment, and persist in the face of adversity.[2] These qualities are remarkably similar to what we want in our business leaders. Some 15,000 managers from Europe, the United States, and Australia report that they most admire superiors who are honest, forward-looking, inspiring, and competent.[3]

There are three important features of virtues. First, virtues are interwoven into the inner life of leaders. They are not easily developed or discarded but persist through time. Second, virtues shape the way leaders both see and behave. Being virtuous makes them sensitive to ethical issues and encourages them to act morally. Third, virtues operate independently of the situation. A virtue may be expressed differently depending on the context (what's prudent in one situation may not be in the next). Yet virtuous leaders will not abandon their principles to please followers or demonstrate courage only when supported by peers.[4]

Aristotle and Plato identified the primary virtues as prudence (discernment, discretion), justice (righteousness, integrity), courage (strength in the face of adversity), and self-restraint (temperance). When the Christians came along, they added faith, hope, and love. Other virtues, such as empathy, compassion, generosity, hospitality, modesty, and civility, were derived from the original seven. The number of virtues has multiplied in modern times. One recent list, for example, identifies 45 positive character traits, including such qualities as resourcefulness, liveliness, magnanimity, and decency.

Coming up with a single, universal list of virtues is not as important as blending a set of desirable qualities together to form a strong, ethical character. This is far from easy, of course. At times, our personal demons will overcome even our best efforts to keep them at bay. We're likely to make progress in some areas while lagging in others. We may be persistent yet tactless, compassionate yet humorless, honest yet impatient. No wonder some prominent leaders reflect both moral strength and weakness. The Reverend Martin Luther King Jr. showed great courage and persistence in leading the civil rights movement but engaged in extramarital relationships. Franklin Delano Roosevelt was revered by many of his contemporaries but had a long-standing affair with Lucy Mercer. She (not Eleanor Roosevelt) was even present when he died. The poor personal behavior of political leaders has sparked debate about personal and public morality. One camp argues that the two cannot be separated. Another camp makes a clear distinction between the public and private arena. According to this second group, we can be disgusted by the private behavior of a politician such as Bill Clinton but vote for him anyway on the basis of his performance in office.

I suspect that the truth lies somewhere between these extremes. We should expect contradictions in the character of leaders, not be surprised by them. Private lapses don't always lead to lapses in public judgment. On the other hand, it seems artificial to compartmentalize private and public ethics. Private tendencies can and do cross over into public decisions. FDR tried to deceive the public as well as his wife and family. He proposed expanding the number of Supreme Court justices from 9 to 15, claiming that the justices were old and overworked. In reality, he was angry with the Court for overturning many New Deal programs and wanted to appoint new justices who would support him. Roosevelt's dishonest attempt to pack the Supreme Court cost him a good deal of his popularity. In a similar fashion, Bill Clinton's moral weaknesses overshadowed many of his political accomplishments.

Fostering character is a lifelong process requiring sustained emotional, mental, and even physical effort. In the remainder of this chapter, I'll introduce a variety of factors that encourage the development of leadership virtues. These include understanding the components of moral action, the identification of role models, learning from hardship, cultivation of habits, creating a personal mission statement, and clarifying values.

▣ Character Building

Components of Moral Action

James Rest at the Center for Ethical Development at the University of Minnesota identifies four thought processes or components that lead to ethical behavior.[5] Component 1 is *moral sensitivity*. We first need to recognize that an ethical problem exists. In addition, we must identify possible courses of action and determine the consequences of each strategy. Component 2 is *moral judgment or reasoning*, deciding which course of action is the right one to follow. Component 3 is *moral motivation*. The desire to follow moral principles generally conflicts with other values such as security, social acceptance, and wealth. Ethical behavior will result only if moral considerations take precedence over competing values. Component 4 is *moral action*, the implementation stage of the model. Being motivated is not enough. Opposition, distractions, fatigue, and other factors make it tough to follow through. Overcoming these obstacles takes persistence and determination; a positive, optimistic attitude ("I can and will succeed"); and interpersonal skills.

Rest presents the four processes in a logical sequence but notes that they don't always occur in this order in real life. For example, what we define as immoral (Component 2) will influence our sensitivity to moral issues (Component 1). Further, we're likely to be strong in some components and weak in others. Some individuals are sensitive to the slightest hint of impropriety. Others have to be told that a potential ethical problem exists.

Ethical breakdowns occur when one or more of the components malfunction. We can demonstrate moral sensitivity and judgment but not carry through if (a) other values become more important than moral values and (b) we lack the necessary will power and skills. Consider the case of supervisors who want to tell the truth but hesitate to confront marginal employees about their poor performance. Their commitment to honesty may be subverted by their desire to avoid conflict and their inability to manage confrontations. As a result, they practice a form of deception by keeping unpleasant truths to themselves.

Identifying your strengths and weaknesses is the first step in character formation. Rest's model can help you determine where you should focus your efforts. You may need to become more sensitive to moral problems and possible solutions. Perhaps you lack the desire to do the right thing or want to further develop virtues, such as persistence, courage, optimism, and determination, that will enable you to implement your moral choices. With your goals in mind, you can seek out leaders who model these qualities.

Finding Role Models

Some attempts to promote character development are as blatant as displaying lists of the virtues in prominent places. On recent visits to the Midwest, for example, I saw "virtue banners" hanging from the fence of an elementary school playground in a small Iowa town as well as from the lobby ceiling in an inner-city Chicago high school. Deliberate moralizing (telling children how to behave) is less effective with older students, however. Character appears to be more "caught than taught." More often than not, we learn what it means to be virtuous by observing and imitating exemplary leaders. That makes role models crucial to developing high moral character.[6] One positive role model is described in Case Study 3.1 below. A negative example is found in Case Study 3.2 at the end of the chapter.

Government ethics expert David Hart argues that it is important to distinguish between different types of moral examples or exemplars.[7] Dramatic acts, such as rescuing a child from danger, capture our attention. To develop worthy character, however, we need examples of those who demonstrate virtue on a daily basis. Hart distinguishes between *moral episodes* and *moral processes*. Moral episodes are made up of *moral crises* and *moral confrontations*. Moral crises are dangerous, and Hart calls

(text continues on p. 56)

CASE STUDY 3.1

The Hero as Optimist:
Explorer Ernest Shackleton

The early 20th century has been called the Heroic Age of Polar Exploration. Teams of adventurers from Norway and Great Britain competed to see who would be first to reach the South Pole. Antarctic expeditions faced temperatures as low as −100° Fahrenheit and gale force winds up to 200 miles an hour. Britain's Captain Robert Scott tried unsuccessfully to claim Antarctica for the Crown in 1901. Ernest Shackleton, who had accompanied Scott on his first journey, came within 100 miles of the Pole in 1909 but had to turn back to save his party. Scott and his companions died during their second expedition launched in 1911. Norwegian Roald Amundsen, who set out at the same time as Scott, succeeded in reaching the southernmost point on earth in January 1912.

Undeterred by Amundsen's success, Shackleton decided to launch "one last great polar journey" aimed at crossing the entire Antarctic continent. Author and museum curator Caroline Alexander describes this adventure in her book titled *The* Endurance: *Shackleton's Legendary Antarctic Expedition.* Shackleton and his crew of 27 men set sail on their wooden sailing ship—the *Endurance*—in August 1914, just days before World War I broke out. Soon, the last great polar journey turned into one of the world's most incredible tales of survival.

The *Endurance* was trapped by pack ice at the end of January, stranding the party. When the ice melted the following October (springtime in the Southern Hemisphere), it crushed and sank the ship. The crew relocated to ice floes. At the end of April, 15 months after being marooned, the group abandoned camp on the shrinking ice packs and made it to an uninhabited island in three small dories.

Shackleton and five companions then set out in one of the small boats (only 22 feet long) to reach the nearest whaling station on South Georgia Island 800 miles away. This voyage would later be ranked as one of the greatest sea journeys of all time. The odds were against the small party from the beginning. They were traveling in the dead of winter on one of the roughest oceans in the world. Darkness made navigation nearly impossible, and they survived a severe storm, one that sank a much bigger tanker sailing at the same time in the same waters. The crew overcame these hurdles and, frostbitten and soaked to the skin, reached South Georgia Island. Yet even then, their suffering was far from over. Shackleton and two colleagues had to cross a series of ridges and glaciers before reaching the whaling camp. Alexander describes how the survivors looked when they finally reached help.

CASE STUDY 3.1 (Continued)

At three in the afternoon, they arrived at the outskirts of Stromness Station. They had traveled for thirty-six hours without rest. Their bearded faces were black with blubber smoke, and their matted hair, clotted with salt, hung almost to their shoulders. Their filthy clothes were in tatters.... Close to the station they encountered the first humans outside their own party they had set eyes on in nearly eighteen months—two small children, who ran from them in fright. (p. 164)

It would be another 4 months before Shackleton could reach the rest of his crew stranded on the first island. Amazingly, not one member of the party died during the entire 22-month ordeal.

Many qualities made Shackleton an effective leader. He had great strength and physical stature that enabled him to endure extreme conditions and to deal with rebellious followers. He understood the skills and limitations of each expedition member and made the most of each person's abilities. Shackleton was both accessible and firm. He mixed easily with his men but, at the same time, enforced discipline in a fair, evenhanded manner. Whatever the setting, he quickly established a routine and made every effort to maintain the group's morale, planning songfests, lectures, dog races, and other activities for his men.

Alexander suggests that Shackleton's character was the key to his success. In 1909, Shackleton could have been the first to reach the South Pole, but he turned back to save the life of his companions. As the supply of food dwindled, he made expedition member Frank Wild (who would join him on the *Endurance* voyage) eat one of his (Shackleton's) daily ration of four biscuits. "I do not suppose that anyone else in the world can thoroughly realize how much generosity and sympathy was shown by this," the grateful Wild later wrote. "I DO by GOD I shall never forget it."

Shackleton continued to demonstrate concern and compassion for the needs of his followers on his trans-Antarctic voyage. When the most unpopular crew member was laid up with a bad back, the commander let him use his own cabin and brought him tea. He made sure that those of lower rank got the warmest clothes and sleeping bags. During the perilous trip to South Georgia Island, Shackleton kept an eye out for those who were growing weak but never embarrassed anyone by singling him out for special help. If one sailor appeared on the verge of collapse, he made sure that everyone got warm milk or food. Shackleton himself valued optimism above all other virtues. "Optimism," he said, "is true moral courage." Relentless optimism kept him going during the hard times, and he had little patience for those who were anxious about the future.

CASE STUDY 3.1 (Continued)

Alexander sums up the essential quality of Ernest Shackleton's leadership this way:

> At the core of Shackleton's gift for leadership in crisis was an adamantine con-
> viction that quite ordinary individuals were capable of heroic feats if the circum-
> stances required; the weak and the strong could and *must* survive together. The
> mystique that Shackleton acquired as a leader may partly be attributed to the
> fact that he elicited from his men strength and endurance they had never imag-
> ined they possessed; he ennobled them. (p. 194)

Discussion Probes

1. What is the relationship between optimism and courage? Can we be optimistic without courage? Can we be courageous without being optimistic?
2. Generate a list of the virtues demonstrated by Shackleton on the *Endurance* voyage.
3. Do dangerous situations such as polar exploration put a premium on some aspects of
   character that would be less important in other, more routine contexts?
4. Who are our true, modern-day heroes? What character qualities do they possess?
5. What leadership lessons can we draw from the life of Ernest Shackleton?

SOURCE: Alexander, C. (1999). *The Endurance: Shackleton's legendary Antarctic expedition.* New York: Knopf.

those who respond to them "moral heroes." Oskar Schindler was one
such hero who risked his life and fortune to save his Jewish workers during World War II (see the movie featured in Box 3.1). Moral confrontations aren't dangerous, but they do involve risk and call for "moral
champions." Marie Ragghianti emerged as a moral champion when, as
chair of the parole board in Tennessee, she discovered that the governor
and his cronies were selling pardons and reported their illegal activities
to the FBI.

Moral processes consist of *moral projects* and *moral work.* Moral projects are designed to improve ethical behavior during a limited time and
require "moral leaders." A moral leader sets out to reduce corruption in
government, for example, or to improve the working conditions of
migrant farmworkers. Moral work, in contrast to a moral project, does
not have a beginning or end but is continuous. The "moral worker"
strives for ethical consistency throughout life. This moral exemplar
might be the motor vehicle employee who tries to be courteous to

---

BOX 3.1 Leadership at the Movies: *Schindler's List*

Key cast members: Liam Neeson, Ben Kingsley, Ralph Fiennes

Synopsis:

This screen adaptation of Thomas Keneally's novel tells the story of Oskar Schindler, a German industrialist who set up an enamelware factory in Poland during the German occupation in World War II. Schindler (played by Neeson) hoped to get rich but lost his entire fortune while saving the lives of 1,100 of his Jewish workers. Schindler is not your typical moral role model. A hedonist at heart, he drove fast cars, wore fine clothes, drank heavily, and kept mistresses. Yet he found Nazi policies abhorrent and, with the encouragement of his Jewish accountant (Kingsley), risked everything to do good. Many consider this to be director Steven Spielberg's finest film.

Rating: R for mature subject matter

Themes: Moral motivation and courage, sacrifice, altruism, ethical inconsistency, evil, suffering

---

everyone who comes to the DMV office or the neighbor who volunteers to coach youth soccer.

Hart argues that the moral worker is the most important category of moral exemplar. He points out that most of life is lived in the daily valleys, not on the heroic mountain peaks. Because character is developed through time by a series of moral choices and actions, we need examples of those who live consistently moral lives. Those who engage in moral work are better able to handle moral crises. Andre and Magda Trocme, for example, committed themselves to a life of service and nonviolence as pastors in the French village of Le Chambon. When the German occupiers arrived, the Trocmes didn't hesitate to protect the lives of Jewish children and encouraged their congregation to do the same. This small community became an island of refuge to those threatened by the Holocaust.[8]

In the introduction, I argued that we could learn about leadership ethics from fictional characters as well as from real-life persons. Ethics professor C. David Lisman offers several reasons why the ethical models contained in literature can provide a moral education that helps us to nurture our virtues.[9] Lisman focuses on literature, but his observations also apply to other forms of fiction (films, plays, television shows). Fiction, in Lisman's estimation, helps us understand our possibilities and limits. We can try to deny the reality of death, our aging, and factors outside our control. Novels and short stories, however, force us to confront these issues. Literature explores many common human themes such as (a) freedom of choice, (b) moral responsibility, (c) conflict between individual and society, (d) conflict between individual conscience and society's rules, and (e) self-understanding. Fiction writers help us escape our old ways of thinking and acting. Their best works also expand our emotional capacity, enabling us to better respond to the needs of others. In sum, almost any story about leaders, whether real or fictional, can teach us something about ethical and unethical behavior. Moral exemplars can be found in novels, television series, and feature films as well as in news stories, biographies, documentaries, and historical records.

Hardship

Hardship and suffering also play a role in developing character. The leaders we admire the most are often those who have endured the greatest hardships. Nelson Mandela, Vaclav Havel, and Aleksandr Solzhenitsyn served extended prison terms, for instance, and English parliamentarian William Wilberforce worked for 46 years to bring about the elimination of slavery in the British Empire.

Perhaps no other American leader has faced as much hardship as did Abraham Lincoln. He was defeated in several elections before winning the presidency. Because of death threats, he had to slip into Washington, D.C., to take office. He presided over the slaughter of many of his countrymen and women, lost a beloved son, and was ridiculed by Northerners (some in his cabinet) and Southerners alike. All these trials, however, seemed to deepen both his commitment to the Union and his spirituality. His Second Inaugural Address is considered to be one of the finest political and theological statements ever produced by a public official.

Trainers at the Center for Creative Leadership (CCL) have identified hardship as one of the factors contributing to leadership development. Leaders develop the fastest when they encounter situations that stretch or challenge them. Hardships, along with novelty, difficult goals, and conflict, challenge individuals. CCL staffer Russ Moxley believes that hardships differ from other challenging experiences because they are unplanned, are experienced in an intensely personal way, and involve loss:

> At the core of any hardship experience is a sense of loss: of credibility, a sense of control, self-efficacy, a former identity. . . . The loss provokes confrontation with self, and in dealing with loss and the pain accompanying it, learning results.
>
> This sense of loss causes people who usually live in an external world to turn inward. What did I do wrong? Do I not measure up? What could I have done differently? Could I have done anything to prevent it?"[10]

Research conducted by the CCL reveals that leaders experience five common categories of hardship events. Each type of hardship can drive home important lessons.

1. *Business mistakes and failures.* Examples of business hardships include the loss of an important client, failed products and programs, broken relationships, and bankruptcies. These experiences help leaders build stronger working relationships, recognize their limitations, and profit from their mistakes.

2. *Career setbacks.* Missed promotions, unsatisfying jobs, demotions, and firings make up this hardship category. Leaders faced with these events lose (a) control over their careers, (b) their sense of self-efficacy or competence, and (c) their professional identity. Career setbacks function as wake-up calls, providing feedback about weaknesses. They encourage leaders to take more responsibility for managing their careers and to identify the type of work that is most significant to them.

3. *Personal trauma.* CCL investigators were surprised to find that many hardships unrelated to the job teach lasting leadership lessons. Examples of personal trauma include divorce, cancer, death, and difficult children. These experiences, which are a natural part of life, drive home the point that leaders (who are used to being in charge) can't control the world around them. As a result, they may strike a better balance between work and home responsibilities, develop coping strategies, and persist in the face of adversity.

4. *Problem employees.* Troubled workers include those who steal, defraud, can't perform, or perform well only part of the time. In dealing with problem employees, leaders may learn how important it is to hold followers to consistently high standards. They may become more skilled at confronting subordinates.

5. *Downsizing*. Downsizing has much in common with career setbacks, but in this type of hardship, leaders lose their jobs through no fault of their own. Downsizing can help leaders develop coping skills and force them to take stock of their lives and careers. Those carrying out the layoffs can also learn from the experience by gaining a deeper understanding of how their organizations operate and by developing greater empathy for the feelings of followers.

Being exposed to a hardship is no guarantee that you'll learn from the experience. Some ambitious leaders never become reconciled to being passed over for a promotion, for instance, and become embittered and cynical. To maximize the chances that you'll benefit from adversity, recognize that hardships are inevitable. See them as opportunities for leadership development.

Habits

No one has done more to popularize virtue or character ethics than business consultant Stephen Covey. Not only is he the author of the best-selling book *The Seven Habits of Highly Effective People*, but thousands of businesses, nonprofit groups, and government agencies have participated in workshops offered by the Covey Center.[11] Covey argues that effectiveness is based on such character principles as integrity, fairness, service, excellence, and growth. The habits are the tools that enable leaders and followers to develop these characteristics. Covey defines a habit as a combination of knowledge (what to do and why to do it), skill (how to do it), and motivation (wanting to do it). Leadership development is an "inside-out" process that starts within the leader and then moves outward to influence others. The seven habits of effective/ethical leaders are these:

Habit 1: Be proactive. Proactive leaders realize that they can choose how they respond to events. When faced with a career setback, they try to grow from the experience instead of feeling victimized by it. Proactive individuals also take the initiative by opting to attack problems instead of accepting defeat. Their language reflects their willingness to accept, rather than avoid, responsibility. A proactive leader makes such statements as "Let's examine our options" and "I can create a strategic plan." A reactive leader makes comments such as "The organization won't go along with that idea," "I'm too old to change," and "That's just who I am."

Habit 2: Begin with the end in mind. This habit is based on the notion that "all things are created twice." First, we get a mental picture of what we want to accomplish, and then we follow through on our plans. If we're unhappy with the current direction of our lives, we can generate new mental images and goals, a process Covey calls "rescripting." Creating personal and organizational mission statements is one way to identify the results we want and thus control the type of life we create. (I'll talk more about how to create a mission statement in the next section.) Covey urges leaders to center their lives on inner principles such as fairness and human dignity, rather than on such external factors as family, money, friends, or work.

Habit 3: Put first things first. A leader's time should be organized around priorities. Too many leaders spend their days coping with emergencies, mistakenly believing that urgent means important. Meetings, deadlines, and interruptions place immediate demands on their time, but other less pressing activities, such as relationship building and planning, are more important in the long run. Effective leaders carve out time for significant activities by identifying their most important roles, selecting their goals, creating schedules that enable them to reach their objectives, and modifying these plans when necessary. They also know how to delegate tasks and have the courage to say "no" to requests that don't fit their priorities.

Habit 4: Think win-win. Those with a win-win perspective take a cooperative approach to communication, convinced that the best solution benefits both parties. The win-win habit is based on these dimensions: (a) character (integrity, maturity, belief that the needs of everyone can be met); (b) trusting relationships committed to mutual benefit; (c) performance or partnership agreements that spell out conditions and responsibilities; (d) organizational systems that fairly distribute rewards; and (e) principled negotiation processes in which both sides generate possible solutions and then select the one that works best.

Habit 5: Seek first to understand, then to be understood. Ethical leaders put aside their personal concerns to engage in empathetic listening. They seek to understand, not to evaluate, advise, or interpret. Empathetic listening is an excellent way to build a trusting relationship. Covey uses the metaphor of the emotional bank account to illustrate how trust develops. Principled leaders make deposits in the emotional bank account by showing kindness and courtesy, keeping commitments, paying attention to details, and seeking to understand. These strong relational reserves help prevent misunderstandings and make it easier to resolve any problems that do arise.

Habit 6: Synergize. Synergy creates a solution that is greater than the sum of its parts and uses right brain thinking to generate a third, previously undiscovered, alternative. Synergistic, creative solutions are generated in trusting relationships (those with high emotional bank accounts) in which participants value their differences.

Habit 7: Sharpen the saw. Sharpening the saw refers to continual renewal of the physical, mental, social-emotional, and spiritual dimensions of the self. Healthy leaders care for their bodies through exercise, good nutrition, and stress management. They encourage their mental development by reading good literature and by writing thoughtful letters and journal entries. They create significant relationships with others and nurture their inner or spiritual values through study, meditation, and/or time in nature. Continual renewal, combined with the use of the first six habits, creates an upward spiral of character improvement.

Mission Statements

Developing a mission statement is the best way to keep the end or destination in mind. Leaders who cast light have a clear sense of what they hope to accomplish and seek to achieve worthwhile goals. For example, Abraham Lincoln was out to preserve the union, Nelson Mandela wanted to abolish apartheid, and Mother Teresa devoted her whole life to reducing suffering.

Author and organizational consultant Laurie Beth Jones believes that useful mission statements are short (no more than a sentence long), easily understood and communicated, and committed to memory.[12] Developing a personal mission statement, according to Jones, begins with personal assessment. Take a close look at how your family has influenced your values and interests. Identify your strengths and determine what makes you unique (what Jones calls your "unique selling point"). Once you've isolated your gifts and unique features, then examine your motivation. What situations make you excited or angry? Chances are, your mission will be related to those factors that arouse your passion or enthusiasm (teaching, writing, coaching, or selling, for example).

Jones outlines a three-part formula for constructing a mission statement. Start with the phrase "My mission is to" and record three action verbs that best describe you (e.g., accomplish, build, finance, give, discuss). Next, plug in a principle, value, or purpose that you could commit the rest of your life to (joy, service, faith, creativity, justice). Finish by identifying the group or cause that most excites you (real estate, design, sports, women's issues). Your final statement ought to inspire you and should direct all your activities, both on and off the job.

Leadership consultant Juana Bordas offers an alternative method or path for discovering personal leadership purpose based on Native American culture. Early Native Americans discovered their life purposes while on vision quests, a practice that continues today. Vision cairns guide members of some tribes. These stone piles served both as directional markers and as reminders that others have passed this way before. Bordas identifies nine cairns or markers for creating personal purpose.[13]

Cairn 1: Call your purpose; listen for guidance. All of us have to be silent to listen to our intuition. Periodically, you will need to withdraw from the noise of everyday life and reflect on such questions as "What am I meant to do?" and "How can I best serve?"

Cairn 2: Find a sacred place. A sacred place is a quiet place of reflection. It can be officially designated as sacred (a church or meditation garden, for example) or merely be a spot that encourages contemplation, such as a stream, park, or favorite chair.

Cairn 3: See time as continuous; begin with the child and move with the present. Our past has a great impact on where we'll head in the future. Patterns of behavior are likely to continue. Bordas suggests that you should examine the impact of your (a) family composition, (b) gender, (c) geography, (d) cultural background, and (e) generational influences. A significant purpose will be anchored in the past but will remain responsive to current conditions such as diversity, globalization, and technological change.

Cairn 4: Identify special skills and talents; accept imperfections. Take inventory by examining your major activities and jobs and evaluating your strengths. For example, how are your people skills? Technical knowledge? Communication abilities? Consider how you might further develop your aptitudes and abilities. Also take stock of your significant failures. What did they teach you about your limitations? What did you learn from them?

Cairn 5: Trust your intuition. Sometimes, we need to act on our hunches and emotions. You may decide to turn down a job that doesn't "feel right," for instance, to accept a position that seems to be a better fit.

Cairn 6: Open the door when opportunity knocks. Be ready to respond to opportunities that are out of your control, such as a new job assignment or a request to speak or write. Ask yourself if this possibility will better prepare you for leadership or fit in with what you're trying to do in life.

Cairn 7: Find your passion and make it happen. Passion energizes us for leadership and gives us stamina. Discover your passion by imagining the following scenarios: If you won the lottery, what would you still do? How would you spend your final 6 months on earth? What would sustain you for a hundred more years?

Cairn 8: Write your life story; imagine a great leader. Turn your life into a story that combines elements of reality and fantasy. Imagine yourself as an effective leader and carry your story out into the future. What challenges did you overcome? What dreams did you fulfill? How did you reach your final destination?

Cairn 9: Honor your legacy, one step at a time. Your purpose is not static but will evolve and expand through time. If you're a new leader, you're likely to exert limited influence. That influence will expand as you develop your knowledge and skills. You may manage only a couple of individuals now, but in a few years, you may be responsible for an entire department or division.

Values

If a mission statement identifies our final destination, then our values serve as a moral compass to guide us on our journey. Values provide a frame of reference, helping us set priorities and determine right or wrong. There are all sorts of values. For example, I value fuel economy (I like spending less on gas), so I drive a small, fuel-efficient pickup truck. Ethical decision making, however, is primarily concerned with identifying and implementing moral values. Moral values are directly related to judgments about what's appropriate or inappropriate behavior. I value honesty, for instance, so I choose not to lie. I value privacy, so I condemn Internet retailers who gather personal information about me without my permission.

There are two ways to identify or clarify the values you hold. You can generate a list from scratch or rate a list of values supplied by someone else. If brainstorming a list of important values seems a daunting task, you might try the following exercise developed by James Kouzes and Barry Posner. The credo memo asks you to spell out the important values that underlie your philosophy of leadership.

Imagine that your organization has afforded you the chance to take a six-month sabbatical, all expenses paid. You will be going to a beautiful island where the average temperature is about eighty degrees Fahrenheit during the day. The sun shines in a brilliant sky, with a few wisps of clouds. A gentle breeze cools the island down in the evening, and a light rain clears the air. You wake up in the morning to the smell of tropical flowers.

You may not take any work along on this sabbatical. And you will not be permitted to communicate to anyone at your office or plant—not by letter, phone, fax, e-mail, or other means. There will be just you, a few good books, some music, and your family or a friend.

But before you depart, those with whom you work need to know something. They need to know the principles that you believe should guide their actions in your absence. They need to understand the values and beliefs that you think should steer their decision making and action taking.

You are permitted no long reports, however. Just a one-page memorandum.

If given this opportunity, what would you write on your one-page credo memo? Take out one piece of paper, and write that memo.[14]

Examples of values that have been included in credo memos include "operate as a team," "listen to one another," "celebrate successes," "seize the initiative," "trust your judgment," and "strive for excellence." These values can be further clarified by engaging in dialogue with coworkers. Many discussions in organizations (how to select subcontractors, when to fire someone, how to balance the needs of various stakeholders) have an underlying values component. Listen for the principles that shape your opinions and the opinions of others.

Working with a list of values can also be useful. Psychologist Milton Rokeach developed the most widely used value system.[15] He divided moral values into two subcategories. *Instrumental values* are a means to an end. Diligence and patience are valuable, for example, because they enable us to reach difficult goals such as completing a degree program or remodeling a house. *Terminal values* generally reflect our lifelong aspirations, such as becoming wise, experiencing happiness, or living comfortably. They stand by themselves. Rokeach's list of instrumental and terminal values is found in Box 3.2. Take a moment and rank the items on both lists.

Comparing our responses with other individuals and groups opens the way for additional dialogue about priorities. We may discover that we don't fit in as well as we would like with the rest of the group and decide to leave or work for change. (More on the importance of shared

---

BOX 3.2 Instrumental and Terminal Values

Instructions

Rank the values on each list from 1 (most important) to 18 (least important) to you. Rate the instrumental values first and then rank order the terminal values. You will end up with two lists. A low ranking doesn't mean that a value is insignificant; it means only that the item is less important to you than other, more highly rated values.

Terminal Values

Freedom (independence, free choice)
Self-respect (self-esteem)
A sense of accomplishment (lasting contribution)
Mature love (sexual and spiritual intimacy)
An exciting life (activity)
A comfortable life (prosperity)
Family security (taking care of loved ones)
True friendship (close companionship)
Social recognition (respect, admiration)
Wisdom (an understanding of life)
Happiness (contentedness)
Inner harmony (freedom from inner conflict)
Equality (brotherhood, equal opportunity for all)
A world at peace (free of war and conflict)
A world of beauty (beauty of nature and art)
Pleasure (an enjoyable, leisurely life)
National security (protection from attack)
Salvation (saved, eternal life)

Instrumental Values

Loving (affection, tenderness)
Independent (self-reliant, self-sufficient)
Capable (competent, effective)
Broad-minded (open-minded)
Intellectual (intelligent, reflective)
Honest (sincere, truthful)
Responsible (dependable, reliable)
Ambitious (hard-working, aspiring)
Imaginative (daring, creative)
Helpful (working for the welfare of others)
Forgiving (willing to pardon others)
Self-controlled (restrained, self-disciplined)
Logical (consistent, rational)
Courageous (standing up for your own beliefs)
Cheerful (light-hearted, joyful)
Polite (courteous, well-mannered)
Obedient (dutiful, respectful)
Clean (neat, tidy)

SOURCE: Reprinted with the permission of The Free Press, a Division of Simon & Schuster, Inc., from *The nature of human values* (p. 28), by Milton Rokeach. Copyright © 1973 by The Free Press.

BOX 3.3 Comparing Terminal Values

Judge surveyed 91 CEOs (all males, average age 54) using Rokeach's values survey. He found that the executives, representing 57 industries, had a significantly different set of terminal values than a sample of adult Americans from the 1960s (see the chart below). The instrumental values of the management executives, however, were virtually identical to the broader sample. The only difference? The CEOs rated courage more highly than other U.S. residents.

Comparison of CEOs' Terminal Values With
American Adults' Terminal Values

Terminal Value	CEOs' Composite Rank (N = 91)	Adult Americans' Rank[a] (N = 1,409)
Sense of accomplishment	1	10
Family security	2	12
Self-respect	3	5
Salvation	4	8
Happiness	5	4
Wisdom	6	6
Freedom	7	3
An exciting life	8	18
A comfortable life	9	9
Mature love	10	14
True friendship	11	11
Inner harmony	12	13
A world at peace	13	1
National security	14	2
Social recognition	15	16
Equality	16	7
A world of beauty	17	15
Pleasure	18	17

SOURCE: Judge, W. A. (1999). *The leader's shadow.* Thousand Oaks, CA: Sage, p. 68. Used by permission.
a. Based on a national sample of American adults during the mid-1960s (Rokeach, 1973).

organizational values in Chapter 9.) Researchers can also use a list of values to determine if different classes of people have different priorities and how values change through time. University of Tennessee management professor William Judge compared the values of CEOs with those of a cross section of the U.S. population from the 1960s. His results are reported in Box 3.3.

Some well-meaning writers and consultants make values the end-all of ethical decision making. They assume that groups will prosper if they develop a set of lofty, mutually shared values. As we saw earlier, however, having worthy values doesn't mean that individuals, groups, or organizations will live by these principles. Other factors—time pressures, faulty assumptions, corrupt systems—undermine their influence. Values, although critical, have to be translated into action. Further, our greatest struggles come from choosing between two good values. Many corporate leaders value both customer service and product quality, but what do they do when reaching one of these goals means sacrificing the other? Pushing to get a product shipped to satisfy a customer may force the manufacturing division into cutting corners to meet the deadline. Resolving dilemmas such as these takes more than values clarification; we also need some standards for determining ethical priorities. With that in mind, I'll identify ethical decision-making principles in Chapters 5 and 6. But first, we need to confront one final inner monster—evil—in Chapter 4.

▣ Implications and Applications

- Our inner fears and insecurities can't be eliminated, but they can be managed through development of positive qualities or virtues (integrity, perseverance, courage) that make up a moral character.

- Strive for consistency, but don't be surprised by contradictions in your character or in the character of others. Become more tolerant of yourself and other leaders.

- Moral action is the product of sensitivity, judgment, motivation, and implementation. Use these components to pinpoint your ethical strengths and weaknesses.

- Never underestimate the power of a good story. Be on the lookout for real and fictional ethical role models.

- Hardships are an inevitable part of life and leadership. The sense of loss associated with these events can provide important feedback, spur self-inspection, encourage the development of coping strategies, force you to reorder your priorities, and nurture your compassion.

- Adopting habits can speed the development of character. Seek to be proactive, begin with the end in mind, organize around priorities, strive for cooperation, listen for understanding, develop synergistic solutions, and engage in continual self-renewal.

- Having an ultimate destination will encourage you to stay on your ethical track. Develop a personal mission statement that reflects your strengths and passions. Use your values as a moral compass to keep you from losing your way.

□ For Further Exploration, Challenge, and Self-Assessment

1. Can the private and public morals of leaders be separated? Try to reach a consensus on this question in a group.
2. Brainstorm a list of moral exemplars. What does it take to qualify for your list? How would you classify these role models according to the types described in the chapter?
3. Create your own list of hardships common to leaders. How does it compare with the one provided by the Center for Creative Leadership? What hardships have you faced, and what have you learned from them?
4. Examine the role that hardship has played in the life of a prominent leader. Summarize your findings in an oral presentation and/or research paper.
5. Rate yourself on each of the seven habits of effective people and develop a plan for addressing your weaknesses. Explore the habits further through reading and training seminars.
6. Develop a personal mission statement using the guidelines provided by Jones and/or Bordas.
7. How do your terminal values compare with those reported in Box 3.3? Are you comfortable with your rankings? Why or why not?
8. Complete the credo memo exercise on page 65 if you haven't already done so. Encourage others in your work group organization to do the same; compare your statements. Use this as an opportunity to dialogue about values.

CASE STUDY 3.2

Chapter End Case: "Chainsaw" Al Dunlap

During the 1990s, Al Dunlap may have been the most admired and the most hated CEO in America. Dunlap earned the name "Chainsaw" for aggressively cutting costs at troubled companies. He didn't shy away from tough decisions but would close plants, lay off employees, and sell assets to improve the bottom line. At the Lily-Tulip disposable cup and plate company, for example, he cut 20% of the staff and half the management team along with 40% of the firm's suppliers. At Scott Paper, Dunlap laid off more than 11,000 workers, deferred maintenance costs, slashed the research budget, and eliminated donations to charity. These cost reductions drove the stock price up 225% and made Scott Paper an attractive takeover candidate. When Kimberly-Clark bought the firm in 1995, Dunlap pocketed $100 million through the sale of his stock options. Dunlap then moved to the Sunbeam Corporation in 1996 and started another round of cutbacks. He hoped to once again reap millions by boosting the company's stock value and then selling out.

The media and Wall Street investors loved Al Dunlap. He was readily available to the press, and his forthright style made him a good interview. Chainsaw became the "poster child" of shareholder capitalism. Shareholder capitalists believe that publicly held corporations serve the interests of only one group—stockholders. Other constituencies, such as customers, employees, and local communities, don't matter. According to Dunlap, "Stakeholders are total rubbish. It's the shareholders who own the company" (Byrne, 1999, pp. xiv-xv). He made investors, particularly the large investors who sat on the boards of Scott and Sunbeam, lots of money.

Company insiders had an entirely different opinion of Dunlap. Those who lost their jobs despised him, whereas those who survived the cuts viewed him as a tyrant. Remaining employees had to work long hours to reach impossible production and sales goals. *Business Week* writer and author John Byrne (1999) offers this description of life under Dunlap.

> Working on the front lines of a company run by Albert Dunlap was like being at war. The pressure was brutal, the hours exhausting, and the casualties high. Dunlap and his consultants had imposed such unrealistic goals on the company that virtually everyone understood he was engaged in a short-term exercise to pretty up the business for a quick sale.
>
> By sheer brutality, he began putting excruciating pressure on those who reported to him, who in turn passed that intimidation down the line. It went beyond the ordinary pressure to do well in a corporation. People were told, explicitly and implicitly, that either they hit the number or another person

CASE STUDY 3.2 (Continued)

would be found to do it for them. Their livelihood hung on making numbers that were not makeable.

At Sunbeam Dunlap created a culture of misery, an environment of moral ambiguity, indifferent to everything except the stock price. He did not lead by intellect or by vision, but by fear and intimidation. (pp. 153-154)

Dunlap's dream of selling Sunbeam and cashing in began to collapse when the firm's stock price went too high to interest corporate buyers. Shortly thereafter, the firm began falling short of its income projections. The company inflated 1997 sales figures by convincing dealers to sign up for merchandise that was then stored in Sunbeam warehouses. This maneuver allowed the corporation to count these "sales" as immediate income before customers had even paid for the products. By 1998, large accounts such as Wal-Mart and Costco were glutted with inventory, and this accounting trick no longer worked. Sunbeam couldn't reverse the slide because Dunlap had fired essential employees, eliminated profitable plants and product lines, and alienated vendors. Share prices then dropped dramatically, and Dunlap was forced out. Following his ouster, the company defaulted on a major loan payment, and the Securities and Exchange Commission began to audit the company's books.

Chainsaw Al had few of the virtues we associate with high moral character. To his credit, he was decisive, hardworking, and loyal to a few business associates and subordinates. He was, however, also bullying, angry, abusive (to family members as well as employees), egotistical, sensitive to the slightest criticism, vengeful, inconsistent, uncaring, and cowardly (he rarely fired anyone himself).

Working for Al could be hell on earth. Why, then, was he so successful, and why did people continue to work for him? As I noted earlier, he appeared to get results (at least in the short term) and got lots of favorable attention in the press. If he hadn't fallen short of earnings projections, he probably would still be at Sunbeam despite his shabby treatment of employees and other stakeholder groups. High-level executives continued to work for Sunbeam in hopes of getting rich and out of fear. They would make millions from their stock options if the company succeeded and were afraid to stand up to the boss. Said one vice president who had often considered quitting: "But it was like being in an abusive relationship. You just didn't know how to get out of it."

Summing up the career of Chainsaw Al, Byrne concludes,

At Sunbeam, he eluded all the safeguards of a public corporation: a well-meaning board of directors, independent, outside auditors, and an army of honest and talented executives. Every system depends on people, people who will say no even

---

CASE STUDY 3.2 (Continued)

when faced with the threat of losing a job or a business. Dunlap worked so hard at creating fear, dependence, and guilt that no one dared to defy him—until it was too late. It is a lesson no one should ever forget. (p. 354)

Discussion Probes

1. How important are investors compared with other stakeholders?
2. How do you define success? Was Al Dunlap successful according to your definition?
3. What responsibility should followers share for the actions of Dunlap? How would you evaluate the character of those who decided to stay and work for him?
4. How much blame do you place on the company directors who hired Dunlap and were supposed to oversee his activities?
5. How can we prevent future Al Dunlaps from taking over companies and other organizations?
6. What leadership lessons do you gain from the rise and fall of Chainsaw Al?

Source: Byrne, J. A. (1999). *Chainsaw: The notorious career of Al Dunlap in the era of profit-at-any-price.* New York: HarperBusiness.

Notes

1. Johannesen, R. L. (1999). *Ethics in human communication* (4th ed.). Prospect Heights, IL: Waveland, Ch. 1.

2. Johannesen, R. L. (1991). Virtue ethics, character, and political communication. In R E. Denton (Ed.), *Ethical dimensions of political communication* (pp. 69-90). New York: Praeger.

3. Kouzes, J. M., & Posner, B. Z. (1993). *Credibility: How leaders gain and lose it, why people demand it.* San Francisco: Jossey-Bass.

4. My discussion of virtue ethics draws from a variety of sources, including

Alderman, H. (1997). By virtue of a virtue. In D. Statman (Ed.), *Virtue ethics* (pp. 145-164). Washington, DC: Georgetown University Press.

Hart, D. K. (1994). Administration and the ethics of virtue. In T. C. Cooper (Ed.), *The handbook of administrative ethics* (pp. 107-123). New York: Marcel Dakker.

Luke, J. S. (1994). Character and conduct in the public service. In T. C. Cooper (Ed.), *The handbook of administrative ethics* (pp. 391-412). New York: Marcel Dakker.

Meilander, G. (1986). Virtue in contemporary religious thought. In R. J. Neihaus (Ed.), *Virtue: Public and private* (pp. 7-30). Grand Rapids, MI: Eerdmans.

Solomon, R. (1988). Internal objections to virtue ethics. *Midwest Studies in Philosophy, 8,* 428-441.

5. Rest, J. (1986). *Moral development: Advances in research and theory.* New York: Praeger; Rest, J. R. (1994). Background: Theory and research. In J. R. Rest & D. Narvaez

(Eds.), *Moral development in the professions: Psychology and applied ethics* (pp. 1-25). Hillsdale, NJ: Lawrence Erlbaum; Rest, J. R. (1993). Research on moral judgment in college students. In A. Garrod (Ed.), *Approaches to moral development* (pp. 210-211). New York: Teachers College Press.

    6. MacIntyre, A. (1984). *After virtue: A study in moral theory* (2nd ed.). Notre Dame, IN: University of Notre Dame Press; Hauerwas, S. (1981). *A community of character*. Notre Dame, IN: University of Notre Dame Press.

    7. Hart, D. K. (1992). The moral exemplar in an organizational society. In T. L. Cooper & N. D. Wright (Eds.), *Exemplary public administrators: Character and leadership in government* (pp. 9-29). San Francisco: Jossey-Bass.

    8. Hallie, P. (1979). *Lest innocent blood be shed: The story of the village of Le Chambon and how goodness happened there.* New York: Harper & Row.

    9. Lisman, C. D. (1996). *The curricular integration of ethics: Theory and practice.* Westport, CT: Praeger.

    10. Moxley, R. S. (1998). Hardships. In C. D. McCauley, R. S. Moxley, & E. Van Velsor (Eds.), *Handbook of leadership development* (pp. 194-213). San Francisco: Jossey-Bass, p. 194.

    11. Covey, S. (1989). *The seven habits of highly effective people.* New York: Simon & Schuster.

    12. Jones, L. B. (1996). *The path: Creating your mission statement for work and for life.* New York: Hyperion.

    13. Bordas, J. (1995). Becoming a servant-leader: The personal development path. In L. Spears (Ed.), *Reflections on leadership* (pp. 149-160). New York: John Wiley.

    14. Kouzes, J. M., & Posner, B. Z. (1995). *Credibility: How leaders gain and lose it, why people demand it.* San Francisco: Jossey-Bass.

    15. Rokeach, M. (1973). *The nature of human values.* New York: Free Press.

    16. Judge, W. (1999). *The leader's shadow: Exploring and developing executive character.* Thousand Oaks, CA: Sage.

4

 Combating Evil

Evil, in whatever intellectual framework, is by definition a monster.
—Essayist Lance Morrow

Without forgiveness there is no future.
—South African Archbishop Desmond Tutu

◻ What's Ahead

This chapter wrestles with the most dangerous monster of all—evil. The first section surveys some of the forms or faces of evil. The second section examines the role of forgiveness in breaking cycles of evil. The third section probes the relationship between spirituality and leadership, highlighting spiritual development and spiritual disciplines.

◻ The Faces of Evil

We can't combat evil until we first understand our opponent. Contemporary Western definitions of evil emphasize its destructiveness.[1] Evil inflicts pain and suffering, deprives innocent people of their humanity, and creates feelings of hopelessness and despair. The ultimate product of evil is death. Evil destroys self-esteem, physical and emotional well-being, relationships, communities, and nations.

We can gain some important insights into the nature of evil by looking at the various forms or faces it displays. In this section, I'll introduce five perspectives on evil and then talk about how each approach can help us better deal with this powerful, destructive force.

Evil as Dreadful Pleasure

University of Maryland political science professor C. Fred Alford defines evil as a combination of dread and pleasure. Alford recruited 60 respondents from a variety of ages and backgrounds to talk about their experiences with evil. He discovered that people experience evil as a deep sense of uneasiness, "the dread of being human, vulnerable, alone in the universe and doomed to die."[2] They do evil when, instead of coming to grips with their inner darkness, they try to get rid of it by making others feel "dreadful." Inflicting this pain is enjoyable. Part of the pleasure comes from being in charge, of being the victimizer instead of the victim.

Evil as Deception

Psychiatrist Scott Peck identifies evil as a form of narcissism or self-absorption.[3] Mentally healthy adults submit themselves to something beyond themselves such as God or love or excellence. Submission to a greater power encourages them to obey their consciences. Evil people, on the other hand, refuse to submit and try to control others instead. They consider themselves above reproach and project their shortcomings, attacking anyone who threatens their self-concepts. Evil individuals are consumed with keeping up appearances. Peck calls them "the people of the lie" because they deceive themselves and others in hopes of projecting a righteous image. Peck believes that truly evil people are more likely to live in our neighborhoods than in our jails. They generally hide their true natures and appear to be normal and successful. Inmates, on the other hand, land in prison because they've been morally inconsistent or stupid.

Evil as Bureaucracy

The 20th century was the bloodiest period in history. More than 100 million people died as the direct or indirect result of wars, genocide, and other violence. According to public administration professors Guy Adams and Danny Balfour, the combination of science and technology made the 1900s so destructive.[4] Scientific and technological developments (tanks, airplanes, chemical warfare, nuclear weapons) made killing highly efficient. At the same time, belief in technological progress encouraged government officials to take a rational approach to problems. The combination of these factors produced *administrative evil*. In administrative evil, ordinary people commit heinous crimes while carrying out their daily tasks. Balfour and Adams argue that the true nature of administrative evil is masked or hidden from participants. Officials are rarely asked to engage in evil; instead they inflict pain and suffering while fulfilling their job responsibilities.

The Holocaust provides the most vivid example of administrative evil in action. Extermination camps would not have been possible without the willing cooperation of thousands of civil servants engaged in such functions as tax collection, municipal government, and running the social security system. These duties may seem morally neutral, but in carrying them out, public officials condemned millions to death. Government authorities defined who was undesirable and then seized their assets. Administrators managed the ghettos, built concentration camp latrines, and employed slave labor. Even the railway authority did its part. The SS had to pay for each prisoner shipped by rail to the death camps. Railroad officials billed the SS at third-class passenger rates (one way) for adult prisoners with discounts for children. Guards were charged round-trip fares. Adams and Balfour note, "It was in this routine, matter-of-fact way that whole communities were transported to their deaths."[5]

Evil as Sanctioned Destruction

Social scientists Nevitt Sanford and Craig Comstock believe that widespread evil occurs when victimizers are given permission or sanction to attack groups that have been devalued or dehumanized.[6] Sanctions can be overt (a direct statement or order) or disguised (a hint, praise for others engaging in aggressive behavior). Once given, sanctions open the door to oppression because targeted groups no longer enjoy the protections given to the rest of society. American history is filled with examples of devalued peoples. Native Americans were targeted for extinction; African Americans were routinely lynched for, among other reasons, public entertainment; Chinese laborers were denied citizenship. (For a closer look at how sanctioned behavior contributed to a particularly heinous act, see Case Study 4.2 on My Lai at the end of this chapter.)

Evil as a Choice

Any discussion of good and evil must consider the role of human choice. Just how much freedom we have is a matter of debate, but a number of scholars have argued that we become good or evil through a series of small, incremental decisions. In other words, we never remain neutral but are moving toward one pole or the other. Medieval scholar C. S. Lewis draws on the image of a road to illustrate this point.[7] On a journey, we make a decision about which direction to take every time we come to a fork in the road. We face a similar series of decisions throughout our lives. We can't correct poor decisions by continuing on but must go back to the fork and take the other path.

Psychologist Erich Fromm makes the same argument as Lewis. Only those who are very good or very bad have no choice; the rest of us do. Each choice we make, however, reduces our options.

> Each step in life which increases my self-confidence, my integrity, my courage, my conviction also increases my capacity to choose the desirable alternative, until eventually it becomes more difficult for me to choose the undesirable rather than the desirable action. On the other hand, each act of surrender and cowardice weakens me, opens the path for more acts of surrender, and eventually freedom is lost. Between the extreme when I can no longer do a wrong act and the other extreme when I have lost my freedom to right action, there are innumerable degrees of freedom of choice. In the practice of life the degree of freedom to choose is different at any given moment. If the degree of freedom to choose the good is great, it needs less effort to choose the good. If it is small, it takes a great effort, help from others, and favorable circumstances.[8]

Fromm uses the story of Israel's exodus from ancient Egypt to illustrate what happens when leaders make a series of evil choices. Moses repeatedly asks Pharaoh to let his people go, but the Egyptian ruler turns down every request. Eventually, the king's heart is "hardened," and he and his army are destroyed.

Facing Evil

Each of the perspectives described above provides insights into how we as leaders can come to grips with evil. The dreadful pleasure approach highlights both the origins of evil and the attraction of doing evil, forcing us to examine our motivations. We need to ask ourselves: Am I projecting my insecurities onto others? Am I punishing subordinates because of their poor performance or because exercising coercive power makes me feel strong? Am I making a legitimate request or merely demonstrating that I have the authority to control another person?

The evil as deception viewpoint makes it clear that people aren't always as they seem. Evil individuals appear, on the surface, to be successful and well-adjusted. In reality, they exert tremendous energy keeping up appearances. Deceit and defensiveness can serve as warning signs. If we routinely lie to protect our images, refuse constructive feedback, and always blame others, we may be engaged in evil. The same may be true of other leaders and followers who display these behaviors. Peck, like Parker Palmer, believes that to master our inner demons, we must first name them. Once we've identified these tendencies, we can then begin to deal with them by examining our will. We should determine if we're willing to submit to a positive force (an ideal, authority) that is greater than we are. Peck urges us to respond to the destructive acts of others with love. Instead of attacking evildoers, we can react with goodness and thereby "absorb" the power of evil.

The administrative evil perspective introduces a new type of evil, one based on technology and logic. Modern evil has greater capacity for destruction, and its face may be masked or hidden from those who participate in it. We need to be aware of how our activities contribute to good or evil. Claiming that we were "just carrying out orders" (as did Nazi war criminal Adolf Eichmann) is no excuse.

The evil as sanction approach should alert us to the danger of dehumanizing any segment of the population. Language is one of the evildoers' most powerful tools. It is much easier to persecute others who have been labeled as "nerds," "pigs," "scum," "Moslem extremists," or "tree huggers." We need to challenge and eliminate these labels (whether we or others use them). Also, be alert to disguised sanctions. If you don't respond to racial slurs, for example, you legitimize these behaviors and encourage future attacks.

The final perspective, evil as a choice, puts the ethical burden squarely on our shoulders. Group and organizational pressures may contribute to our wrongdoing. We make the decision, however, to participate in evil acts. Further, the choices we make now will limit our options in the future. Every moral decision, no matter how insignificant it seems at the time, has lasting consequences.

◻ Making a Case for Forgiveness

Breaking the Cycle of Evil

Scott Peck is not alone in arguing that loving acts can overcome evil. A growing number of social scientists believe that forgiving instead of retaliating can prevent or break cycles of evil. In a cycle of evil, aggressive acts provoke retaliation followed by more aggression. When these destructive patterns characterize relations between ethnic groups (Turks vs. Armenians, Serbs vs. Croatians), they can continue for hundreds of years. Courageous leaders can end retaliatory cycles, however, through dramatic acts of reconciliation. Former Egypt Prime Minister Anwar Sadat engaged in one such conciliatory gesture when he traveled to Jerusalem to further the peace process with Israel. Pope John Paul II went to the jail cell of his would-be assassin to offer forgiveness. Archbishop Desmond Tutu and Nelson Mandela prevented a bloodbath in South Africa by creating the Truth and Reconciliation Commission. This body, composed of both blacks and whites, investigates crimes committed during the apartheid era and allows offenders to confess their guilt and ask for pardon.

The concept of forgiving evildoers is controversial. (See Case Study 4.1 for a closer look at some of the issues raised by forgiveness.) Skeptics worry that guilty parties will get off without paying for their crimes, that forgiveness is impossible in some situations, that forgiveness can't be offered until after the offender asks for it, and that no leader has the right to offer forgiveness on behalf of other victims. Each of these concerns is valid. You will have to decide if forgiveness is an appropriate response to

CASE STUDY 4.1

To Forgive or Not to Forgive?

Like many other European Jews, Simon Wiesenthal endured unimaginable suffering at the hands of the Nazis. Eighty-nine of his relatives perished in the Holocaust, and Wiesenthal himself spent the war in a concentration camp. Hunger, torture, and death were his constant companions.

One day, a nurse called Wiesenthal away from his work detail, which was removing rubbish from a hospital, to hear the confession of an SS officer named Karl who had been severely wounded by an artillery shell. Blind and near death, Karl told how he had rejected his Catholic upbringing to join the Hitler youth. Later, he volunteered for the SS. Posted to the Russian front, he participated in a massacre in a small town named Dnepropetrovsk. Jews from the area were crammed into a house that was set on fire. All who tried to escape, including small children, were shot. This incident haunted Karl, and now he wanted to confess his crime to Wiesenthal as a representative of the Jewish race. He begged for forgiveness so that he could die in peace. Wiesenthal pondered the request and then left without saying a word.

Prisoner Wiesenthal had mixed feelings about his decision, asking companions if he had made the right choice. He went to Karl's home after the war ended and met Karl's mother, who still believed that her son was a "good boy." To protect Karl's reputation, Wiesenthal did not tell her that her son had become a murderer. Later, Wiesenthal would become the world's most famous Nazi hunter, bringing more than 1,100 war criminals to justice.

Wiesenthal describes his encounter with the SS soldier in *The Sunflower*. In the first half of the book, he recounts the story. In the second half, he asks 42 theologians, political leaders, writers, Holocaust survivors, and others what they would have done in his place. Must we forgive when asked? Can we forgive on behalf of other people? Does forgiveness diminish the seriousness of the crime? What does forgiveness do to the victim? To the perpetrator?

As you might imagine, responses to this moral dilemma vary widely. Some respondents argue that forgiveness is a form of "cheap grace" that diminishes the enormity of the crime and the suffering of the victims. Even God can't forgive some atrocities, they argue. Others believe that only the offended can forgive the offenders; no one can offer mercy on their behalf. Still others claim that genuine remorse deserves forgiveness. They believe that mercy in the face of honest repentance is the way to break the cycle of retribution and to help victims regain control over their lives.

What would you have done had you been in Wiesenthal's place? Why?

evil deeds. Before you make that determination, however, I want to describe the forgiveness process and identify some of the benefits that come from extending mercy to others.

The Forgiveness Process

There are lots of misconceptions about what it means to forgive another person or group of people. According to Robert Enright, professor of educational psychology and president of the International Forgiveness Institute at the University of Wisconsin, forgiveness is *not* the following:[9]

- Forgetting past wrongs to "move on"
- Excusing or condoning bad, damaging behavior
- Reducing the severity of offenses
- Offering a legal pardon
- Pretending to forgive to wield power over another person
- Ignoring the offender
- Dropping our anger and becoming emotionally neutral

Enright and his colleagues define forgiving as "a willingness to abandon one's right to resentment, negative judgment, and indifferent behavior toward one who unjustly injured us, while fostering the undeserved qualities of compassion, generosity, and even love toward him or her."[10] This definition recognizes that (a) the wronged party has been unjustly treated (slandered, betrayed, imprisoned); (b) the offended person willingly chooses forgiveness regardless of the offender's response; (c) forgiving involves emotions, thoughts, and behavior; and (d) forgiveness is a process that takes place through time.

Enright and his colleagues offer a four-stage model to help people forgive. In the first phase—*uncovering*—a victim may initially deny that a problem exists. When the individual does acknowledge the hurt, however, he or she may experience intense feelings of anger, shame, and betrayal. The victim invests a lot of psychic energy in rehashing the offense and comparing his or her condition with that of the offender. Feeling permanently damaged, the individual may believe that life is unfair.

BOX 4.1 Leadership Ethics at the Movies:
Dead Man Walking

Key cast members: Susan Sarandon, Sean Penn

Synopsis:

Based on the book of the same name, this film is the sobering story of
Sister Helen Prejean, a nun in Louisiana who becomes the spiritual
adviser for an inmate on death row. The condemned man (Penn) has
been convicted of the brutal torture and murder of two teenagers.
Sister Prejean, played by Sarandon (who won an Oscar for her performance), ministers to Penn and his family at the same time that she tries
to understand the needs of the victims' parents. Penn finally admits
his guilt on the way to his lethal injection. One set of parents appears
ready to consider forgiveness, but the other couple remains locked in
hate. "Dead man walking" is what the guards call out as they escort an
inmate to the death chamber.

Rating: R for strong subject matter

Themes: Evil, forgiveness, personal responsibility, spirituality, the
death penalty, compassion versus justice, courage

During the second phase—*decision*—the injured party recognizes
that he or she is paying a high price for dwelling on the injury, considers
the possibility of forgiveness, and commits him- or herself to forgiving.

Forgiveness is accomplished in stage three—*work*. The wronged
party tries to understand (not condone) the victimizer's background
and motivation. He or she may experience empathy and compassion for
the offender. Absorbing pain is the key to this stage. The forgiver decides
to endure suffering rather than pass it on, thereby breaking the cycle of
evil. Viewed in this light, forgiveness is a gift of mercy to the wrongdoer.
(For a closer look at the hard work of forgiveness, see the movie described in Box 4.1.)

The fourth and final phase—*deepening*—describes the outcomes of
forgiving. A forgiver may find deeper meaning in suffering, realize his
or her need for forgiveness, and come to a greater appreciation for support groups (friends, congregations, classmates). In the end, the person
offering forgiveness may develop a new purpose in life and find peace.

The four-stage model has been used successfully with a variety of audiences: survivors of incest, inmates, college students deprived of parental love, and older women suffering from depression. In each case, forgivers experienced significant healing. Enright emphasizes that personal benefits should be a by-product, not the motivation, for forgiving. Nonetheless, forgiveness can pay significant psychological, physical, and relational dividends.[11] Those who forgive are released from resentments and experience less depression and anxiety. Overall, they enjoy a higher sense of well-being. By releasing their grudges, forgivers experience better physical health. Reducing anger, hostility, and hopelessness lowers the risks of heart attack and high blood pressure while increasing the body's resistance to disease. Acting mercifully toward transgressors also maintains relationships between friends and family members.

The social-scientific study of forgiveness is relatively recent, but results so far are extremely encouraging. Forgiving does appear to absorb or defuse evil. If this is the case, then as leaders we should practice forgiveness when treated unjustly by followers, supervisors, peers, or outsiders. We may even need to follow the example of Anwar Sadat and Nelson Mandela and offer forgiveness on behalf of the group, hoping to bring reconciliation with a long-standing enemy. When we give offense ourselves, we will need to apologize and ask for mercy.

In sum, I believe that forgiveness is one of a leader's most powerful weapons in the fight against evil. To use the central metaphor of this text, forgiving is one of the ways that leaders cast light, rather than shadow. We must face our inner darkness, particularly our resentments and hostilities, to offer genuine forgiveness. By forgiving, we short-circuit or break the shadowy, destructive cycles that poison groups, organizations, and societies. Offering forgiveness brightens our lives by reducing our anxiety and enhancing our sense of well-being.

▣ Spiritual Resources

Spirituality and Leadership

Coming to grips with evil is hard work. We must always be on the lookout for evil whatever form it takes, continually evaluate our motivations and choices, and make a conscious effort to forgive by reshaping our thoughts, emotions, and behaviors. All the elements introduced in the last chapter—virtues, habits, hardships, purpose, and values—can equip us for these tasks. Many leaders also look to spirituality for help when addressing the shadow side of leadership. Spirituality has to do with our deepest yearnings and emotions as well as our connection to larger forces such as God and nature. Religion professor Clark Roof offers this definition: "Spirituality gives expression to the yearning that is in us; it has to do with feelings, with the power that comes from within, with knowing our deepest selves and what is sacred to us, with . . . 'heart-knowledge.'"[12] Religion and spirituality overlap but are not identical. Religious institutions encourage and structure spiritual experiences, but spiritual encounters can occur outside formal religious channels.

If spirituality seems to be a strange topic to discuss in a book about leadership ethics, consider the recent explosion of interest in spirituality in the workplace. According to William Judge, an estimated 4,000 chaplains work for private corporations (excluding hospitals, jails, and colleges). Meditation rooms and reflective gardens are part of many company headquarters. Judge argues that the number of business books on the subject provides the clearest sign of corporate interest in spirituality. He identifies 19 popular books on spirituality published in one recent 8-year span.[13]

In his study of 91 top executives at publicly held companies cited in the last chapter, Judge found that "spirituality is central to executive character."[14] Most of the CEOs he surveyed were connected with religious denominations and engaged in regular spiritual activities such as prayer. All reported some sort of trigger event, generally a major setback, which convinced them that they were not in control and deepened their faith in God. Judge's findings are consistent with those of other researchers who report that middle- and upper-level managers are more religious than the population as a whole.

The recent surge of interest in spirituality in the workplace has been fueled, in large part, by the growing importance of employers. For better or for worse, the work organization has replaced other groups (family, church, social groups) as the dominant institution in society. Work takes up increasing amounts of our time and energy. As a result, we tend to develop more friendships with coworkers and fewer with individuals outside the organization. Many of us want a higher return on this investment of time and energy, seeking purposeful tasks and relationships that serve higher purposes.

Spiritual Development

It's one thing to acknowledge that spiritual resources can help leaders; figuring out how to develop them is quite another. Fortunately, we don't have to start from scratch. Emory University professor James Fowler provides one description of the process of spiritual development or spiritual formation.[15] Fowler believes that we as individuals go through spiritual or faith phases in the same way that we pass through stages of physical and emotional development. Each stage focuses on a particular set of spiritual concerns and poses its own unique set of challenges. Individuals shift or "convert" from one stage to another. When their current worldview doesn't seem to explain events, they abandon it for the next. Chronological age is a necessary precondition for spiritual formation but in and of itself does not bring spiritual maturity. Spiritual development can stop as physical development continues. Fowler's seven stages of spiritual growth are these:

1. *Primal faith (infancy).* Before children begin to speak, they learn to trust in parents and other caregivers.

2. *Intuitive-projective faith (early childhood).* Guided by their feelings and imaginations, young children develop images of good and evil powers based on stories and symbols.

3. *Mythic-literal faith (childhood and beyond).* Older children develop the ability to think logically and thus bring order to their worlds. They can determine cause and effect, measure time and space, and so on. They also adopt the beliefs and values of their families.

4. *Synthetic-conventional faith (adolescence and beyond).* In this stage, individuals build a unified sense of the self. Most of the beliefs and values that make up the self-concept or personal story are uncritically borrowed from others, however, making this an age of conformity.

5. *Individuative-reflective faith (young adulthood and beyond).* This is a period of critical reflection during which persons think carefully about personal beliefs and values, see their place in the larger system, and internalize standards. Doubts and questions are common. Individuals consciously choose which beliefs, values, and commitments to hold.

6. *Conjunctive faith (midlife and beyond).* People in this stage learn to recognize and live with opposites or paradoxes. Common paradoxes include the need to have both masculine and feminine qualities, the joy of life and the reality of death, and the recognition of personal strengths and weak-

nesses. Those with conjunctive faith are open to the truths of other traditions while remaining committed to their own beliefs.

7. *Universalizing faith (midlife and beyond).* The few who reach this final state show little concern for themselves. Instead, they commit themselves at great personal cost to serving larger purposes and forces such as love and nonviolence. The moral exemplars I described in the last chapter fit into this category, as would Gandhi, Mother Teresa, Martin Luther King Jr., and German theologian and resistance leader Dietrich Bonhoeffer.

The seven-stage model is the story of how people, in general, develop spiritually. Fowler says we also need to develop our personal stories of spiritual formation within this larger narrative. Our individual stories revolve around our vocation. By vocation, Fowler means a sense of calling. This calling should incorporate our careers but extend to all aspects of our lives. Teachers, for example, may exercise their vocations through their jobs in schools, as mentors to their grandchildren, and as volunteers in local literacy centers.

Vocation and the stages of spiritual formation move in tandem. Individuals modify and refine their sense of vocation as they move through the phases of life. Young adults are occupied with identifying their vocations. Middle-aged adults, in contrast, must reevaluate their vocations in light of their experiences, acknowledging that some of their earlier dreams may never be fulfilled. They may experience burnout because they denied their vocations to make money or to meet the expectations of other people. Older adults don't have to be as concerned about career success as do younger people and can take on new roles and projects. Their example can be an inspiration to those just starting on their vocations or reevaluating their choices.

Fowler has been criticized for developing a theory that promotes Christianity and identifies one stage—universalizing—as superior to the others. Fowler responds to these charges by noting that adherents of all religions seem to follow the same general spiritual path as they seek the same goal. For example, the state of enlightenment, the goal of Buddhist spiritual development, appears to be a form of universalizing faith.

The debate about what constitutes the highest level of spiritual growth should not diminish the importance of Fowler's model and others like it.[16] Any spiritual training must take developmental differences into account by addressing the unique needs of various age groups.

Spiritual issues at age 20 (critical examination of beliefs, identifying a vocation) will be replaced by other concerns in middle age (balancing contradictions, facing death, reevaluation and deepening of vocation). The developmental approach should also put to rest the mistaken belief that spiritual formation is quick and easy. There may be periods when we find ourselves caught in the transition between levels, disillusioned with the past stage but not yet at home in the next.

Fowler's discussion of spiritual growth enriches our understanding of personal mission and hardship, two concepts introduced in the last chapter. The ultimate goal of vocation is service, not personal success and achievement. We would do well to incorporate this outward focus in our mission statements. Fowler's research also suggests that spiritual development, like other forms of leadership development, is a by-product of hardship. Failures, setbacks, personal trauma, and downsizing can reveal the inadequacies of our current faith system and move or convert us to another.

Spiritual Disciplines

Practicing spiritual disciplines is one way to promote our spiritual progress. Richard Foster, director of the Renovaré spiritual renewal movement, identifies 12 disciplines or practices that have been used for centuries by such spiritual seekers as Augustine, Madame Guyon, Brother Lawrence, George Fox, and Thomas Merton. Foster focuses on their use in the Judeo-Christian tradition, but adherents of other faiths also engage in these practices. Fasting plays an important role in Islam, for instance, and meditation is central to Zen Buddhism. Foster divides the spiritual disciplines into three categories: inward, outward, and corporate.[17]

Inward Disciplines

The first group of disciplines encourages us to explore the inner dimension of spirituality. They tend to be "invisible" because they are practiced in private.

1. *The discipline of meditation.* Meditation is quiet contemplation aimed at making a connection with God (Western tradition) or emptying

the mind (Eastern religious tradition). Foster makes these suggestions for productive meditation. Take 5 to 10 minutes to "center down" (quiet your mind). Then reflect on some aspect of creation and/or spiritual reading. You might visualize yourself in a beautiful setting or interacting with God, for example.

2. *The discipline of prayer.* Prayer is often seen as the best means of getting something from a higher spiritual power—physical recovery, improved relationships, a better job. Foster points out, however, that more often than not, it is the person praying who changes as a result of seeking God. Prayer brings a different perspective. We begin to see the big picture, feel more compassion for those who have wronged us (see the earlier discussion of forgiveness), and become more patient.

3. *The discipline of fasting.* Fasting is going without food for spiritual purposes. For example, we might fast to signal our spiritual commitment, to draw closer to our spiritual center, to increase our concentration on spiritual matters, or to provide more time for meditation and prayer.

4. *The discipline of study.* Study is designed to change the way we think about reality. Meditation is reflective, but study is analytical. Changing our perspectives through study requires repeated effort, concentrated focus, and careful reflection on what we have learned. We can uncover important spiritual principles by reading, observing nature, analyzing relationships, and uncovering the underlying values of society. You might want to study the primary texts of the world's faiths and philosophies (the *Tao Te Ching,* the Koran, the Bible, the *Analects of Confucius*) or seek out spiritual classics that have withstood the test of time. In Christian tradition, spiritual classics include the writings of Augustine, Martin Luther, Søren Kierkegaard, and Teresa of Avila.[18]

Outward Disciplines

The outward disciplines are visible to others and have an impact on our relationships with others and society at large. The outward disciplines include these:

5. *The discipline of simplicity.* Simplicity means putting spiritual goals first by relegating material goods to a secondary position in our lives. "Simple" individuals don't worry about status or protecting their assets.

Instead, they speak plainly and honestly, give things away, and avoid excessive debt.

6. *The discipline of solitude.* Setting aside time to be alone may seem selfish. After we've been silent, however, we listen more effectively to others and are more attentive to their needs. Unfortunately, most of us (including me) avoid silence like the plague. Even when we're alone, we listen to music or watch television. Foster suggests that we take advantage of the "little solitudes" that occur during the average day. These include the first few moments after waking up, our morning cup of coffee or tea, being stuck in traffic, or walking to an appointment. Create a space at home or work (a room, chair, corner of the garage) for silence and set aside 3 to 4 hours several times a year to reexamine and reset your goals.

7. *The discipline of submission.* Submission means putting aside our need to always have our way. With this attitude, we can decide to give up our rights for the benefit of other people. Acts of submission include

- Yielding to God
- Following the tenets of sacred texts
- Having commitment to other family members
- Performing acts of kindness toward neighbors
- Helping those who are disadvantaged
- Recognizing our commitment to an interdependent world and future generations

8. *The discipline of service.* Foster makes a clear distinction between "self-righteous" and "true" service. Self-righteous service looks for immediate visible results and wants public recognition. Those engaged in this type of service pick who they want to serve and when. They serve only when they feel like it. True service is motivated by need, not mood. It is a lifestyle that quietly goes about caring for others on a regular basis. True service produces humility in the server. Ways to serve include protecting the reputation of coworkers, using common courtesy, practicing hospitality, listening empathetically, and sharing spiritual insights. I'll have more to say about the relationship between service and leadership in Chapter 6.

Corporate Disciplines

The final set of disciplines recognizes that for most of us, our spiritual formation takes place in the context of a larger community (church, synagogue, temple, worship group). Corporate disciplines are what believers do together to foster the spiritual growth of the entire group.

9. *The discipline of confession.* Confession plays an important role in forgiveness (see the earlier discussion). An honest confession requires careful self-examination, genuine sorrow for the act, and a strong desire to not offend again. When receiving a confession, don't act shocked or pry for further details. Instead, listen quietly, accept the confession, and, if appropriate, pray with the offender.

10. *The discipline of worship.* Worship occurs when seekers gather together for singing, praise, prayer, and teaching. Effective worship takes preparation. Those coming to the gathering must be prepared to listen and should expect to be spiritually strengthened. The inward disciplines are excellent preparation for the corporate expression of faith. Engage in meditation and prayer, for instance, before joining with others for worship.

11. *The discipline of guidance.* Wise leaders recognize the importance of receiving feedback from the larger group when making significant individual decisions. They're willing to delay or adjust their plans on the basis of the feedback they receive. Quakers call "meetings for clearness" to seek collective input on important questions such as what job an individual should take, the suitableness of a couple for marriage, and how to address social concerns. Corporate guidance can also come through a mentor. Recognizing this fact, members of Catholic religious orders appoint spiritual directors to assist younger priests and nuns.

12. *The discipline of celebration.* "Celebration is central to all the Spiritual Disciplines," according to Foster.[19] A joyful spirit breathes life into the rest of the practices and is the product of a spiritually disciplined life. Joy encourages us to be disciplined, and spiritual development is something worth celebrating. Celebration (a) relaxes us, (b) acts as an antidote to sadness and depression, (c) gives a new perspective (we can laugh at ourselves), (d) levels out status differences, (e) frees us from judgmental attitudes, and (f) increases the likelihood of more celebration ("joy begets joy"). We can celebrate through music, dance, fantasy

and play, family gatherings, major holidays, and rituals of our own creation.

🔲 Implications and Applications

- Evil takes a variety of forms or faces, including a sense of dreadful pleasure, deception, rational administration, sanctioned devaluation, and a series of small but fateful decisions. Whatever face it displays, evil is a destructive force that inflicts pain and suffering and ends in death.
- Ultimately, the choice of whether to do or participate in evil is yours.
- Forgiveness is one way to defuse or absorb evil. As a leader, you need to seriously consider the role of forgiveness in your relations with followers, peers, supervisors, and outsiders.
- Forgiving does *not* mean forgetting or condoning evil. Instead, forgivers hold offenders accountable for their actions at the same time that they offer mercy. Forgiving takes a conscious act of the will, unfolds through time, and replaces hostility and resentment with empathy and compassion.
- Forgiveness breaks cycles of evil and restores relationships. You, however, may gain the most from extending mercy. Forgiving can heighten your sense of well-being, give you renewed energy, and improve your health.
- Spiritual resources can equip you for the demanding work of confronting evil. Spirituality looks both inward and outward, touching your deepest feelings while connecting you with larger forces such as God, nature, and humanity.
- Spiritual development is a continuing, lifelong process. Expect to face new challenges and concerns throughout your life span. Anticipate that the nature of your spiritual beliefs and commitments will change.
- Engaging in spiritual disciplines can help your spiritual progress. Common spiritual practices fall into three categories: (a) *inward* (meditation, prayer, fasting, study); (b) *outward* (simplicity, solitude, submission, service); and (c) *corporate* (confession, worship, guidance, celebration).

🔲 For Further Exploration, Challenge, and Self-Assessment

1. Which of the perspectives on evil described in the chapter is most useful to you? How does it help you better understand and prevent evil?

CASE STUDY 4.2

Chapter End Case:
Collective Evil at My Lai

Certain historic figures, such as the Roman emperor Caligula, Rasputin, and Hitler, seem to personify evil. Yet more often than not, evil is a group phenomenon. Scott Peck uses the My Lai massacre during the Vietnam War as a case study in group evil. On the morning of March 16, 1968, troops from Task Force Baker moved into the Quang Ngai province of South Vietnam looking for Vietcong solders. They expected opposition but found only unarmed women, children, and elderly men. Members of several platoons then murdered between 500 and 600 civilians. They fired into huts and shot down those who tried to escape, or rounded up villagers and then slaughtered them.

The killing went on for several hours, and only one person, a helicopter pilot, tried to stop it. He talked to the troops on the ground and radioed headquarters. When his efforts were unsuccessful, he gave up and went back to flying. Approximately 50 soldiers actually engaged in the killing; 200 witnessed what occurred. A year passed before the atrocities came to light because of the efforts of a former soldier who had heard about the incident from friends. Military authorities considered bringing charges against 25 soldiers, but only 6 were brought to trial. One, Lieutenant William Calley, was convicted.

What accounts for the My Lai atrocity and its subsequent cover-up? Specialization certainly played a role. Large organizations such as the Pentagon fragment responsibility, letting members pass the "moral buck." Peck, who consulted at the Pentagon at the time of the Vietnam War, asked officers about the morality of what they did and found that each department ducked responsibility. Ordinance officials, those who manufactured napalm, argued that they only supplied the weapons and weren't in charge of how they were used. Those who identified military targets claimed, in turn, that they were merely following directions from the White House.

Peck believes that moral insensitivity played the greatest role in perpetuating the evil of My Lai. The soldiers involved did not confess their crimes because they weren't aware that they had done anything wrong, although the Geneva Convention and Army policy forbid killing unarmed civilians. Many members of the Task Force Baker had volunteered for the war and were specially trained to kill on behalf of larger society. They were under constant stress (random attacks, mines, sleep and food deprivation) and became numb to the suffering of others. Military discipline promoted obedience, whereas allegiance to the group fostered hatred of the enemy (described as "gooks," "dinks," and "animals"). Any soldier reporting the crime would be ostracized and could be killed.

CASE STUDY 4.2 (Continued)

The killers weren't the only ones suffering from ethical blindness. The military was frustrated because it was failing to achieve the one objective for which it had been created—to win at war. American society as a whole was committed to the idea that communism was a monolithic force to be defeated at all costs. The public allowed President Johnson to wage an undeclared war for several years. According to Peck, citizens let political and military leaders have their way while pursuing their personal interests. Too few took the effort to learn about either the purpose of the war or the nation we were supposed to be helping.

Combating group evil begins with the individual, according to Peck. Even the humblest team member can have some impact on the direction of the group. It is our personal responsibility to acknowledge and combat the laziness and narcissism that lead to evil. We should resist the temptation to let the larger group or group leader make ethical decisions for us.

Discussion Probes

1. How did the military and larger society sanction the evil that took place at My Lai?
2. What other similar cases of group evil can you find in American history?
3. How can the U.S. military prevent similar atrocities in the future?
4. What is moral laziness, and how does it contribute to collective evil?

SOURCE: Peck, S. (1983). *People of the lie: The hope for healing human evil.* New York: Touchstone, Ch. 6.

2. Develop your own definition of forgiveness. Does your definition set boundaries that limit when forgiveness can be offered? What right do leaders have to offer or accept forgiveness on behalf of the group?
3. Consider a time when you forgave someone who treated you unjustly. Did you move through the stages identified by Enright and his colleagues? What benefits did you experience? Conversely, describe a time when you asked for and received forgiveness. What process did you go through? How did you and the relationship benefit?
4. Develop your own forgiveness case study based on the life of a leader who prevented or broke a cycle of evil through an act of mercy or reconciliation.

5. What should be the role of spirituality in leadership? Try to reach a consensus on this question in a group.

6. Break your life into 4- to 5-year increments and chart your spiritual development. Note the ups and downs. Does your life history reflect the stages of faith described in the last part of the chapter? Why or why not?

7. Design a strategy for encouraging your spiritual growth as a leader using as many of the 12 spiritual disciplines as possible.

Notes

1. Definitions of evil can be found in the following sources. There are, of course, a host of other definitions offered by major religions and philosophical systems.

Hallie, P. (1997). *Tales of good and evil, help and harm.* New York: HarperCollins.

Katz, F. E. (1993). *Ordinary people and extraordinary evil: A report on the beguilings of evil.* Albany: State University of New York Press.

Peck, M. S. (1983). *People of the lie: The hope for healing human evil.* New York: Touchstone.

Sanford, N., & Comstock, C. (Eds.). (1971). *Sanctions for evil.* San Francisco: Jossey-Bass.

2. Alford, C. F. (1997). *What evil means to us.* Ithaca, NY: Cornell University Press, p. 3.

3. Peck (1983), *People of the lie.*

4. Adams, G. B., & Balfour, D. L. (1998). *Unmasking administrative evil.* Thousand Oaks, CA: Sage. See also Arendt, H. (1964). *Eichmann in Jerusalem: A report on the banality of evil.* New York: Viking.

5. Adams & Balfour (1998), *Unmasking administrative evil,* p. 67.

6. Sanford & Comstock (1971), *Sanctions for evil.*

7. Lewis, C. S. (1946). *The great divorce.* New York: Macmillan.

8. Fromm, E. (1964). *The heart of man: Its genius for good and evil.* New York: Harper & Row, p. 136.

9. Material on the definition and psychology of forgiveness is taken from the following:

Enright, R. D., Freedman, S., & Rique, J. (1998). The psychology of interpersonal forgiveness. In R. D. Enright & J. North (Eds.), *Exploring forgiveness* (pp. 46-62). Madison: University of Wisconsin Press.

McCullough, M. E., Pargament, K. I., & Thoresen, C. E. (2000). The psychology of forgiveness: History, conceptual issues, and overview. In M. E. McCullough, K. I. Pargament, & C. E. Thoresen (Eds.), *Forgiveness: Theory, research, and practice* (pp. 1-14). New York: Guilford.

Thomas, G. (2000, January 10). The forgiveness factor. *Christianity Today, 44*(1), 38-43.

10. Enright et al. (1998), "Psychology of interpersonal forgiveness," pp. 46-47.

11. For information on the by-products of forgiveness, see Casarjian, R. (1992). *Forgiveness: A bold choice for a peaceful heart.* New York: Bantam; Enright et al. (1998), "Psychology of interpersonal forgiveness"; McCullough, M. E., Sandage, S. J., & Worthington, E. L. (1997). *To forgive is human: How to put your past in the past.* Downers Grove, IL: InterVarsity Press.

Thoresen, C. E., Harris, H. S., & Luskin, F. (2000). Forgiveness and health: An unanswered question. In M. E. McCullough, K. I. Pargament, & C. E. Thoresen (Eds.), *Forgiveness: Theory, research, and practice* (pp. 254-280). New York: Guilford.

12. Roof, W. C. (1993). *A generation of seekers: The spiritual journeys of the baby boom generation.* San Francisco: HarperCollins, p. 64.

13. Judge, W. Q. (1999). *The leader's shadow: Exploring and developing executive character.* Thousand Oaks, CA: Sage. See also

Laabs, J. (1995, September). Balancing spirituality and work. *Personnel Journal, 74*(9), 60-76.

Mitroff, I. I., & Denton, E. A. (1999, Summer). A study of spirituality in the workplace. *Sloan Management Review, 40*(4), 83-93.

14. Judge (1999), *Leader's shadow,* p. 108.

15. Information on Fowler's stages of faith and discussion of vocation are drawn from the following:

Fowler, J. W. (1981). *Stages of faith: The psychology of human development and the quest for meaning.* San Francisco: Harper & Row.

Fowler, J. W. (1984). *Becoming adult, becoming Christian.* New York: Harper & Row.

Fowler, J. W. (1991). The vocation of faith development theory. In J. W. Fowler, K. E. Nipkow, & F. Schweitzer (Eds.), *Stages of faith and religious development: Implications for church, education, and society* (pp. 19-36). New York: Crossroad.

Fowler, J. W. (1991). *Weaving the new creation: Stages of faith and the public church.* San Francisco: HarperSanFrancisco.

Fowler, J. W. (1996). *Faithful change: The personal and public challenges of postmodern life.* Nashville, TN: Abingdon.

16. Fritz Oser of Switzerland offers an alternative developmental approach to faith. See Oser, F. (1991). Toward a logic of religious development. In J. W. Fowler, K. E. Nipkow, & F. Schweitzer (Eds.), *Stages of faith and religious development* (pp. 37-64). New York: Crossroad.

17. Foster, R. J. (1978). *Celebration of discipline: The path to spiritual growth.* New York: Harper & Row.

18. Foster provides one set of spiritual classics in Foster, R. J., & Smith, J. B. (Eds.). (1993). *Devotional classics: Selected readings for individuals and groups.* San Francisco: HarperSanFrancisco.

19. Foster (1978), *Celebration,* p. 164.

PART III

Ethical Standards and Strategies

5

 General Ethical Perspectives

Leaders are truly effective only when they are motivated by a concern for others.

—McGill University business professors
Rabindra Kanungo and Manuel Mendonca

▣ What's Ahead

This chapter surveys widely used ethical perspectives that can be applied to the leadership role. These approaches include utilitarianism, Kant's categorical imperative, communitarianism, and altruism.

Leaders, as we saw in Chapter 2, may unintentionally cast shadows because they lack ethical knowledge, skills, and experience. In this section of the text, I'll address each of these ethical deficiencies. Chapters 5 and 6 describe approaches that can help you determine your moral priorities. Chapter 7 outlines decision-making formats that can be applied to ethical dilemmas and concludes with a set of practice scenarios. All three chapters have a similar structure. After describing each perspective or format, I'll provide a balance sheet that identifies its advantages and disadvantages.

The ethical dilemmas we face as leaders may be unique. We can meet these challenges, however, with the same tools that we apply to other ethical problems. I've labeled the ethical approaches or theories described in the pages that follow as "general" because they were developed for all types of moral choices. Yet they have much to say to those of us in leadership positions.

◻ Utilitarianism: Do the Greatest Good for the Greatest Number of People

Utilitarianism is based on the premise that ethical choices should be based on their consequences. Individuals have probably always considered the likely outcomes of their decisions when determining what to do. This process, however, wasn't formalized and given a name until the 18th and 19th centuries. English philosophers Jeremy Bentham (1748-1832) and John Stuart Mill (1806-1873) argued that the best decisions (a) generate the most benefits as compared with their disadvantages and (b) benefit the largest number of people.[1] In sum, utilitarianism is attempting to do the greatest good for the greatest number of people. Utility can be based on what is best in a specific case (act utilitarianism) or on what is generally best in most contexts (rule utilitarianism). We can decide, for example, that telling a specific lie is justified in one situation (to protect someone's reputation) but as a general rule believe that lying is wrong because it causes more harm than good.

Leaders frequently take a utilitarian approach to ethical decision making. America's nuclear weapons program, for instance, was the product of a series of utilitarian decisions. Harry Truman decided to drop the atomic bomb on Japan after determining that the benefits of shortening the war in the Pacific (reduction in the loss of American lives) outweighed the costs of destroying Hiroshima and Nagasaki and ushering in the nuclear age. Federal energy officials later decided that the benefits of nuclear weapons testing—improved national security—outweighed the risks to citizens in Nevada and Utah. On the basis of this calculation, the Nuclear Energy Commission conducted a series of aboveground nuclear tests in the 1940s and 1950s. Local citizens were

---

CASE STUDY 5.1

The Reference Letter

Being asked to write a letter of reference can pose a thorny ethical dilemma. Writing or giving a reference for a competent, well-liked employee or student is not a problem. Deciding what to do in the case of a marginal or poor performer is a different matter. On the one hand, as a supervisor or professor, you don't want to exaggerate or lie about the person's qualifications. On the other hand, refusing the request may alienate the person and endanger your relationship. Writing a critical letter could provoke a lawsuit. That's why many former employers will confirm only the dates that an individual worked for their organization. Further complicating matters is the possibility that writing the letter may help you get rid of a marginal follower, saving you the hassle of having to fire or demote this individual.

Imagine that you are a college professor. What would you do if a marginal (C-) student asked you for a job reference? For a reference to another university or to another program at your school? Would your response be different if this were a bad (D and F) student?

Imagine that you are a supervisor. What would you do if a marginal employee (one who barely meets minimal work standards) asked you for a letter of reference to seek another position or a transfer to another division of your corporation? What would you say if another employer called and asked you to comment on someone you had fired earlier?

Once you've made your decisions, identify the consequences you weighed when making these choices. Describe how the benefits outweighed the costs in each case.

---

not warned in advance, and their exposure to radiation led to abnormally high cancer rates.

Balance Sheet

Advantages (+s)
>Is easy to understand
>Is frequently used
>Forces us to examine the outcomes of our decisions

Disadvantages (–s)
>Is difficult to identify and evaluate consequences
>May have unanticipated outcomes
>Decision makers may reach different conclusions

The notion of weighing outcomes is easy to understand and to apply. We create a series of mental balance sheets for all types of decisions (see Case Study 5.1). Focusing on outcomes encourages us to think through our decisions, and we're less likely to make rash, unreasoned choices. The ultimate goal of evaluating consequences is admirable—to maximize benefits to as many people as possible. Utilitarianism is probably the most defensible approach in a medical combat unit such as the one portrayed on the television show *MASH*, for example. Surgeons give top priority to those who are most likely to survive. It does little good to spend time with a terminal patient while another soldier who would benefit from treatment dies.

Identifying possible consequences can be difficult, particularly for leaders who represent a variety of constituencies or stakeholders. Take the case of a college president who must decide what academic programs to cut in a budget crisis. Many groups have a stake in this decision, and each will likely reach a different conclusion about potential costs and benefits. Every department believes that it makes a valuable contribution to the university and serves the mission of the school. Powerful alumni may be alienated by the elimination of their majors. Members of the local community might suffer if the education department is terminated and no longer supplies teachers to local schools, or if plays and concerts end because of cutbacks in the theater and music departments. Unanticipated consequences further complicate the choice. If student enrollments increase, the president may have to restore programs that were eliminated earlier. Yet failing to make cuts can put the future of the school in jeopardy.

Even when consequences are clear, evaluating their relative merits can be daunting. As I noted in Chapter 2, we tend to favor ourselves when making decisions. Thus, we are likely to put more weight on consequences that most directly affect us. It's all too easy to confuse the "greatest good" with our selfish interests.

On the basis of the difficulty of identifying and evaluating potential costs and benefits, utilitarian decision makers sometimes reach different conclusions when faced with the same dilemma. Historians still debate the wisdom of dropping the atomic bomb on Japan. Some argue that the war would have ended soon without the use of nuclear weapons and that no military objective justifies such widespread destruction.

Kant's Categorical Imperative:
Do What's Right No Matter What the Cost

In sharp contrast to the utilitarians, German philosopher Immanuel Kant (1724-1804) argued that individuals should do what is morally right no matter what the consequences.[2] (The term *categorical* means "without exception.") His approach to moral reasoning is the best known example of deontological ethics. Deontological ethicists argue that we ought to make choices based on our duty (*deon* is the Greek word for duty) to follow universal truths that are imprinted on our consciences. Guilt is an indication that we have violated these moral laws.

According to Kant, "What is right for one is right for all." We need to ask ourselves one question: Would I want everyone else to make the decision I did? If the answer is yes, the choice is justified. If the answer is no, the decision is wrong. On the basis of this reasoning, certain behaviors such as truth telling and helping the poor are always right. Other acts, such as lying, cheating, and murder, are always wrong. Testing and grading would be impossible if everyone cheated, for example, and cooperation would be impossible if no one could be trusted to tell the truth. Kant lived well before the advent of the automobile, but violations of his decision-making rule could explain why law enforcement officials now have to crack down on motorists who run red lights. So many Americans regularly disobey traffic signals (endangering pedestrians and other drivers) that some communities have installed cameras at intersections to catch violators. Drivers have failed to recognize one simple fact. They may save time by running lights, but they shouldn't do so because the system breaks down when large numbers of people ignore traffic signals.

Balance Sheet

Advantages (+s)
> Promotes persistence and consistency
> Is highly motivational

Disadvantages (–s)
> Exceptions exist to nearly every "universal" law
> Actors may have warped consciences
> Is demonstrated through unrealistic examples
> Is hard to apply, particularly under stress

Emphasis on duty encourages persistence and consistent behavior. Those driven by the conviction that certain behaviors are either right or wrong no matter what the situation are less likely to compromise their personal ethical standards. They are apt to "stay the course" despite group pressures and opposition and to follow through on their choices. Transcendent principles serve as powerful motivational tools. Seeking justice, truth, and mercy is more inspiring than pursuing selfish concerns.

Most attacks on Kant's system of reasoning center on his assertion that there are universal principles that should be followed in every situation. In almost every case, we can think of exceptions. For instance, many of us believe that lying is wrong yet would lie or withhold the truth to save the life of a friend. Countries regularly justify homicide during war. Then, too, how do we account for those who seem to have warped or dead consciences, such as serial killers Jeffrey Dahmer and Ted Bundy? They didn't appear to be bothered by guilt. Psychological factors and elements of the environment, such as being born to a crack addict or to abusive parents, can blunt the force of conscience.

Despite the significant differences between the categorical and utilitarian approaches, both theories involve the application of universal rules or principles to specific situations. Dissatisfaction with rule-based approaches is growing.[3] Some contemporary philosophers complain that these ethical guidelines are applied to extreme situations, not the types of decisions we typically make. Few of us will be faced with the extraordinary scenarios (stealing to save a life or lying to the secret police to protect a fugitive) that are frequently used to illustrate principled decision making. Our dilemmas are less dramatic. Should I confront a coworker about a sexist joke? Tell someone the truth and hurt their feelings? We also face time pressures and uncertainty. In a crisis, we don't always have time to carefully weigh consequences or to determine which abstract principle to follow.

Communitarianism: Shoulder Your Responsibilities/Seek the Common Good

The modern communitarian movement began in 1990 when a group of 15 ethicists, social scientists, and philosophers led by sociologist Amatai Etzioni met in Washington, D.C., to express their concerns about

---

BOX 5.1 Leadership Ethics at the Movies: *Quiz Show*

Key cast members: John Turturro, Rob Morrow, Ralph Fiennes,
                    Paul Scofield

Synopsis:

This film tells the story of the quiz show scandal of the late 1950s. To boost ratings, producers made sure that certain contestants would win by providing them with the questions and answers in advance. Professor Charles Van Doren (Fiennes), son of one of the country's most prominent scholars, participates in the fraud. The scheme collapses when a congressional investigator (Morrow) follows up on allegations raised by a disgruntled loser (Turturro). Although Van Doren and his family suffer, the creators of the program, the show's sponsor, and NBC escape punishment. The film is particularly relevant now that quiz shows, led by *Who Wants to Be a Millionaire?*, once again appear in prime time on the major television networks.

Rating: PG 13, primarily for language

Themes: Deception, conflicting loyalties, character flaws, situational pressures, the power of television, parental love

---

the state of American society. Members of this gathering took the name "communitarian" to highlight their desire to shift the focus of citizens from individual rights to communal responsibilities. The next year, the group started a journal and organized a teach-in that produced the communitarian platform. In 1993, Etzioni published the communitarian agenda in a book titled *The Spirit of Community: The Reinvention of American Society.*[4] Etzioni argues that we ought to (a) institute a moratorium on the generation of new rights such as the right to higher education or the right to drive a motorcycle without a helmet; (b) recognize that citizenship means taking on civic responsibilities (serving on a jury) along with rights and privileges (the right to a trial by jury); (c) accept that some duties, such as protecting the environment, may not bring any immediate payoffs but benefit future generations; and (d) adjust some of our legal rights to improve public safety and health. For example, sobriety checkpoints mean less personal freedom but are justified because they can significantly reduce traffic deaths.

Many communitarians resemble evangelists more than philosophers. They are out to recruit followers to their movement that promotes moral revival. American society is fragmenting and in a state of moral decline, they proclaim. Evidence of this decay is all around us, in the form of high divorce and crime rates, campaign attack ads, and the growing influence of special interest groups in politics. The United States needs renewal that can come only through the creation of a series of communities centered on shared meanings and values. Healthy communities are created by what organizational consultants Juanita Brown and David Isaacs call the "Seven Cs" of community building: commitment, competence, contribution, collaboration, continuity, conscience, and continuity.[5]

> *Commitment.* Commitment comes when people work together in neighborhoods, organizations, volunteer groups and other settings to reach goals that they value. Along the way they learn together, develop a common language and symbols, master adversity, and build trust.
>
> *Competence.* In healthy communities, citizens individually and collectively engage in learning and improvement. For example, group members envision the future they want, surface their assumptions, identify new ways to work together, and learn to see the broader picture. Continual learning and development enable them to actively shape events instead of merely reacting to them.
>
> *Contribution.* People want to contribute to a worthwhile cause. Vital communities help citizens use their talents in pursuit of significant goals such as restoring a blighted neighborhood. To achieve this objective, lawyers, contractors, real estate agents, police officers, city planners, and others must work together, blending their skills to rid the area of slumlords, to build new housing, and to attract new businesses and industry.
>
> *Collaboration.* Collaboration involves identifying and mobilizing the various stakeholder groups on behalf of a larger cause (improving schools, reducing teen pregnancy, producing a valuable product, cleaning up a polluted river). Leaders provide lots of information to all citizens and encourage face-to-face communication that builds relationships.
>
> *Continuity.* A community can't survive without some continuity. Encouraging people to put down roots is one way to ensure that a community doesn't lose its collective memory. Leaders can also build in continuity

through training, mentoring, rituals, and other means. An organization, for instance, can pass along important traditions through new employee orientation, pairing mentors and protégés, and annual ceremonies and celebrations.

Conscience. Conscience refers to the ways that communities publicize and then live out their values, principles, and ethical standards. Groups with a highly developed conscience make sure that citizens and outsiders understand their key values and recognize that they are connected to other communities.

Conversation. Conversation builds community. Citizens make and share common values and meanings, build relationships, share information, solve problems, and perform a host of other tasks through talk. Leaders of successful communities make sure that followers have ample opportunities to engage in honest conversation that both reflects differing perspectives and serves the needs of the group as a whole.

The social fabric of a nation and the world as a whole can be seen as a web of intersecting communities—families, neighborhoods, towns, nations, voluntary associations, work groups, unions, and professional associations. These communities often have different moral standards that clash with one other. Consider the conflict about flying the Confederate battle flag in South Carolina's state capital. Many white South Carolinians consider the flag to be part of their cultural heritage. Minorities (as well as many white citizens in other parts of the country) see the flag as a symbol of racial discrimination. During the 2000 presidential primary season, Republican candidates said it was up to state residents to decide what to do with the flag; Democratic presidential hopefuls urged the South Carolina governor to remove it. Later, the flag was moved from the capitol building to another public location in the same complex. Civil rights leaders continue to object to the flag's presence on state property.

Communitarian thinkers have offered a number of suggestions or criteria for resolving conflicts such as these.[6] The first criterion— community agreement—respects local values because they reflect the unique history of the group. These principles should be given more weight if they have been developed through careful deliberation and have been adopted by most, if not all, citizens. Consensus, however, doesn't equate with morality. A community can adopt values that are immoral. After all, segregation was the norm in the South until the civil rights movement. This leads to the need for a second criterion—societal values. In addition to reflecting local preferences, values need to be accountable to those of the larger society or community. Attempts to deny blacks the right to vote, for instance, were eventually overturned because they violated rights guaranteed by the U.S. Constitution. The third criterion—cross-societal moral dialogues—comes into play when dealing with members of other nations. The same type of dialogues that occur within communities (those characterized by openness, equality, and honesty) need to take place with individuals of other cultural groups. The fourth criterion—global community—seeks to identify core values that are common to all societies. (I'll have more to say about universal values in Chapter 10.)

According to Amatai Etzioni, the most important values are moral order and autonomy. Moral order refers to commitment to shared values and purposes that preserve human life and stability. Blatant disregard of gun safety laws would violate this standard, for example, because such behavior endangers others. Autonomy refers to individual rights and freedoms. Autonomous individuals are free to make their own choices about where they should live, their careers, their hobbies, and so on. On the basis of this value, severe restrictions on the freedom of speech are immoral because they limit personal rights. Etzioni creates a new "golden mean or rule" that embraces both moral order and autonomy. As a test case, he applies his rule to speed limits. These laws are justified because they preserve the life of the individual driver (autonomy) while preventing accidents that would endanger passengers and other motorists (social order).

Before weighing the pros and cons of communitarianism, I want to highlight the movement's concern for the common good. Selfishness destroys community. If each group looks out only for its own welfare, the community as a whole suffers. Competing interests make it difficult for the federal government to improve health care, for example. HMOs, drug manufacturers, lawyers, doctors, hospital administrators, and patients all want the health care system to serve the needs of their particular group. As a result, the nation as a whole suffers as medical costs escalate at the same time that millions remain uninsured. Communitarians address the problems posed by competing interests by urging leaders and followers to put the needs of the broader community above the needs of any one individual, group, or organization.

Balance Sheet

Advantages (+s)
> Fosters stronger connections between people
> Discourages selfish individualism
> Encourages collaboration
> Promotes character development

Disadvantages (−s)
> Evangelistic fervor of its leaders
> Promotion of one set of values in a pluralistic society
> Possible erosion of individual rights
> Failure to resolve conflicting moral standards

Communitarianism is a promising new approach to moral reasoning, particularly for leaders. First, the movement addresses the shortcomings of individualism. Members of individualistic cultures pay a high price for autonomy. U.S. citizens enjoy a great deal of freedom but are far more likely to be lonely, depressed, and divorced than are people in collectivist societies such as Japan and Venezuela. We would likely experience richer, fuller lives if we were to forge stronger connections to others in our communities. Second, communitarianism addresses selfishness head on, encouraging us to put responsibilities above rights and to seek the common good. We're less tempted to abuse power or to accumulate leadership perks, for example, if we remember that we have obligations both to our immediate followers and to the broader communities in which we live. Lying, polluting, or manufacturing dangerous products may serve our needs or the needs of the organizations we lead. Such actions are unethical, however, because they rarely benefit society as a whole.

Third, communitarianism encourages a collaborative approach to communication and problem solving, which facilitates effective decision making. Communities identify and promote their values through conversation within and among groups. Ethical leaders encourage open, honest discussion of moral questions. Fourth, the rise of communitarianism coincides with renewed interest in virtue ethics, the focus in Chapter 3. Both are concerned with the development of moral character. The communitarian movement fosters the development of the virtues by promoting strong families, schools, religious congregations, and governments. A "virtue cycle" is created. Virtuous citizens build moral communities that in turn encourage further character formation.

The communitarian movement has its share of detractors. Some critics are uncomfortable that its founders are out to make converts. Others worry about promoting one set of values in a pluralistic society. Who decides, for example, which values are taught in the public schools? Christians want the Ten Commandments displayed in classrooms, but Buddhists, Moslems, and other religious groups object. Still other critics fear that focusing on the needs of the community will erode individual rights.

Competing community standards may pose the greatest threat to the communitarian movement. The criteria for resolving these disputes leave many unanswered questions. Is communitarianism deficient because decision makers must ultimately rely on universal principles to make these choices? Why should autonomy and moral order be the primary values? What happens when leaders apply the same criteria but reach different conclusions? In the case of the South Carolina flag controversy, some whites claim that completely removing the Confederate banner would violate their freedom of self-expression and that this symbol is an integral part of the state's history (social order). Opponents claim that prominently displaying the Confederate flag is unethical because it reduces the autonomy of minority citizens (who are offended by its presence on public property) and creates tension and disorder.

▣ Altruism: Love Your Neighbor

Advocates of altruism argue that love of neighbor is the ultimate ethical standard. People are never a means to an end; they *are* the ends. Our actions should be designed to help others whatever the personal cost. The altruistic approach to moral reasoning, like communitarianism, shares much in common with virtue ethics. Many of the virtues that characterize people of high moral character, such as compassion, hospitality, empathy, and generosity, reflect concern for other people. Clearly, virtuous leaders are other, not self, centered.

Altruism appears to be a universal value, one promoted in cultures from every region of the world. The Dalai Lama urges followers to practice an ethic of compassion, for instance, and Western thought has been greatly influenced by the altruistic emphasis of Judaism and Christianity. The command to love God and to love others as we love ourselves is the most important obligation in Judeo-Christian ethics. Because humans are made in the image of God and God is love, individuals have an obligation to love others no matter who they are and no matter what their relationship. Jesus drove home this point in the parable of the Good Samaritan.

A man was going down from Jerusalem to Jericho, when he fell into the hands of robbers. They stripped him of his clothes, beat him and went away, leaving him half dead. A priest happened to be going down the same road, and when he saw the man, he passed by on the other side. So too, a Levite, when he came to the place and saw him, passed by on the other side. But a Samaritan, as he traveled, came where the man was; and when he saw him he took pity on him. He went to him and bandaged his wounds, pouring on oil and wine. Then he put the man on his own donkey, took him to an inn and took care of him. The next day he took out two silver coins and gave them to the innkeeper. "Look after him," he said, "and when I return, I will reimburse you for any extra expense you hay have."

Which of these three do you think was a neighbor to the man who fell into the hands of robbers?

The expert replied, "the one who had mercy on him."

Jesus told him, "Go and do likewise." (Luke 10:30-37, New International Version)

Mother Teresa's religious order in India practices the type of unconditional love portrayed in the story of the Good Samaritan. These nuns minister to the needs of every stranger who comes in for help, regardless of the person's social or religious background. They provide help at significant personal cost and don't expect anything in return.

Concern for others promotes healthy social relationships. Society as a whole functions more effectively when individuals help one another in their daily interactions.[7] Altruism is the driving force behind all types of movements and organizations designed to help the less fortunate and to eliminate social problems. Name almost any nonprofit group, ranging from a hospital or medical relief team to a youth club or crisis hotline, and you'll find that it was launched by someone with an altruistic motive. In addition, when we compare good with evil, altruistic acts generally come to mind. Moral heroes and moral champions shine so brightly because they ignore personal risks to battle evil forces.

From the discussion above, it's easy to see why altruism is a significant ethical consideration for all types of citizens. Management professors Rabindra Kanungo and Manuel Mendonca believe, however, that concern for others is even more important for leaders than it is for followers.[8] By definition, leaders exercise influence on behalf of others. They can't understand or articulate the needs of followers unless they focus on the concerns of constituents. To succeed, leaders may have to take risks and sacrifice personal gain. According to Kanungo and Mendonca, leaders intent on benefiting followers will pursue organizational goals, rely on referent and expert power bases, and give power away. Leaders intent on benefiting themselves will focus on personal achievements; rely on legitimate, coercive, and reward power bases; and try to control followers.

Balance Sheet

Advantages (+s)
> Ancient yet contemporary
> Important to society and leaders
> Powerful and inspiring

Disadvantages (–s)
> Failure of many who profess to love their neighbor to act as if they do
> Many different, sometimes conflicting forms

Altruism is an attractive ethical perspective for several reasons. First, concern for others is an ancient yet contemporary principle. Two thousand years have passed since Jesus told the story of the Good Samaritan. We're still faced, however, with the same type of dilemma as the characters in the story. Should we stop to help a stranded motorist or drive on? Should we ignore or give our spare change to the homeless person on the street? Do we help a fallen runner in a 10K race or keep running? (The Parable of the Sadhu in Case Study 5.2 at the end of the chapter is a modern version of the Samaritan dilemma, one that may have involved life or death consequences.) Second, as I noted earlier, altruism is essential to the health of society in general and leaders in particular. In recognition of this fact, social scientists have joined theologians and philosophers in studying the roots of altruistic behavior.[9] Third, altruism is both powerful and inspiring. Acting selflessly counteracts the effects of evil and inspires others to do the same.

Although attractive, love of neighbor is not an easy principle to put into practice. Far too many people who claim to follow the Christian ethic fail miserably, for instance. They come across as less, not more, caring then those who don't claim to follow this approach. Some of the bitterest wars are religious battles fought by believers who seemingly ignore the altruistic values of their faiths. There's also disagreement about what constitutes loving behavior. For example, committed religious leaders disagree about the legitimacy of war. Some view military service as an act of love, one designed to defend their families and friends. Others oppose the military, believing that nonviolence is the only way to express compassion for others.

▣ Ethical Pluralism

I've presented these four ethical perspectives as separate and sometimes conflicting approaches to moral reasoning. In so doing, I may have given you the impression that you should select one theory and ignore the others. That would be a mistake. Often, you'll need to combine perspectives (practice *ethical pluralism*) to resolve an ethical problem. As seen in the discussion of communitarianism, conflicting community standards can be resolved only by appealing to broader rules or principles such as those described by Immanuel Kant and other deontological ethicists. I suggest that you apply all four approaches to the same problem and see what insights you gain from each one. You might find that a particular perspective is more suited to some types of ethical dilemmas than others. For example, when discussing the Sadhu case at the end of the chapter, you may conclude that communitarianism is less helpful than utilitarianism or the categorical imperative. I'll return to the importance of multiple approaches in the examination of ethical decision-making formats in Chapter 7.

◻ Implications and Applications

- Well-established ethical systems can help you set your ethical priorities as a leader.
- Utilitarianism asks you to weigh the possible costs and benefits of moral choices. Seek to do the greatest good for the greatest number of people.
- The categorical imperative urges you to do what's right no matter what the consequences. By this standard, some actions (lying, cheating, murder) are always wrong.
- Communitarians focus your attention on your responsibility to the larger community and the need to make decisions that support the common good.
- Altruism encourages you to put others first no matter what the personal cost.
- Don't expect perfection from any ethical perspective. Ethical approaches, like leaders themselves, have their critics, strengths, and weaknesses.
- Two well-meaning leaders can use the same ethical system and reach different conclusions.
- Whenever possible, practice ethical pluralism by applying more than one perspective to the same problem.

◻ For Further Exploration, Challenge, and Self-Assessment

1. Can you think of any absolute moral laws or duties that must be obeyed without exception?
2. Reflect on one of your recent ethical decisions. What ethical system(s) did you follow? Were you satisfied with your choice?
3. What items can you add to each of the balance sheets in this chapter?
4. Create your own ethics case based on your personal experience or on current or historical events. Describe the key ethical issues raised in the case and evaluate the characters in the story according to each of the four ethical standards.
5. Apply each of the four perspectives to the Sadhu case either on your own or in a group. Write your conclusions.

CASE STUDY 5.2

Chapter End Case: The Parable of the Sadhu

The following case first appeared in the September-October 1983 issue of *Harvard Business Review*. Since that time, it has been discussed in thousands of business schools, churches, and corporations. The author, business professor Bowen H. McCoy, believes that the story of the Sadhu reminds us of the constant tension between reaching our goals and the claims of strangers.

The Sadhu

The Nepal experience was more rugged than I had anticipated. Most commercial treks last two or three weeks and cover a quarter of the distance we traveled.

My friend Stephen, the anthropologist, and I were halfway through the sixty-day Himalayan part of the trip when we reached the high point, an 18,000-foot pass over a crest that we'd have to traverse to reach the village of Muklinath, an ancient holy place for pilgrims.

Six years earlier, I had suffered pulmonary edema, an acute form of altitude sickness, at 16,500 feet in the vicinity of Everest base camp—so we were understandably concerned about what would happen at 18,000 feet. Moreover, the Himalayas were having their wettest spring in twenty years; hip-deep powder and ice had already driven us off one ridge. If we failed to cross the pass, I feared that the last half of our once-in-a-lifetime trip would be ruined.

The night before we would try the pass, we camped in a hut at 14,500 feet. In the photos taken at that camp, my face appears wan. The last village we'd passed through was a sturdy two-day walk below us, and I was tired.

During the late afternoon, four backpackers from New Zealand joined us, and we spent most of the night awake, anticipating the climb. Below, we could see the fires of two other parties, which turned out to be two Swiss couples and a Japanese hiking club.

To get over the steep part of the climb before the sun melted the steps cut in the ice, we departed at 3:30 a.m. The New Zealanders left first, followed by Stephen and myself, our porters and Sherpas, and then the Swiss. The Japanese lingered in their camp. The sky was clear, and we were confident that no spring storm would erupt that day to close the pass.

CASE STUDY 5.2 (Continued)

At 15,500 feet, it looked to me as if Stephen were shuffling and staggering a bit, which are symptoms of altitude sickness. (The initial stage of altitude sickness brings a headache and nausea. As the condition worsens, a climber may encounter difficult breathing, disorientation, aphasia, and paralysis.) I felt strong—my adrenaline was flowing—but I was very concerned about my ultimate ability to get across. A couple of our porters were also suffering from the height, and Pasang, our Sherpa sirdar (leader), was worried.

Just after daybreak, while we rested at 15,500 feet, one of the New Zealanders, who had gone ahead, came staggering down toward us with a body slung across his shoulders. He dumped the almost naked, barefoot body of an Indian holy man—a sadhu—at my feet. He had found the pilgrim lying on the ice, shivering and suffering from hypothermia. I cradled the sadhu's head and laid him out on the rocks. The New Zealander was angry. He wanted to get across the pass before the bright sun melted the snow. He said, "Look, I've done what I can. You have porters and Sherpa guides. You care for him. We're going on!" He turned and went back up the mountain to join his friends.

I took a carotid pulse and found that the sadhu was still alive. We figured he had probably visited the holy shrines at Muklinath and was on his way home. It was fruitless to question why he had chosen this desperately high route instead of the safe, heavily traveled caravan route through the Kali Gandaki gorge. Or why he was shoeless and almost naked, or how long he had been lying in the pass. The answers weren't going to solve our problem.

Stephen and the four Swiss began stripping off their outer clothing and opening their packs. The sadhu was soon clothed from head to foot. He was not able to walk, but he was very much alive. I looked down the mountain and spotted the Japanese climbers, marching up with a horse.

Without a great deal of thought, I told Stephen and Pasang that I was concerned about withstanding the heights to come and wanted to get over the pass. I took off after several of our porters who had gone ahead.

On the steep part of the ascent where, if the ice steps had given way, I would have slid down about 3,000 feet, I felt vertigo. I stopped for a breather, allowing the Swiss to catch up with me. I inquired about the sadhu and Stephen. They said that the sadhu was fine and that Stephen was just behind them. I set off again for the summit.

Stephen arrived at the summit an hour after I did. Still exhilarated by victory, I ran down the slope to congratulate him. He was suffering from altitude sickness—walking fifteen steps, then stopping, walking fifteen steps, then stopping. Pasang accompanied him all the way up. When I reached them, Stephen glared at me and said: "How do you feel about contributing to the death of a fellow man?"

I did not completely comprehend what he meant. "Is the sadhu dead?" I inquired.

"No," replied Stephen, "but he surely will be!"

CASE STUDY 5.2 (Continued)

After I had gone, followed not long after by the Swiss, Stephen had remained with the sadhu. When the Japanese had arrived, Stephen had asked to use their horse to transport the sadhu down to the hut. They had refused. He had then asked Pasang to have a group of our porters carry the sadhu. Pasang had resisted the idea, saying that the porters would have to exert all their energy to get themselves over the pass. He believed they could not carry a man down 1,000 feet to the hut, reclimb the slope, and get across safely before the snow melted. Pasang had pressed Stephen not to delay any longer.

The Sherpas had carried the sadhu down to a rock in the sun at about 15,000 feet and pointed out the hut another 500 feet below. The Japanese had given him food and drink. When they had last seen him, he was listlessly throwing rocks at the Japanese party's dog, which had frightened him.

We do not know if the sadhu lived or died.

For many of the following days and evenings, Stephen and I discussed and debated our behavior toward the sadhu. Stephen is a committed Quaker with deep moral vision. He said, "I feel that what happened with the sadhu is a good example of the breakdown between the individual ethic and the corporate ethic. No one person was willing to assume ultimate responsibility for the sadhu. Each was willing to do his bit just so long as it was not too inconvenient. When it got to be a bother, everyone just passed the buck to someone else and took off. Jesus was relevant to a more individualistic stage of society, but how do we interpret his teaching today in a world filled with large, impersonal organizations and groups?"

I defended the larger group, saying, "Look, we all cared. We all gave aid and comfort. Everyone did his bit. The New Zealander carried him down below the snow line. I took his pulse and suggested we treat him for hypothermia. You and the Swiss gave him clothing and got him warmed up. The Japanese gave him food and water. The Sherpas carried him down to the sun and pointed out the easy trail toward the hut. He was well enough to throw rocks at a dog. What more could we do?"

"You have just described the typical affluent Westerner's response to a problem. Throwing money—in this case food and sweaters—at it, but not solving the fundamentals!" Stephen retorted.

"What would satisfy you?" I said. "Here we are, a group of New Zealanders, Swiss, Americans, and Japanese who have never met before and who are at the apex of one of the most powerful experiences of our lives. Some years the pass is so bad no one gets over it. What right does an almost naked pilgrim who chooses the wrong trail have to disrupt our lives? Even the Sherpas had no interest in risking the trip to help him beyond a certain point."

Stephen calmly rebutted. "I wonder what the Sherpas would have done if the sadhu had been a well-dressed Nepali, or what the Japanese would have done if the sadhu had been a well-dressed Asian, or what you would have done, Buzz, if the sadhu had been a well-dressed Western woman?"

CASE STUDY 5.2 (Continued)

"Where, in your opinion," I asked, "is the limit of our responsibility in a situation like this? We had our own well-being to worry about. Our Sherpa guides were unwilling to jeopardize us or the porters for the sadhu. No one else on the mountain was willing to commit himself beyond certain self-imposed limits."

Stephen said, "As individual Christians or people with a Western ethical tradition, we can fulfill our obligations in such a situation only if one, the sadhu dies in our care, two, the sadhu demonstrates to us that he can undertake the two-day walk down to the village; or three, we carry the sadhu for two days down to the village and persuade someone there to care for him."

"Leaving the sadhu in the sun with food and clothing—where he demonstrated hand-eye coordination by throwing a rock at a dog—comes close to fulfilling items one and two," I answered. "And it wouldn't have made sense to take him to the village where the people appeared to be far less caring than the Sherpas, so the third condition is impractical. Are you really saying that, no matter what the implications, we should, at the drop of a hat, have changed our entire plan?"

Discussion Probes

1. Which ethical standard did the author of the parable follow? What perspective did Stephen take?

2. Did McCoy make the right choice? How would you evaluate the responses of the other persons in the story?

3. How far should we go to help strangers?

4. What parallels can you draw between the parable of the sadhu and the types of ethical choices made by groups and organizations?

5. Is there any way to prepare ourselves for an ethical crisis such as this one?

6. What leadership lessons do you draw from this case?

Notes

1. See, for example,

Barry, V. (1978). *Personal and social ethics: Moral problems with integrated theory.* Belmont, CA: Wadsworth.

Bentham, J. (1948). *An introduction to the principles of morals and legislation.* New York: Hafner.

Gorovitz, S. (Ed.). (1971). *Utilitarianism: Text and critical essays.* Indianapolis, IN: Bobbs-Merrill.

2. Kant, I. (1964). *Groundwork of the metaphysics of morals* (H. J. Ryan, Trans.). New York: Harper & Row; Christians, C. G., Rotzoll, K. B., & Fackler, M. (1990). *Media ethics* (3rd ed.). New York: Longman; Leslie, L. Z. (2000). *Mass communication ethics: Decision-making in postmodern culture.* Boston: Houghton Mifflin.

3. Meilander, G. (1986). Virtue in contemporary religious thought. In R. J. Nehaus (Ed.), *Virtue: Public and private* (pp. 7-30). Grand Rapids, MI: Eerdmans; Alderman, H. (1997). By virtue of a virtue. In D. Statman (Ed.), *Virtue ethics* (pp. 145-164). Washington, DC: Georgetown University Press.

4. Etzioni, A. (1993). *The spirit of community: The reinvention of American society.* New York: Touchstone. See also

Bellah, N., Madsen, R., Sullivan, W. M., Swidler, A., & Tipton, S. M. (1991). *The good society.* New York: Vintage.

Eberly, D. E. (1994). *Building a community of citizens: Civil society in the 21st century.* Lanham, MD: University Press of America.

Etzioni, A. (Ed.). (1995). *New communitarian thinking: Persons, virtues, institutions, and communities.* Charlottesville: University Press of Virginia.

Etzioni, A. (Ed.). (1995). *Rights and the common good: A communitarian perspective.* New York: St. Martin's, pp. 271-276.

Johnson, C. E. (2000). Emerging perspectives in leadership ethics. In *Selected proceedings: 1999 annual meeting of the International Leadership Association.* College Park, MD: Academy of Leadership Press.

5. Brown, J., & Isaacs, D. (1995). Building corporations as communities: The best of both worlds. In K. Gozdz (Ed.), *Community building: Renewing spirit and learning in business* (pp. 69-83). San Francisco: Sterling.

6. Etzioni, A. (1996). *The new golden rule: Community and morality in a democratic society.* New York: Basic Books.

7. Altruistic behavior can be critical to organizational success. See Organ, D. W. (1988). *Organizational citizenship behavior: The good soldier syndrome.* Lexington, MA: Lexington Books.

8. Kanungo, R. N., & Mendonca, M. (1996). *Ethical dimensions of leadership.* Thousand Oaks, CA: Sage.

9. See, for example,

Eisenberg, N. (Ed.). (1982). *The development of prosocial behavior.* New York: Academic Press.

Kanungo, R. N., & Conger, J. A. (1993). Promoting altruism as a corporate goal. *Academy of Management Executive, 7*(3), 37-49.

Rushton, J. P., & Sorrention, R. M. (Eds.). (1981). *Altruism and helping behavior: Social, personality, and developmental perspectives.* Hillsdale, NJ: Lawrence Erlbaum.

6

▣ Normative
▣ Leadership Theories

The Presidency is . . . preeminently a place of moral leadership.

—Franklin D. Roosevelt

▣ What's Ahead

This chapter continues to look at ethical perspectives but narrows the focus to approaches that directly address the behavior of leaders. These include transformational leadership, the postindustrial model, Taoism, and servant leadership. As in the previous chapter, I'll describe each theory and then offer a balance sheet outlining some of its advantages and disadvantages.

Chapter 5 looked at well-established ethical systems or theories. I referred to them as general perspectives because they can be applied to whatever situation or role in which we find ourselves. This chapter examines what philosopher and ethicist Joanne Ciulla of the University of Richmond calls *normative leadership theories*.[1] Normative leadership theories tell leaders how they ought to act. They are built on moral principles or norms but unlike general ethical perspectives, deal directly with the leader-follower relationship.

▣ Transformational Leadership: Raising the Ethical Bar

Social scientists offered a series of explanations for leadership behavior during the 20th century. Until the 1940s, researchers believed that leaders were born, not made. Only individuals who inherited the necessary mental and physical characteristics (intelligent, extroverted, tall, good-looking) or traits could be leaders. When investigators had trouble isolating one set of traits common to all leaders, this model was largely (but not completely) abandoned. The next group of scholars assumed that to be effective, leaders had to adapt to elements of the situation, such as the nature of the task; the emotional, motivational, and skill level of followers; and the quality of the leader-follower relationship. New workers will need more direction than experienced ones, for example. These situational or contingency theories are still popular but suffer from two major shortcomings. First, they are hard to apply. It's not easy to decide what leadership style to use because so many factors must be taken into consideration. Second, contingency theories give too much weight to contextual factors. Elements of the situation are important, but there are strategies that can be effective in a variety of settings.

The transformational approach addressed the limitations of both the traits and situational perspectives by isolating sets of behaviors (which are learned, not inherited) that can produce positive results in many contexts. Interest in transformational leadership began in 1978 with the publication of *Leadership* by James McGregor Burns, a former presidential adviser, political scientist, and historian.[2] In his book, Burns contrasted traditional forms of leadership, which he labeled *transactional,* with a more powerful form of leadership he called *transforming.* Transactional leaders appeal to lower-level needs of followers, that is, the need for food, shelter, and acceptance. They exchange money, benefits, recognition, and other rewards in return for the obedience and labor of followers. Transformational leaders, in contrast, speak to higher-level needs such as esteem, competency, self-fulfillment, and self-actualization. In so doing, they have a major impact on the people and groups that they lead. Burns points to Franklin Roosevelt and Mahatma Gandhi as examples

---

BOX 6.1 Leadership Ethics at the Movies: *Gandhi*

Key cast members: Ben Kingsley, Candice Bergen, Edward Fox,
                    John Gielgud, Martin Sheen

Synopsis:

This film traces the life of Mohandas Gandhi (played by Ben Kingsley), one of the most powerful transformational leaders of the 20th century. Young Gandhi's career as an activist began in South Africa when he was thrown off a train for refusing to give up his seat to a white passenger. He led the movement to free India from British rule and used hunger strikes to prevent violence between Muslims and Hindus. His life was cut short by an assassin's bullet. Watching this movie will give you a better understanding of Gandhi's commitment to nonviolent resistance, the poor, religious tolerance, and simple living. Although long (approximately 3 hours), the film is well worth the time.

Rating: PG for violence

Themes: Transformational leadership, courage, nonviolence, racial and religious bigotry and tolerance, cultural differences, the power of the press, leadership of social and political movements

---

of leaders who transformed the lives of followers and their societies. (Gandhi's life is profiled in Leadership Ethics at the Movies in Box 6.1.)

Moral commitments are at the heart of Burns's definition of transforming leadership. "Such leadership," states Burns, "occurs when one or more persons *engage* with others in such a way that leaders and followers raise one another to higher levels of motivation and morality."[3] Transactional leaders emphasize instrumental values, such as responsibility, fairness, and honesty, that make routine interactions go smoothly. Transformational leaders, on the other hand, focus on terminal values such as liberty, equality, and justice. They want to achieve significant goals and, in the process, help followers move into leadership roles.

In a series of studies, leadership expert Bernard Bass and his colleagues identified the factors that characterize transactional and transformational forms of leadership.[4] They found that transactional leaders engage in *contingent reward* and *management-by-exception*. Transactional leaders reward followers for reaching objectives and discipline them when they fall short. In extreme cases, such leaders don't exert much influence at all. Transformational leaders engage in *charismatic leadership (idealized influence)* and *inspirational motivation*. They become role models for followers, set high standards and goals, create shared visions, provide meaning, and make emotional appeals. In addition, transforming leaders provide *intellectual stimulation* and *individualized consideration*. They stimulate creativity by helping followers question their assumptions and develop new approaches to problems. They provide learning opportunities tailored to the needs of each individual.

Burns believed that leaders display either transactional or transformational characteristics, but Bass found otherwise. Transforming leadership uses both transactional *and* transformational elements. Explains Bass: "Many of the great transformational leaders, including Abraham Lincoln, Franklin Delano Roosevelt, and John F. Kennedy, did not shy away from being transactional. They were able to move the nation as well as play petty politics."[5] The transformational leader uses contingent reward and management-by-exception along with idealized influence, inspirational motivation, cognitive stimulation, and individualized consideration.

The popularity of the transformational approach probably has more to do with practical considerations than with ethical ones. Evidence suggests that transforming leaders are more successful than their transactional counterparts. Their followers are more committed, form stronger bonds with colleagues, work harder, and persist in the face of obstacles.[6] As a result, organizations led by transforming figures often achieve extraordinary results—higher quality, greater profits, improved service, military victories, better win-loss records.

James Kouzes, Barry Posner, Tom Peters, Warren Bennis, and Burt Nanus are just some of the prominent scholars, consultants, and authors who have identified principles and behaviors that characterize highly successful leaders. University of Colorado professor Michael Hackman finds that the characteristics of transformational leaders identified by these researchers are "strikingly similar." Extraordinary leaders are (a) creative (innovative, foresighted); (b) interactive (skilled communicators who use powerful images, metaphors, and models); (c) visionary (develop a concise, motivating description of where the group is headed); (d) empowering (encourage participation and involvement); and (e) passionate (care deeply for their work).[7]

Burns originally believed that the transforming leader is a moral leader because the ultimate product of transformational leadership is higher ethical standards and performance. His definition, however, did not account for the use by some leaders of transformational strategies to reach immoral ends. A leader can act as a role model, provide intellectual stimulation, and be passionate about a cause. Yet the end product of her or his efforts can be evil. Hitler was a charismatic figure who had a clear vision for Germany but left a trail of unprecedented death and destruction.

Acknowledging the difference between ethical and unethical transformational leaders, Bass adopted the term *pseudotransformational* to distinguish between the two categories.[8] Transformational leaders are motivated by altruism; pseudotransformational leaders are self-centered. Mahatma Gandhi and Martin Luther King Jr. deserve to be classified as transformational because they promoted universal brotherhood. Ayatollah Khomeini was pseudotransformational because he taught followers to hate outsiders. A list of the products of transformational and pseudotransformational leadership is found in Box 6.2.

Balance Sheet

Advantages (+s)
> Strives for higher morality
> Is highly effective
> Is inspirational
> Recognizes that leaders are made, not born
> Is not bound by the context

Disadvantages (−s)
> Moral principles often overlooked by practitioners
> Leader centric
> Creates dependency

Transformational leadership rests on a clear ethical foundation. The goal of a transforming leader is to raise the level of morality in a group or organization. Pursuit of this goal will increase the ethical capacity of followers, create a more moral climate, foster independent action, and serve the larger good. In addition, transformational leaders get results. Identify a successful corporation, team, or military unit, many experts say, and you'll find the guiding hand of a transformational leader. This

---

BOX 6.2 **Products of Transformational and Pseudotransformational Leadership**

Transformational Leaders

Raise awareness of moral standards

Highlight important priorities

Increase followers' needs for achievement

Foster higher moral maturity in followers

Create an ethical climate (shared values, high ethical standards)

Encourage followers to look beyond self-interests to the common good

Promote cooperation and harmony

Pseudotransformational Leaders

Promote special interests at the expense of the common good

Encourage dependency of followers and may privately despise them

Foster competitiveness

Pursue personal goals

Forment greed, envy, hate, and deception

Engage in conflict rather than cooperation

SOURCE: Bass, B. M. (1995). The ethics of transformational leadership. In J. Ciulla (Ed.), *Ethics: The heart of leadership* (pp. 169-192). Westport, CT: Praeger.

---

combination of morality and pragmatism makes transformational leadership attractive. After all, who wouldn't want to be an extraordinary leader who is both good and effective?

The transformational approach holds promise for those wanting to become better, more ethical leaders. If transforming leadership consists of a set of practices, then anyone can function as a transformational leader by adopting these behaviors. Further, the same set of practices works in every context. No longer do leaders have to balance a host of situational factors when making decisions. Instead, they display the same set of characteristics that they adapt to their particular setting.

Unfortunately, the ethical assumptions underlying transformational leadership have often been overlooked in the pursuit of greater results. Many writers and researchers appear more interested in what works than in what is right. To them, transformational leadership is another name for successful or effective leadership; leaders are transforming because they achieve extraordinary, tangible results such as rescuing failing corporations or winning battles. These theorists are less concerned with whether leaders foster higher moral standards or if transforming tactics serve ethical ends. Thus, Attila the Hun can be held up as an example of transformational leadership although he pillaged the lands that he conquered.[9]

Writers who fail to distinguish between pseudotransformational and transformational leadership engage in the blind hero worship I criticized in the introduction to this book. There are true leadership heroes, but let's not confuse them with the villains. Remember, too, that all leaders suffer from the uneven character development described in Chapter 3. No leader is perfect; all are a mix of virtues and vices.

Some scholars label transformational theorists as leader centric for paying too much attention to leaders while downplaying the contributions of followers. These skeptics have reason for concern. Burns, Bass, and other proponents of transformative leadership argue that leaders play the most important role in determining group morality and performance. Leaders craft the vision, challenge the status quo, and inspire. At times, they may decide to transform the organization despite, not because of, followers, as in the case of the CEO who overrules her staff to bring about change. Critics of transformational leadership argue that stakeholders are just as important to the success of a group as leaders, if not more so. After all, followers do most of the work.[10]

So much focus on the leader can create dependency. Followers won't act independently if they continually look to the leader for guidance. Leaders may also get an inflated sense of their own importance, tempting them to cast shadows. Bass believes that the distinction between pseudo- and truly transformational leadership addresses these concerns. Transforming leaders are much less prone to ethical abuses, he contends, because they put the needs of others first, treat followers with respect, and seek worthy objectives. You'll need to decide for yourself if transformational theorists have adequately responded to the dangers posed by their perspective.

◻ Postindustrial Leadership:
Ethics in Relational Process

James Rost is one of the most influential opponents of transformational leadership and other modern leadership theories. Rost, a retired professor of leadership studies at the University of San Diego, contends that most definitions of leadership are based on an industrial model. In this model, leaders function as supermanagers. They set the goals and then get followers to reach these objectives. The higher the group's productivity, as measured by such yardsticks as profits, service, and growth, the more effective the leader.

The industrial model of leadership, according to Rost, is ill suited to the new, postindustrial age, which will put a greater value on collaboration, consensus, diversity, and participation. In addition, theories based on this foundation (including the transformational approach) overlook the "essential nature" of what leadership is—the relationship between leaders and followers that enables them to get things done. Rost highlights this partnership in his definition. Leadership, he says, "is an influence relationship among leaders and followers who intend real changes that reflect their mutual purposes."[11] Four elements are key to this definition:

- *The relationship is based on influence.* Leaders influence followers, followers influence leaders, followers influence other followers, and so on. Followers can disagree with their leaders and decide to end the relationship.

- *Leaders and followers are the people in this relationship.* This principle seems self-evident, but Rost wants to highlight that followers are active partners with leaders. At one point, he rejects the *follower* label because it implies passivity, opting instead for such alternative terms as *constituent* and *participant*. Leaders have more power to influence, but they work together with constituents. Rost contends that "followers do not do followership, they do leadership. Both leaders and followers form one relationship that is leadership."[12]

- *Leaders and followers intend real changes.* Real changes are both purposeful and substantive. They don't happen by accident but are designed to make a significant difference in the lives of individuals, group, organizations, and societies. Unlike approaches based on the industrial model, the postindustrial perspective emphasizes process, rather than product. The key is the intent of both parties. Few immediate changes may result, but leadership occurs when leaders and their constituents share the same intentions and engage in the continuing relational process.

■ *Leaders and followers develop mutual purposes.* Leaders and participants don't have to have identical purposes but need to share at least some in common. Purposes are different than goals. Goals are quantifiable, are aimed at producing specific end products, and are achievable. Purposes are broad statements that address the quality of life. They are never reached (and they may change), but they allow leaders and followers to create communities. Leaders don't create purposes and then impose them on followers. Instead, leaders and constituents come to a common agreement about what they hold to be important.

Rost believes that ethicists have not paid enough attention to the interaction between leaders and followers. Leaders need to generate ethical products or content (decisions, policies, programs), but they ought to do so in an ethical manner. The *process* should follow certain criteria. One, influence in the leader-follower relationship should be based on persuasion, not coercion (physical force, psychological intimidation, obedience to authority). Two, influence should flow in both directions. Three, followers must be able to choose whether to participate. Four, goals should be created jointly through discussion and argument. Rost concludes by offering the following ethical standard: "The leadership process is ethical if the people in the relationship (the leaders and followers) *freely* agree that the intended changes *fairly* reflect their mutual purposes."[13]

The developer of the postindustrial model doesn't totally ignore the outcomes of the leadership process. Rost rejects utilitarianism, Kant's categorical imperative, and other popular ethical perspectives as too individualistic. Instead, he believes that leaders and followers must work together to develop ethical standards by which to judge their actions. Rost wants to shift the focus from individual choices to those made by the community. Drawing from communitarianism, he argues that leaders and followers should pursue the common good.

Balance Sheet

Advantages (+s)

    Focuses on persuasion, mutual influence, and joint purposes
    Shifts attention from leaders to followers
    Is highly creative
    Recognizes the importance of ethical leadership process

Disadvantages (–s)
  Blurs the distinction between leaders and followers
  Limits leadership to major change efforts
  Is idealistic
  Discards well-established ethical theories

Rost's postindustrial model generated an enthusiastic response from many leadership scholars when it first came out. Supporters liked its emphasis on process, persuasion, collaboration, mutual influence, and shared purposes. This approach seemed to reverse the trend, reflected in transformational leadership, toward glorifying leaders at the expense of followers. Even casual readers had to be impressed by Rost's thorough review of previous definitions of leadership. The postindustrial model is a creative attempt to develop a new understanding of leadership better suited to a new era. Important ethical values—empowerment, nonviolence, community, honesty, equality—run throughout its definitional elements. Rost rightly recognizes that *how* we carry out our tasks as leaders is extremely important.

The advantages of the postindustrial model must be weighed against a number of significant disadvantages. First, Rost blurs the distinction between leaders and followers (participants or constituents). If followers "do" leadership, how do their roles differ from those of leaders? Second, leaders can intend small, immediate changes in addition to significant, long-term, "real" changes described in the postindustrial model. Third, Rost appears to limit leadership to only those relationships marked by persuasion, mutual purposes, participation, and equality. He doesn't seem to acknowledge the reality that many leaders use coercion to get their way, withhold power and information, put their goals first, and distance themselves from constituents. Even leaders who do want to build partnerships with followers must sometimes punish poor behavior and closely supervise followers who lack skills and experience. Fourth, Rost is too quick to reject well-established ethical perspectives. General ethical perspectives, as shown in the last chapter, can provide plenty of moral guidance to leaders. Rost makes the common good the sole standard for making ethical choices about leadership products. In Chapter 5, my discussion of communitarianism noted that communities often pursue conflicting standards or goods. We need additional criteria, such as those proposed by Amatai Etzioni, to sort through these competing claims.

▣ Taoism: Leading Nature's Way

Taoism (pronounced "Daoism") is one of the world's oldest philosophies, dating to ancient China (600-300 B.C.). The nation had enjoyed peace and prosperity under a series of imperial dynasties but was now a patchwork of warring city-states. Groups of traveling philosophers traveled from one fiefdom to another, offering leaders advice for restoring harmony. The Taoists were one of these "100 Schools of Thought."[14]

The *Tao Te Ching (The Classic of the Way and its Power and Virtue)* is Taoism's major text. According to popular tradition, a royal librarian named Lao-tzu authored this book as he departed China for self-imposed exile. Most scholars, however, believe that this short volume (5,000 words) is a collection of the teachings of several wise men or sages. Taoism divided into philosophical and religious branches by A.D. 200. Religious Taoists sought to extend their lives through diet and exercise and developed a priesthood that presided over elaborate temple rituals. Today, Taoist religious practices are popular in both the East and the West. Those interested in Taoist leadership principles, however, generally draw from the movement's philosophical roots. These principles are described for American audiences in such books as *The Tao of Leadership, The Tao of Personal Leadership,* and *Real Power: Business Lessons From the Tao Te Ching.*[15]

Understanding the Way or Tao is the key to understanding Taoist ethical principles. The Tao is the shapeless, nameless force or Non-Being that brings all things into existence or Being and then sustains them. The Tao takes form in nature and reveals itself through natural principles. These principles then become the standards for ethical behavior. Moral leaders and followers develop their character (*te*) by acting in harmony with the Tao, not by following codes or laws.

Three principles, in particular, lay the groundwork for ethical decision making. The first is complementary opposites (the yin and the yang). Mountains require valleys, there is no life without death, and so on. The world operates as it should when these forces are in balance. The second principle is circular movement or reversion. Plants, animals, rocks, and other forms of matter ultimately return to their natural state.

Living creatures die, for example, and mountains eventually wear down. The third principle is positive inaction or *wu-wei*. "Leave well enough alone" seems to capture the essence of Taoist ethics. Government reflects a distrust of the working of the Tao and of human nature, according to the Taoist sages. When left alone, followers obey natural laws, and harmony is restored to society. They govern best who govern least. Attempting to solve problems often creates new ones because the universe is one interconnected whole. The creation of the interstate highway system demonstrates how problem solving can have unanticipated consequences. Construction of the nation's superhighways began during the Eisenhower administration. Government officials wanted to speed the flow of troops and supplies in case of Communist attack and to tie regions of the nation together. Planners did not anticipate the profound changes that this network of high-speed roads would bring, however. The interstate system destroyed existing neighborhoods and promoted urban sprawl by making travel from the suburbs easier. Our national reliance on the automobile increased dramatically.

Taoists introduce a model of leadership based on images drawn from nature and daily life. The first image is that of an uncarved block. An uncarved block of stone or wood is nameless and shapeless, like the Tao itself. Leaders should also be blocklike, avoiding wealth, status, and glory at the same time they leave followers alone.

The second image is water. Water provides an important insight into how leaders ought to influence others by illustrating that there is great strength in weakness. Given enough time, water cuts through the hardest rock. According to the *Tao Te Ching*,

> *There is nothing softer and weaker than water,*
> *And yet there is nothing better for attacking hard and*
> *Strong things.*
> *For this reason there is no substitute for it.*
> *All the world knows that the weak overcomes the strong and*
> *The soft overcomes the hard.*[16]

Flexibility or pliability is one reason why weakness is so powerful. Water moves around obstacles, and young blades of grass and saplings survive windstorms because they bend, rather than resist as big trees do.

The third image is the valley. Although both the yin and yang are important, Taoists highlight the importance of the yin or feminine side of leadership that is represented by the valley metaphor. Leaders should act humbly, rather than seek celebrity and status.

The fourth image is the clay pot, which celebrates emptiness by elevating nothing to higher status than something. The most useful part of a pot is the emptiness within. Similarly, the most useful part of a room is the empty space between the walls. Leaders ought to empty themselves, putting aside empty words, superficial thinking, technology, and selfishness: "Do not be an embodier of fame; do not be a storehouse of schemes; do not be an undertaker of projects; do not be a proprietor of wisdom. . . . Be empty, that is all."[17]

Balance Sheet

Advantages (+s)

  Provides an alternative to Western approaches
  Is suited to the modern work environment
  Emphasizes inner peace, service, and balance
  Speaks directly to the leader's use of power and relationship to the environment
  Promotes character

Disadvantages (–s)

  Denies reason
  Rejects codes and laws
  Is ambiguous about many moral issues
  Does not adequately explain evil

Nearly all the concepts presented in the typical Western leadership or ethics text are drawn from the United States, Great Britain, and Europe. Taoism is one of the few non-Western approaches to attract much attention. It's easy to see why Taoist thought is catching on with leaders and scholars alike. Taoist principles seem particularly well suited to leaders working in fast-paced, rapidly changing, decentralized work environments. Taoist thinkers encourage us to be flexible and to use "soft" tactics such as collaboration, listening, and negotiation that facilitate teamwork in leaner, flatter organizations. They urge us to develop a sense of inner peace, to serve (see the discussion of servant leadership in the next section), and to strike a better balance between work and home. Focusing on being, rather than doing, encourages leaders to develop character, the emphasis in Chapter 3.

Taoism speaks most directly to the leader's use of power and privilege. It is difficult to imagine that Taoist sages would approve of the vast difference in pay between American executives and employees, for example, or give their blessing to such perks as company jets, private chauffeurs, and executive dining rooms. The Taoist perspective also addresses environmental issues. According to Taoists, we need to work with nature, not attempt to control or manage it. The natural world seems to renew itself when left alone. When cows are kept out of streams, for instance, vegetation returns to the riverbank, providing shade that cools the water and encourages the return of native fish. On the other hand, attempts to manage the environment frequently end in disaster. Consider the attempts to suppress forest fires. Putting out wildfires allows tinder to build up for years. When a blaze does take hold, it is much more likely burn out of control.

There are some serious disadvantages to Taoist ethics. In their attempt to follow nature, Taoists encourage leaders to empty themselves, among other things, of reason. Intuition has its place, but we need to learn how to make more reasoned decisions, not to abandon logic. Taoists are skeptical, and rightly so, about moral codes and laws. Rules alone won't improve behavior. Yet reasonable rules, professional guidelines, and organizational codes of conduct can and do play a role in improving ethical climate (see Chapter 9).

Although Taoism has much to say about the shadow of power and our relationship to the world around us, it is silent on many common ethical dilemmas, such as the case of the manager asked to keep information about an upcoming merger to herself (see Chapter 1). What does it mean to follow nature's example when faced with this decision? Perhaps the manager should keep quiet to keep from intruding into the lives of followers. Nonetheless, withholding information would put her in the position of a mountain instead of a valley, giving her an advantage.

One final concern should be noted before closing this discussion of Taoist ethics. Taoism's firm conviction that humans, in their natural state, will act morally seems to deny the power of evil. My thesis has been that leaders and followers can and do act destructively, driven by the monsters lurking in their shadow side.

▣ Servant Leadership:
Put the Needs of Followers First

Servant leadership has roots in both Eastern and Western thought. The Taoist sages encouraged leaders to be humble valleys; Jesus told his disciples that "whoever wants to become great among you must be your servant, and whoever wants to be first must be slave of all" (Mark 10:43-44, New International Version). Robert Greenleaf sparked contemporary interest in leaders as servants. Greenleaf, who worked for many years as director of research at General Electric, coined the term *servant-leader* in 1970 to describe a leadership model that puts the concerns of followers first.[18] Later, he founded a center, headquartered in Indianapolis, to promote servant leadership. A number of businesses, nonprofit organizations, and community leadership programs have adopted his model. Margaret Wheatley, Peter Block, Max DePree, and James Autry have joined Greenleaf in urging leaders to act like servants.

The basic premise of servant leadership is simple yet profound. Leaders should put the needs of followers before their own needs. By continually asking themselves what would be best for their constituents, servant-leaders are less likely to cast shadows by taking advantage of the trust of followers, acting inconsistently, or accumulating money and power. Larry Spears, executive director of the Greenleaf Center for Servant Leadership, identifies the following set of 10 characteristics as central to servant leadership.[19]

1. *Listening.* Leaders need to back up their speaking and decision-making skills with attentive listening. Listening is both external and internal. Listening to others clarifies the will of the group; listening to the self promotes personal growth. (More information on effective listening can be found in Chapter 8.)

2. *Empathy.* Developing empathy is an extension of listening. Followers need to be accepted and recognized; they should never be rejected as people. Leaders can object, however, to their behavior and performance.

3. *Healing.* Servant leadership has the potential to heal emotional hurts, helping to make followers whole.

4. *Awareness.* Awareness of the self and the situation makes a leader more sensitive to ethical issues and important values. This consciousness also promotes a broader perspective on ethical problems.

5. *Persuasion.* Servant-leaders rely on persuasion, instead of authority. They rarely coerce but convince instead, focusing on building group consensus.

6. *Conceptualization.* Servant leadership involves looking beyond daily activities to dream about the future, to develop a vision for the organization.

7. *Foresight.* Like conceptualization, foresight involves looking ahead, only with a sharper focus on determining the probable outcome of a decision or situation.

8. *Stewardship.* Servant-leaders recognize that they hold their positions on behalf of followers and hold their institutions in trust for the larger society.

9. *Commitment to the growth of people.* Employees are more than workers; they are people, too. Servant-leaders commit themselves to nurturing the professional, personal, and spiritual growth of followers. This commitment takes visible form through such actions as training, soliciting suggestions, and involving employees in decision making.

10. *Building community.* Servant-leaders seek to restore community bonds one group at a time. They believe that a sense of community can be created in businesses and other work organizations.

Balance Sheet

Advantages (+s)
> Altruism
> Simplicity
> Self-awareness

Disadvantages (−s)
> Seems unrealistic
> Encourages passivity
> May not work in every context
> May serve the wrong cause
> Is associated with negative connotation of the term *servant*

Altruism is the first strength of servant leadership. Concern for others, in this case, our followers, comes before concern for self. We can serve only if we commit ourselves to the principle that others should come first.

Simplicity is the second strength of servant leadership. We are far less likely to cast shadows if we approach our leadership roles with one goal in mind—the desire to serve. A great number of ethical abuses, as Chapter 2 emphasized, stem from leaders putting their personal interests first. Servant-leaders promote the growth of followers, use power and privilege wisely, and act as stewards on behalf of the larger community.

Self-awareness is a third strength of servant leadership. Servant-leaders listen to themselves as well as others, take time for reflection, and recognize the importance of spiritual resources.

Despite its strengths, servant leadership has not met with universal approval. Cynicism is often the first response when this model is presented. "Sounds good in principle," listeners respond, "but it would never work at my company, in my family, at my condominium association meeting, or _____ " (fill in the blank). Skeptics report that they have been "walked on" whenever they've tried to be nice to poor performers at work, rebellious teenagers, or nasty neighbors. Others equate a servant attitude with passivity.

Skepticism about servant leadership may stem, in part, from a misunderstanding that equates service with weakness. Servant-leaders need to be tough. Sometimes, the best way to serve someone is to reprimand or fire that individual. Nevertheless, there may be situations in which servant leadership is extremely difficult if not impossible to implement. See Case Study 6.1 for one example of service in one of the world's hardest places.

Misplaced goals are a problem for servant-leaders and followers alike. The butler in the novel *The Remains of the Day* illustrates the danger of misspent service. He devotes his entire life to being the perfect servant who meets the needs of his English employer. Sadly, his sacrifice is wasted because the lord of the manor turns out to be a Nazi sympathizer. The desire to serve needs to be combined with careful reasoning and values clarification. We must carefully examine who and what we serve, asking ourselves such questions as these: Is this group, individual, or organization worthy of our service? What values are we promoting? What is the product of our service—light or darkness?

Finally, members of some minority groups, particularly African Americans, associate the word *servant* with a history of slavery, oppression, and discrimination. The negative connotations surrounding the word *servant* may keep you from embracing the idea of servant

CASE STUDY 6.1

Servant Leadership Behind Bars

A federal penitentiary filled with some of the nation's most notorious criminals seems an unlikely setting for servant leadership. Prison guards must deal with hostile, manipulative inmates. Their jobs are monotonous but quickly become dangerous when prisoners take hostages or riot. Do the principles of servant leadership apply in this situation? That was the challenge that Les, an experienced federal custodial officer, posed after hearing my presentation on servant leadership. He wanted to abandon his old, authoritarian approach to his job but was afraid that inmates would take advantage of him if he adopted a "softer" leadership style.

For the next half hour, the group wrestled with the question of whether Les could serve prisoners in his role as a guard. We concluded that Les could demonstrate at least some of the characteristics of a servant-leader. He could (a) listen more, (b) remember that inmates are valuable human beings, (c) try persuasion first before giving orders or using force, and (d) encourage prisoners to take advantage of educational and training opportunities while in prison.

Evaluate the suggestions of the group. Can Les be a servant-leader? Are there situations in which it is impossible to serve followers?

leadership. You may want to abandon this term and focus instead on related concepts such as altruism and the virtues of concern and compassion.

◻ Implications and Applications

- Many popular leadership theories are built on moral principles. Try to understand a perspective's underlying values and standards before you adopt it as your blueprint for leadership.

- Contrary to popular belief, being ethical makes us more, not less, successful. Being a "good" leader means being both ethical *and* effective.

- Extraordinary leadership is a mix of the practical and the ideal. Blend transaction with transformation. Use rewards, punishments, and exchanges along with idealized influence, inspirational motivation, intellectual stimulation, and individual consideration.

- Pay attention to both the *how* and *what* of leadership. Ethical values should guide your relationships with followers as well as your ultimate goals.

- Don't overlook nature and everyday objects as a source of leadership lessons. You can learn from uncarved blocks, water, valleys, and clay pots.

- Putting the needs of followers first reduces the likelihood that you'll cast ethical shadows.

- Be careful who and what you serve. Make sure that your efforts support worthy people and goals.

▣ For Further Exploration, Challenge, and Self-Assessment

1. What additional advantages and disadvantages can you add for each approach described in the chapter? Which perspective do you find most useful? Why?

2. Brainstorm a list of pseudotransformational and transformational leaders. What factors distinguish the two types of leaders? How do your characteristics compare with those presented in the chapter?

3. Develop a definition of ethical leadership that addresses both leadership processes and products.

4. Discuss the following proposition in a group: "The most successful leaders are also the most ethical leaders." Do you agree? Why or why not?

5. Make a diligent effort to serve followers for a week. At the end of this period, reflect on your experience. Did focusing on the needs of followers change your behavior? What did you do differently? What would happen if you made this your leadership philosophy?

6. Which natural image from Taoism do you find most interesting and helpful? Why? Can you think of additional natural metaphors that would be useful to leaders?

7. Read a popular book on transformational leadership and/or on a transformational leader. Write a review. Summarize the contents for those who have not read it. Next, evaluate the book. What are its strengths and weaknesses from an ethical standpoint? Would you recommend the book to others? Why or why not?

CASE STUDY 6.2

Chapter End Case:
Transforming Clear Lake College

Clear Lake College was in serious trouble in 1982. Enrollment at the midwestern school had dropped from 650 to 600 undergraduates. Because it had no emergency endowment fund, Clear Lake counted on tuition revenue to pay its bills. The loss of so many students threatened to close the 90-year-old school. The college's president, who seemed unable to respond to the crisis, resigned.

The school's board of directors appointed Samuel (Sam) Thomas as the next president. Thomas had a Ph.D. in higher education but came to Clear Lake directly from a marketing position in business. Unlike his predecessor, Thomas didn't hesitate to make bold, sometimes risky decisions. He hired a new admissions staff, convinced faculty to agree to a salary and benefits freeze, and spent several hundred thousand dollars to launch the college's first graduate degree program.

Initially, Clear Lake seemed to go backward, rather than forward, under Sam's direction. Enrollment dropped still further during the first year of his administration, but 1984 saw a surge in new students. The graduate program was a big success, and Sam used his marketing background to improve the college's visibility. An entrepreneur at heart, he encouraged faculty and staff to develop additional programs for new markets. During the next 10 years, enrollment grew to nearly 2,000 students. The college added more graduate degrees and several new undergraduate majors. Clear Lake College earned a national listing as "one of America's educational bargains."

Thomas had many admirable leadership qualities. To begin, he was a "people person" who enjoyed mixing with donors, students, faculty, and administrators at other schools. No one would think of calling him "Dr. Thomas." He was "Sam" to everyone. Second, he was more than willing to tackle tough problems and fire those who weren't performing up to standards. Third, he kept his word to faculty and staff. When the financial picture of the school improved, he raised faculty salaries dramatically. Fourth, he had an uncanny ability to sense new educational markets. He never made a major miscalculation when it came to proposing additional programs.

Yet all was not well under Sam's leadership. His friendly exterior masked an explosive temper. He dressed down faculty and other employees in public meetings and made personnel decisions on his own, based on his instincts rather than on hard data. A number of employees were let go without warning, and many of his hires lasted less than a year. In several instances, the college had to offer generous severance packages to dismissed employees to avoid costly lawsuits. Sam's autocratic style was not limited strictly to personnel decisions. He would change the school's governance structure without consulting faculty who expected to participate in these decisions. In addition, Sam

CASE STUDY 6.2 (Continued)

engaged in micromanagement. He read minutes from every department meeting held on campus, for example, and sent scathing memos if he disagreed with the group's conclusions. Soon, faculty members learned to censor what they put in their meeting notes because they knew that Sam would be reading them.

Sam received lots of accolades for his success at Clear Lake College. He was credited for the school's turnaround and was named as the area's outstanding citizen one year. He was popular with other university presidents, serving on national collegiate boards and commissions. The board of the college was eager to renew his contract despite the concerns of the faculty. Unfortunately, Sam's successes made him less, not more, flexible. Frustrated by faculty criticism, he made even fewer efforts to consult them when making decisions. He began to call students who had offended him into his office to berate them.

By the early 1990s, it looked as if the college had "outgrown" Sam's leadership style. After all, the school was much bigger and more complex then it had been when he took over. Sam had no intention of stepping down, however. He began to refer to Clear Lake as "my" college and continued to be involved in every detail of college life. Sam had to be forced to resign when he contracted Parkinson's disease in 1995. The college has continued to grow under the leadership of a new president who, while maintaining a good deal of decision-making power, relies heavily on his vice presidents and has little input in the day-to-day operations of most departments.

Discussion Probes

1. What elements of transactional and transforming leadership did Sam exhibit?

2. Was Sam a transformational or a pseudotransformational leader?

3. Have you ever had to confront a leader about her or his behavior? What did you say or do? What was the outcome of the encounter? Would you do anything differently next time?

4. Does success make leaders more dangerous, more likely to cast shadows?

5. How do you determine when to remove a leader, particularly one who has a proven track record of success?

Notes

1. Ciulla, J. B. (1995). Ethics: Mapping the territory. In J. B. Ciulla (Ed.), *Ethics: The heart of leadership* (pp. 3-25). Westport, CT: Praeger.

2. Burns, J. M. (1978). *Leadership.* New York: Harper & Row.

3. Burns (1978), *Leadership,* p. 20.

4. See, for example, the following:

Bass, B. M. (1996). *A new paradigm of leadership: An inquiry into transformational leadership*. Alexandria, VA: U.S. Army Research Institute for the Behavioral and Social Sciences.

Bass, B. M., & Avolio, B. J. (1993). Transformational leadership: A response to critiques. In M. M. Chemers & R. Ayman (Eds.), *Leadership theory and research: Perspectives and directions* (pp. 49-60). San Diego, CA: Academic Press.

Waldman, D. A., Bass, B. M., & Yammarino, F. J. (1990). Adding to contingent-reward behavior: The augmenting effect of charismatic leadership. *Group and Organizational Studies, 15*, 381-394.

5. Bass, B. M. (1990). *Bass & Stogdill's handbook of leadership* (3rd ed.). New York: Free Press, p. 53.

6. Many popular leadership books offer anecdotal or statistical evidence that transforming leaders are generally the most successful. Examples include these:

Bennis, W., & Nanus, B. (1985). *Leaders: The strategies for taking charge*. New York: Harper & Row.

Kotter, J. P. (1990). *A force for change: How leadership differs from management*. New York: Free Press.

Kouzes, J. M., & Posner, B. (1995). *The leadership challenge: How to get extraordinary things done in organizations*. San Francisco: Jossey-Bass.

7. Hackman, M. Z., & Johnson, C. E. (2000). *Leadership: A communication perspective* (3rd ed.). Prospect Heights, IL: Waveland, Ch. 4.

8. Bass, B. M. (1995). The ethics of transformational leadership. In J. Ciulla (Ed.), *Ethics: The heart of leadership* (pp. 169-192). Westport, CT: Praeger.

9. Roberts, W. (1987). *Leadership secrets of Attila the Hun*. New York: Warner Books.

10. One particularly vocal critic of leader-centric approaches is Robert Kelley. See Kelley, R. (1992). *The power of followership*. New York: Doubleday/Currency.

11. Rost, J. (1991). *Leadership for the twenty-first century*. New York: Praeger, p. 102; See also Rost, J. (1993). Leadership in the new millennium. *Journal of Leadership Studies, 1*, 92-110.

12. Rost, *Leadership for the twenty-first century*, p. 109.

13. Rost, *Leadership for the twenty-first century*, p. 161.

14. Material on key components of Taoist thought is adopted from the following:

Johnson, C. E. (1997, Spring). A leadership journey to the East. *Journal of Leadership Studies, 4*, 82-88.

Johnson, C. E. (2000). *Emerging perspectives in leadership ethics*. In *Selected proceedings: 1999 annual meeting of the International Leadership Association*. College Park, MD: Academy of Leadership Press.

Johnson, C. E. (2000). Taoist leadership ethics. *Journal of Leadership Studies, 7*, 82-91.

15. Heider, J. (1985). *The Tao of leadership*. New York: Bantam; Dreher, K. (1995). *The Tao of personal leadership*. New York: HarperBusiness; Autry, J. A., & Mitchell, S. (1998). *Real power: Business lessons from the Tao te ching*. New York: Riverhead.

16. Chan, W. (Trans.). (1963). *The way of Lao Tzu*. Indianapolis, IN: Bobbs-Merrill, p. 236.

17. Watson, B. (Trans.). (1996). *Chuang Tzu: Basic writings*. New York: Columbia University Press, p. 95.

18. Greenleaf, R. K. (1977). *Servant leadership*. New York: Paulist Press.

19. Spears, L. (1998). Introduction: Tracing the growing impact of servant leadership. In L. C. Spears (Ed.), *Insights on leadership* (pp. 1-12). New York: John Wiley.

7

As we practice resolving dilemmas we find ethics to be less a goal than a pathway, less a destination than a trip, less an inoculation than a process.

—Ethicist Rushworth Kidder

□ What's Ahead

This chapter introduces systematic approaches to ethical problem solving. We'll take a look at four decision-making formats: (1) Kidder's ethical checkpoints, (2) Potter's box, (3) Nash's 12 questions, and (4) Cooper's active process model. Once again, I'll give you my thoughts about the strengths and weaknesses of each approach.

□ Pick a Format, Any Format

Decision-making guidelines or formats can help us make better ethical choices. Taking a systematic approach encourages teams and individuals to carefully define the problem, gather information, apply ethical

143

standards and values, identify and evaluate alternative courses of action, and follow through on their choices. They're also better equipped to defend their decisions. I'll describe four ethical decision-making formats in the pages to come. All four approaches are useful. You may want to use just one or a combination of all of them. The particular format you use is not as important as taking a systematic approach to moral reasoning. You can practice these guidelines by applying them to the scenarios described at the end of the chapter.

◻ Kidder's Ethical Checkpoints

Ethicist Rushworth Kidder suggests that nine steps or checkpoints can help bring order to otherwise confusing ethical issues.[1]

1. *Recognize that there is a problem.* This step is critical because it forces us to acknowledge that there is an issue that deserves our attention and helps us separate moral questions from disagreements about manners and social conventions. Being late for a party, for example, may be bad manners and violate cultural expectations. This act, however, does not translate into a moral problem involving right or wrong. Deciding whether to accept a kickback from a supplier, on the other hand, is an ethical dilemma.

2. *Determine the actor.* Once we've determined that there is an ethical issue, we then need to decide who is responsible for addressing the problem. I may be concerned that the owner of a local business treats his employees poorly. Nonetheless, unless I work for the company or buy its products, there is little I can do to address this situation.

3. *Gather the relevant facts.* Adequate, accurate, and current information is important for making effective decisions of all types, including ethical ones. Details do make a difference. In deciding whether it is just to suspend a student for fighting, for instance, a school principal will want to hear from teachers, classmates, and the offender to determine the seriousness of the offense, the student's reason for fighting, and the outcome of the altercation. The administrator will probably be more lenient if this is the offender's first offense and the student was fighting in self-defense.

4. *Test for right-versus-wrong issues.* A choice is generally a poor one if it (a) gives you a negative, gut-level reaction (the stench test);

BOX 7.1 Leadership at the Movies: *The Insider*

Key cast members: Russell Crowe, Al Pacino, Christopher Plummer

Synopsis:

Russell Crowe plays Jeffrey Wigand, a former research executive at the Brown & Williamson tobacco company, who wrestles with the decision of whether to go public with what he knows about the industry's cover-up of the health risks of smoking. If he does, he will lose his pension and health benefits as well as any hope of continuing his career in business. *60 Minutes* producer Lowell Bergman (Al Pacino) coaxes him to come forward, but executive producer Don Hewitt, under pressure from CBS lawyers, betrays Wigand by deciding not to air the interview. Belatedly, Hewitt and Mike Wallace (Christopher Plummer) realize that their journalistic integrity has been compromised, and they air the segment. Wigand's wife divorces him, and he becomes a science teacher. Bergman resigns from CBS.

Rating: R, for language

Themes: The costs of whistle-blowing, courage and cowardice, personal integrity, following through on choices, manipulation of the media

---

(b) would make you uncomfortable if it appeared on the front page of tomorrow's newspaper (the front-page test); or (c) would violate the moral code of someone who you care a lot about (the Mom test). If your decision violates any of these criteria, you had better reconsider.

5. *Test for right-versus-right values.* Many ethical dilemmas pit two core values against each other. Determine if two good or right values are in conflict with one another in this situation. Right-versus-right value clashes include

- Truth telling versus loyalty to others and institutions. Telling the truth may threaten our allegiance to another person or to an organization, such as when a leader (such as the one profiled in the Leadership Ethics at the Movies feature in Box 7.1) must determine whether to "blow the whistle" on corporate wrongdoing.
- Personal needs versus the needs of the community. Our desire to serve our immediate group or ourselves can run counter to the needs of the larger group or community.

CASE STUDY 7.1

The Board Chairman's Question

In his position as the number two in a loan organization, Andrew was appointed directly by the board of directors, as was the president. The organization, a nonprofit with some $10 million in assets, had a good record of dispensing loans to families in need. It proved to be a very attractive entity to a similar and slightly larger organization, whose principals approached the president and suggested a merger.

For some months the talks between the organizations continued, with the president as the chief negotiator for Andrew's side. The board of directors was aware of the activity. As the situation seemed to be approaching a decision point, however, the board got cold feet and one day instructed the president to cease and desist in his negotiations, explaining that from now on all contacts with the other organization should flow through the board.

Several days later, the president told Andrew he had invited the senior officers from the other loan organization to town for a day-long site visit, where they could examine the loan files and learn about the procedures of this organization. Andrew was taken aback: Was not this in direct violation, he asked, of the board's directive? The president admitted it was, but asserted that he was tired of being run around by the board. He told Andrew that he was going ahead with plans for what seemed to him a very good merger, not only for the two organizations but for the client base they served. And he asked Andrew to be present for the day-long meeting.

- Short-term benefits versus long-term negative consequences. Sometimes, satisfying the immediate needs of the group (giving a hefty pay raise to employees, for example) can lead to long-term negative consequences (endangering the future of the business).
- Justice versus mercy. Being fair and evenhanded may conflict with our desire to show love and compassion.

Kidder believes that truth versus loyalty is the most common type of conflict involving two deeply held values. He offers the case described in Case Study 7.1 as an example of the tension caused by this type of choice.

6. *Apply the ethical standards/perspectives.* Apply the ethical principle(s) that is most relevant and useful to this specific issue. Is it com-

---

CASE STUDY 7.1 (Continued)

Andrew's initial dilemma was clear. As an appointee of the board, he had more than the usual commitment of a number two to an organization's governing board. Yet he knew that, were he to cross the president on such a matter, his tenure in the organization could be short-lived. What's more, he liked and respected the president. What to do?

He explained to the president that, while he did not feel he could stand in his way, his conscience would not let him participate. So they agreed that he should work at home on the day of the visit. The day came, and Andrew was at home when, early in the afternoon, the phone rang. It was the chairman of the board, who asked why Andrew was at home.

Now the dilemma was immediate. It was right, Andrew knew, to support his president, show the kind of loyalty that he knew the president would show him in similar circumstances, and not play the tattletale. What's more, it would have been easy to create an explanation that was acceptable and unrevealing—pleading, for example, a health-related problem. Yet it was right to tell the truth—especially when the question was a legitimate one, coming from an individual who had every right to know what was happening.

If you were Andrew, how would you answer the board chairman's question? Why?

SOURCE: Kidder, R. M. (1995). *How good people make tough choices: Resolving the dilemmas of ethical living.* New York: Fireside, pp. 124-125. Reprinted by permission of HarperCollins Publishers, Inc.

---

munitarianism? Utilitarianism? Kant's categorical imperative? A combination of perspectives?

7. *Look for a third way.* Seemingly irreconcilable values can sometimes be resolved through compromise or the development of a creative solution. Negotiators frequently seek a third way to bring competing factions together. Such was the case in the deliberations that produced the Camp David peace accord. Egypt demanded that Israel return land on the West Bank seized in the 1967 War. Israel resisted because it wanted a buffer zone to protect its security. The dispute was settled when Egypt pledged that it would not attack Israel again. Assured of safety, the Israelis agreed to return the territory to Egypt.

8. *Make the decision.* At some point, we need to step up and make the decision. This seems a given (after all, the point of the whole process is to reach a conclusion). We may be mentally exhausted from wrestling

with the problem, however, get caught up in the act of analysis, or lack the necessary courage to come to a decision. In Kidder's words,

> At this point in the process, there's little to do but decide. That requires moral courage—an attribute essential to leadership and one that, along with reason, distinguishes humanity most sharply from the animal world. Little wonder, then, that the exercise of ethical decision-making is often seen as the highest fulfillment of the human condition.[2]

9. *Revisit and reflect on the decision.* Learn from your choices. Once you've moved on to other issues, stop and reflect. What lessons emerge from this case that you can apply to future decisions? What ethical issues did it raise?

Balance Sheet

Advantages (+s)
>Is thorough
>Considers problem ownership
>Emphasizes the importance of getting the facts straight
>Recognizes that dilemmas can involve right-right as well as right-wrong choices
>Encourages the search for creative solutions
>Sees ethical decision making as a learning process

Disadvantages (–s)
>Not easy to determine who has the responsibility to solve a problem
>Facts not always available or insufficient time to gather them
>Decisions don't always lead to action

A lot can be said for Kidder's approach to ethical decision making. For one thing, he seems to cover all the bases, beginning with defining the issue all the way through to learning from the situation after the "dust has settled." He acknowledges that there are some problems that we can't do much about and that we need to pay particular attention to gathering as much information as possible. The ethicist recognizes that some decisions involve deciding between two "goods" and leaves the door open for creative solutions. Making a choice can be an act of courage, as Kidder points out, and we can apply lessons learned in one dilemma to future problems.

On the flip side, some of the strengths of Kidder's model can also be seen as weaknesses. In an increasingly interdependent world, determining responsibility or ownership of the problem is getting harder. Who is responsible for poor labor conditions in Third World countries, for instance? The manufacturer? The subcontractor? The store that sells the products made in sweatshops? Those who buy the items? Kidder also seems to assume that leaders will have the time to gather necessary information. Unfortunately, in crises, time is in short supply. When an employee goes public with a charge of sexual harassment against a manager, the supervisor must decide immediately whether to fire or suspend the accused, what information to release to the press, and so on. Finally, the model seems to equate deciding with doing. As the discussion of moral action in Chapter 3 noted, we can decide on a course of action but not follow through. Kidder is right to say that making ethical choices requires courage. It takes even more courage, however, to put the choice into effect.

▣ Nash's 12 Questions

Ethics consultant Laura Nash offers 12 questions that can help businesses and other groups identify the responsibilities involved moral choices.[3] She argues that discussions based on these queries can be useful even if the group doesn't reach a conclusion. Managers who answer the questions surface ethical concerns that might otherwise remain hidden, identify common moral problems, clarify gaps between stated values and performance, and explore a variety of alternatives.

1. *Have you defined the problem accurately?* The ethical decision-making process begins with assembling the facts. Determine how many employees will be affected by layoffs, how much the cleanup of toxic materials will cost, or how many people have been injured by faulty products. Finding out the facts can help defuse the emotionalism of some issues (perhaps the damage is not as great as first feared). Experts may disagree, however, as to what the facts really are. In the Bhopal disaster profiled in Chapter 10, for example, estimates of the dead and injured are much higher in India than in the United States.

2. *How would you define the problem if you stood on the other side of the fence?* Asking how others might feel forces self-examination. From a

company's point of view, expanding a local plant may make good sense by increasing production and efficiency. Government officials and neighbors might have a different perspective. A larger plant means more workers clogging already overcrowded roads and contributing to urban sprawl.

3. *How did this situation occur in the first place?* This question separates the symptoms from the disease. Strained labor relations and customers who lie and cheat are generally symptoms of deeper problems. Firing an employee for unethical behavior is a temporary solution. Probe to discover the underlying causes. Many dubious accounting practices, for example, are the result of pressure to produce high quarterly profits.

4. *To whom and to what do you give your loyalties as a person or group and as a member of the organization?* Conflicts of loyalty, as noted in Chapter 1, are hard to sort through. Wrestling with the problem of ultimate loyalty (work group? family? self? corporation?), however, can clarify the values operating in an ethical dilemma.

5 and 6. *What is your intention in making this decision? How does this intention compare with the likely results?* These questions probe both the group's intentions and the likely results. Honorable motives don't guarantee positive results. Make sure that the outcomes reflect your motivations.

7. *Whom could your decision or action injure?* Too often, groups consider possible injury only after being sued. Try, in advance, to determine harmful consequences. What will happen if customers ignore label warnings and spread your pesticide indiscriminately, for example? Will the guns you manufacture end up in the hands of urban gang members? On the basis of these determinations, you may decide to abandon your plans to make these items or revise the way they are marketed.

8. *Can you engage the affected parties in a discussion of the problem before you make your decision?* Talking to affected parties is one way to make sure that you understand how your actions will affect them. Few of us want other people to decide what is in our best interest. Yet we often push forward with projects that assume we know what is in the best interests of others.

9. *Are you confident that your position will be as valid for a long period as it seems now?* Make sure that your choice will stand the test of time. What seems like a compelling reason for a decision may not seem so im-

portant months or years later. Consider the U.S. decision to attack Iraq during the Gulf War, for instance. Americans were outraged over atrocities against Kuwaiti citizens and wanted to topple Saddam Hussein. Reporters discovered later that many reports of atrocities were false, and the Iraqi leader remains in power. Our decision to wage this war doesn't appear as justified now as it did in the months leading up to the conflict.

10. *Could you disclose without qualm your decision or action to your boss, your CEO, the board of directors, your family, or society as a whole?* No ethical decision is too trivial to escape the disclosure test. If you or your group wouldn't want to disclose this action, then you'd better reevaluate your choice.

11. *What is the symbolic potential of your action if understood? Misunderstood?* What you intend may not be what the public perceives (see questions 5 and 6). If your company is a notorious polluter, contributions to local arts groups may be seen as an attempt to divert attention from your firm's poor environmental record, not as a generous civic gesture.

12. *Under what conditions would you allow exceptions to your stand?* Moral consistency is critical, but is there any basis for making an exception? Dorm rules might require that visiting hours end at midnight on weekdays. As a resident assistant, however, is there any time when you would be willing to overlook violations? During finals week? On the evening before classes start? When dorm residents and visitors are working on class projects?

Balance Sheet

Advantages (+s)
  Highlights the importance of gathering facts
  Encourages perspective taking
  Forecasts results and consequences through time
Disadvantages (–s)
  Is extremely time-consuming
  May not always reach a conclusion
  Ignores implementation

Like Kidder's ethical checkpoints, Nash's 12 questions highlight the importance of problem identification and information gathering. They go a step further, however, by encouraging us to engage in perspective taking. We need to see the problem from the other party's view, consider the possible injury we might cause, invite others to give us feedback, and consider how our actions will be perceived. Perspective-taking skills will play a critical role in managing ethical-cultural diversity, the subject of Chapter 10. We also need to envision results and take a long-term perspective, imagining how our decisions will stand the test of time. Stepping back can keep us from making choices we might regret later. For example, the decision to test nuclear weapons without warning citizens may have seemed justified to officials waging the Cold War. Now, however, even the federal government admits that these tests were immoral.

I suspect that some groups will be frustrated by the time it takes to answer the 12 questions. Not only is the model detailed, but discussing the problem with affected parties could take a series of meetings lasting weeks and months. Complex issues such as determining who should clean up river pollution involve a great variety of constituencies with different agendas (e.g., government agencies, company representatives, citizen groups, conservation clubs). Some decision makers may also be put off by the model's ambiguity. Nash admits that experts may define problems differently, that there may be exceptions to the decision, and that groups may use the procedure and never reach a conclusion. Finally, none of the questions use the ethical standards identified in Chapter 5 or address the problem of implementing the choice once it is made.

◙ Potter's Box

Ralph Potter of Harvard University developed the Potter box, but much of the credit for publicizing his model goes to media ethicists Clifford Christians, Kim Rotzoll, and Mark Fackler. Christians and his colleagues introduce the Potter box in their text *Media Ethics: Cases and Moral Reasoning* as a means of analyzing ethical issues in reporting, advertising, public relations, and entertainment. The model, however, seems well suited for all types of ethical cases, not just those in the media.[4]

A diagram of the Potter model is found in Figure 7.1. As you can see, it contains four quadrants or dimensions. I'll use the example provided by Christians and his coauthors in their text to illustrate how the process works. They describe the case of a fire at a metropolitan theater, known "as the best spot in town for gay film buffs." Sixteen men, including a politician, banker, and minister, were killed in the blaze. The city's two

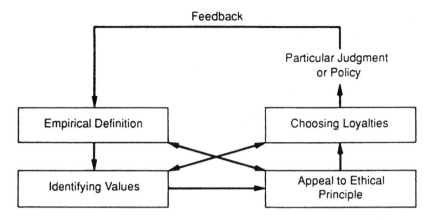

Figure 7.1. The Potter Box
SOURCE: Christian, C. G., Rotzoll, K. B., & Fackler, M. (1991). *Media Ethics: Cases and Moral Reasoning* (3rd ed.). New York: Longman, p. 4. Copyright Ralph Potter; used by permission.

newspapers—the *Sentry-Citizen* and the *News-Print*—would normally report the names of the deceased in such a tragedy. In this instance, however, the *Sentry-Citizen* printed the names and addresses (claiming legitimate reader interest), whereas the *News-Print* did not (claiming to protect the innocent, both victims and survivors). The *Sentry-Citizen* defined the story as a community news item, while the *News-Print* defined the incident as the deaths of 16 prominent men under questionable circumstances. The first paper valued professional credibility. The second viewed homosexuality as wrong and detrimental to the welfare of the community, giving more weight to privacy and protecting the innocent. The two papers also followed different ethical principles and loyalties. *Sentry-Citizen* editors decided to disclose the information following Kant's imperative to tell the truth at whatever the cost. They put their loyalty to the general public first. *News-Print* staff appealed to the virtue of compassion instead. They gave top priority to the needs of the survivors.

Christians and his colleagues urge decision makers to view the quadrants as a circle. Go through the box one time, focusing particularly on values. Return to it a second time to examine important principles and so on. The authors conclude that leaders (editors in this case) can use the Potter model and reach different conclusions. In the case of the gay theater fire, editors of both newspapers can justify their decisions on the basis of their definition of the situation, their values, ethical principles, and loyalties.

Christians and his colleagues point out that conflicting loyalties are particularly troubling for professionals. Those in the professions, whether leaders or followers, must consider five duties when making moral choices. These include (1) duty to ourselves (integrity, conscience); (2) duty to those who pay the bills (clients of a firm, subscribers to a magazine or cable service, donors to a nonprofit group); (3) duty to the organization or firm; (4) duty to professional colleagues (those doing similar work); and (5) duty to society (social responsibility). The last duty is becoming increasingly important in modern society. To illustrate this fact, consider the public response following crises at the Johnson & Johnson Company and at Exxon Oil. Johnson & Johnson CEO Raymond Burke and his staff put the public good first when bottles of its most profitable product—Tylenol—were poisoned. The company recalled the product not once but twice, eventually replaced capsules with caplets, worked with law enforcement agencies, and cooperated with the press. Sales of Tylenol soon rebounded, and the firm is frequently cited as a model corporate citizen. In contrast, President Lawrence (John) Rawl and his managers at Exxon were slow to respond to the *Valdez* oil spill and appeared more interested in blaming the press and federal agencies than in cleaning up the mess. There are still consumers who refuse to buy gas at the company's service stations on the basis of their perception that the company failed to accept full responsibility for its actions.

Balance Sheet

Advantages (+s)
>   Explicitly identifies values, principles, and loyalties as part of the ethical decision-making process
>   Produces a well-reasoned, defensible decision
>   Recognizes that we can legitimately reach different conclusions about the same ethical problem

Disadvantages (–s)
>   Leaves some ethical conflicts unresolved
>   Doesn't encourage the search for creative solutions
>   Overlooks implementation of the decision

The Potter box can be a powerful tool for addressing ethical issues of all types. If you carefully apply this system (considering each element and repeatedly cycling through the box), you should be on solid ground when asked to defend your ethical conclusion. The Potter model acknowledges what many of us have discovered through personal experience. When debating the merits and demerits of a controversial issue such as abortion or assisted suicide, thoughtful, informed people often reach opposite conclusions. Finally, Christians, Rotzoll, and Fackler rightly emphasize duty to society, recognizing the importance of putting the public good ahead of narrow interests.

I suspect that some will find the model dissatisfying precisely because it leaves ethical dilemmas unresolved. What do we do in these cases? Christians and his coauthors say we ought to appeal to "ultimate values, metaphysics, or theology."[5] But whose ultimate values and theology? What do we do when public policy (as in the case of abortion) is involved? Groups may reach conflicting conclusions on issues such as these, but one group or the other "wins" by having its policy put into law. The Potter model may actually encourage a win-lose approach by failing to encourage creative, mutually satisfying ethical solutions. The Potter grid, like the Kidder checklist and Rush's list of questions, also seems to end with the decision step, ignoring implementation.

▣ Cooper's Active Process Model

Ethics professor Terry Cooper developed his decision-making system for public administrators, but leaders in other fields will also find it useful.[6] Cooper believes that government officials develop their ethical character through solving a series of ethical dilemmas. As leaders encounter a series of ethical challenges, both large and small, they form an "ethical identity." They can strengthen their ethical identities by understanding how to best make ethical choices and then by practicing their skills.

According to Cooper, we typically respond to ethical problems at four levels: expressive, moral rules, ethical analysis, and postethical. The lowest level—*expressive*—is our emotional response to ethical situations. Our first reaction to an ethical dilemma may be to vent our frustrations: "How could they do that?" "Why do I always get stuck with these types of decisions?" At the next level—*moral rules*—we begin to consider alternatives and consequences. Imagine that you're a low-level manager at a construction company who suspects that your supervisor is using substandard building materials on a major building project to reduce costs. Should you ignore the violations? Confront your supervisor? Go directly to your boss's boss? Report your suspicions directly to city building inspectors? Moral rules play a key role in solving these types of dilemmas. You may decide that honesty is the best policy (so you decide to confront the problem) and that you should always follow the organizational chain of command (you first take your concerns directly to your supervisor). Most ethical problems are resolved at this level. Further analysis is required if (a) the moral rules don't seem to apply, (b) they conflict with one another, or (c) the actions just don't feel right.

At the level of *ethical analysis,* we link our values with specific actions and determine our priorities. Let's say that you value integrity above all else, followed by fairness and loyalty. As the construction manager in our example, you determine that you must air your concerns no matter what the cost. To be fair, however, you will first give your supervisor an opportunity to dispel your fears. To display loyalty, you will try to resolve the problem internally before going to the press or outside regulators. You come up with a plan of action that begins with confronting your boss and, if he or she doesn't provide a satisfactory explanation, working your way up the company chain of command. You will go to inspectors and/or the press only as a last resort.

The *postethical* level of decision making occurs in cases when we are faced with particularly thorny problems. We ask ourselves, "Why should I act morally?" "What's so important about integrity or truth or loyalty?" We may then turn to religion or philosophy for answers to these questions. This level comes to a close when we identify a motive for striving to be ethical.

Cooper emphasizes that decision makers routinely move between the levels. They may react emotionally, search for moral reasons, get frustrated, and then move on to in-depth analysis. They may reach a decision and stop to ponder why morality matters. It's important to recognize that group members may be functioning at different levels at the same time. One may be ready to apply moral rules, while others are still venting, for instance.

Emotions do play a role in ethical decision making, but leaders must have a reasoned justification for their actions. To that end, Cooper offers the following steps to help leaders move beyond the expressive level to careful analysis.

Examining the ethical issue. Too often, public administrators (and likely the rest of us) define moral problems as practical ones instead. In Chapter 1, for instance, I described the ethical quandary faced by the manager who knows about an upcoming merger but has been ordered to keep silent. If she focuses on how to please her boss or her followers, she'll overlook that this is an ethical dilemma involving deception.

Identifying alternative courses of action. Many choice makers fall into the either-or trap, believing that the right course of action consists of either one action or another. Leaders sometimes reinforce this mode of thinking by insisting on obedience ("my way or the highway"). Keep from falling into this trap by first brainstorming lists of alternatives and consequences.

Projecting the probable consequences. After identifying a variety of alternatives, project the anticipated positive and negative consequences of each one. This requires "moral imagination"—visualizing what might happen, complete with characters, script, and vivid imagery. In the construction case, this would mean mentally rehearsing your encounters with each party. What will you say? How will they react? How will you feel if they ignore your concerns? Threaten you? What will happen to the firm if you succeed or fail in your attempts to focus attention on this problem?

Finding a fit. No alternative will be perfect. The key, instead, is to find a balance between four elements. First, determine which moral rules support each course of action. Second, consider how the decision can be defended. How would the company feel, for example, if it had to defend its choice to ignore evidence of faulty materials on the local news? Third, consider which ethical principles and their priorities come into play. How can the firm give higher priority to earning profits than public safety? Fourth, consider how the decision fits with your self-image. How would you feel about yourself if you chose to keep silent about your supervisor's illegal activity? How will you feel about yourself if you turn your supervisor in to the authorities? The more satisfied you are with your choices, the more inclined you'll be to act in a similar way in the future. If you consistently combine sound reasoning with positive feelings about your choices, you will develop a strong sense of ethical autonomy.

Balance Sheet

Advantages (+s)

    Acknowledges the expressive or emotional element in ethical decision making

    Recognizes that some decisions will be more serious than others and require a deeper level of analysis

    Links action and character; character emerges from patterns of ethical behavior through time

    Highlights the role of moral imagination

    Admits that ethical decision making is an imperfect process; strives for balance

Disadvantages (–s)

    Puts action before reflection

    Ignores implementation

The active process approach adds some elements that are missing from the other three models. The first new component is emotion. Our gut-level reactions shouldn't drive our choices, but it's okay to vent and to check our emotions to see if we're comfortable with our decisions. The second new component is level of ethical difficulty. Some decisions are going to be more taxing than others and will take more concentrated analysis to resolve. The third additional component is a link between action and character. Cooper argues that our character emerges from patterns of ethical behavior that unfold through extended periods. The fourth new component is the notion of moral imagination, of visualizing the likely consequences of decisions. The fifth and final additional component is balance. We shouldn't expect to find a perfect solution but strive, instead, to reach one that fits well with our moral rules, can be adequately defended, reflects our ethical principles and priorities, and is congruent with our self-image.

Cooper's model broadens our understanding of moral reasoning by adding the elements listed above. Its creator, however, seems to put action before reflection. According to Cooper, we wrestle with the question of *why* we ought to be moral only when faced with particularly difficult dilemmas. This ought to be the first, not the last, level of ethical analysis. Making reasoned ethical choices is hard, time-consuming work. We need to determine early on that moral reasoning is worth the effort. Only then will we be willing to invest the time and energy we need to improve our ethical fitness. Cooper also omits the implementation step. Once we've found a decision that fits, we need to put it into effect.

◻ Implications and Applications

- The particular format you choose to follow is not as important as taking a systematic approach to ethical problem solving.

- Possible ethical decision-making formats include Kidder's ethical checkpoints, Nash's 12 questions, Potter's box, and Cooper's active process model.

- Get your facts straight. Make every effort to gather in-depth, current, and accurate information.

- Creativity is vital in ethical decisions as it is to generating new products and programs. Sometimes, you can come up with a "third way" that resolves ethical conflicts.

- Moral dilemmas often involve clashes between two core (good) values. Common right-versus-right dilemmas are truth versus loyalty, short-term versus long-term, individual versus community, and justice versus mercy.

- Action is the ultimate test of leadership ethics. You can make reasoned moral choices, but they'll do little practical good unless you put them to into practice.

- Think of ethical deliberation as a continuing process. You may go through a sequence of steps and use them again. Return to your decision later to evaluate and learn from it. As soon as one ethical crisis passes, there's likely to be another on the horizon.

- Emotions play a subservient but significant role in ethical decision making. Use your feelings as one yardstick to determine if you're satisfied with a particular action.

- Don't expect perfection. As a leader, make the best choice you can after thorough deliberation but recognize that sometimes you may have to choose between two flawed alternatives.

◻ For Further Exploration, Challenge, and Self-Assessment

1. How do you typically go about making ethical choices? How effective is this strategy?

(text continued on p. 162)

CASE STUDY 7.2

Chapter End Case:
Ethical Scenarios for Analysis

Scenario A: The Sting

Since 1997, the U.S. Department of Agriculture has cross-listed food stamp recipients with law enforcement records of outstanding felony warrants. Authorities in at least 30 cities have then used the names generated by matching the lists to trap fugitives. Typically, suspects receive letters promising a cash bonus to them if they meet with a "program specialist" at a local courthouse or other facility. Most receiving the letters are wanted for drug use or theft, but a few are wanted for rape and other violent crimes. Once the suspects show up, they are placed under arrest.

Department of Agriculture and local law enforcement officials are relieved that police officers don't have to put themselves in danger to catch offenders. On the other hand, critics view these operations with concern. They note that there is no indication on the food stamp application form that personal information will be shared with law enforcement agencies. Further, sting operations such as these destroy people's trust in government. No wonder citizens were concerned that information collected during the census would be shared with other federal agencies.

If you were a local law enforcement or a food stamp program manager, would you participate in this type of sting?

SOURCE: Wentz, P. (2000, February 2). Cuffs with those fries? Willamette Week, p. 15.

Scenario B: Campus Bookstore Protest

You are the bookstore manager on your college or university campus. Although not required to make a profit, your store is to break even, generating enough sales to match expenses. Next to textbooks, clothing items with the school name and logo bring in the most revenue. These items have a high profit margin and are particularly popular among alumni who come to campus for games, Parents Day, graduation, and other public events. Recently, students at the University of Michigan and other campuses around the country have protested the sale of licensed school clothing (sweatshirts, t-shirts, hats, shorts) made by suppliers who manufacture their garments in deplorable conditions in Third World countries. Your clothing line is manufactured by one of the firms accused of unfair labor practices.

CASE STUDY 7.2 (Continued)

It's 2 weeks before homecoming (which attracts one of the largest crowds of alumni). A representative from the student government comes to your office to announce that unless you stop selling your current line of licensed apparel, protestors will picket the bookstore during the upcoming festivities. In addition, students will be urged to buy their books through the Internet and from other sources. There is no way you can replace your current clothing stock in time for homecoming. Besides, you will lose thousands of dollars if you do. Your supervisor is out of town but is noted for a "get tough" attitude toward student protests. You, however, are bothered by the idea of selling products produced in sweatshops and are sympathetic to the students' concerns.

What would you do?

Scenario C: The Hiring Decision

You are the male owner of a small company that installs printer cables and services printers at automotive dealerships. With the exception of receptionists and billing clerks, few women work at the stores that buy your parts and services. In this male-dominated atmosphere, women are treated as second-class citizens, and sexist humor is common. Your former service person, Mike, was quite at home in this environment. He kept his clients entertained with a constant stream of dirty jokes and was accepted as "one of the guys."

Mike has given notice that he is going to quit, and you're searching for a replacement. The job market is tight for cable installers, and you can't match the salaries paid by larger firms in the area. After a monthlong search, you finally locate an enthusiastic applicant. Sue, a recent college graduate, has limited experience but appears to be a go-getter who mixes well with all types of people. Most important, she holds a Class C low voltage license that qualifies her to do all types of installation and maintenance work.

You worry about hiring a young woman for this particular job. Not only do you wonder if she will be as successful as Mike, but you fear that she may be the target of sexist humor. Sue doesn't seem to be easily offended, but you wonder if you could be sued later if she claims sexual discrimination. After all, you would be sending her into a potentially hostile working environment.

Would you hire Sue for this position?

CASE STUDY 7.2 (Continued)

Scenario D: The Terminal Patient

Determining what to tell patients with life-threatening illnesses is one of the most difficult challenges facing physicians. American doctors have been told to be more honest with patients in recent years, but they have plenty of reasons for concealing or softening the truth. Some of their motivations may be self-serving, as when they don't want to admit that a disease has defeated them or that they misdiagnosed a medical condition. Doctors are also motivated by altruism, however. They know that patients are more likely to survive operations and live longer if they are hopeful and optimistic. This holds true even when they are given false hope. European doctors have even criticized their U.S. counterparts for being *too truthful* in many such situations, believing that brutal honesty does the patient little good.

Imagine that you are the chief surgeon on an emergency room team. An ambulance has rushed a patient to your hospital following a serious accident. Initial X-rays indicate that the victim is suffering from multiple fractures; damage to his heart, liver, and kidneys; and internal bleeding. Chances are the patient will not live through the night, but you prepare to operate anyway. As you leave the examination room to prep for surgery, the injured man beckons you back to his bedside to ask, "Will I make it?"

What would you say to the accident victim? What would you say to his family waiting in the lobby?

SOURCE: Ford, C. V. (1996). *Lies! Lies! Lies! The psychology of deceit.* Washington, DC: American Psychiatric Press, Ch. 1.

2. Which of the four formats do you find most useful? Why?
3. Brainstorm a list of possible ethical dilemmas faced by a college student. How many of these problems involve a clash between two important values (right vs. right)? Identify which values are in conflict in each situation.
4. Apply each of the formats to one of the chapter end scenarios. Do you reach different conclusions depending on the system you follow? To enhance the experience, first reach your own conclusions and then discuss the situation in a group. See if you can reach a consensus. Make note of the important factors dividing or uniting group members.

5. Use a format from the chapter to analyze an ethical decision faced by society (assisted suicide, cloning, Internet music sites). Write your analysis and conclusions.

Notes

1. Kidder, R. M. (1995). *How good people make tough choices: Resolving the dilemmas of ethical living.* New York: Fireside.

2. Kidder (1995), *How good people make tough choices,* p. 186.

3. Nash, L. L. (1989). Ethics without the sermon. In K. R. Andrews (Ed.), *Ethics in practice: Managing the moral corporation* (pp. 243-257). Boston: Harvard Business School Press.

4. Christians, C. G., Rotzoll, K. B., & Fackler, M. (1991). *Media ethics: Cases and moral reasoning* (3rd ed.). New York: Longman. See also Potter, R. B. (1972). The logic of moral argument. In P. Deats (Ed.), *Toward a discipline of social ethics* (pp. 93-114). Boston: Boston University Press.

5. Christians et al. (1991), *Media ethics,* p. 9.

6. Cooper, T. C. (1998). *The responsible administrator* (4th ed.). San Francisco: Jossey-Bass.

PART IV

**Shaping
Ethical Contexts**

8

▫▫▫ Building an Effective, ▫▫▫ Ethical Small Group

A monologue is not a decision.

—Former British Prime Minister Clement Attlee

▫ What's Ahead

This chapter examines ethical leadership in the small group context. Groups are often charged with making ethical decisions because they have the potential to make better choices than individuals. To make the most of the small group advantage, however, leaders must resist groupthink and engage in productive (enlightening) communication patterns.

Parker Palmer, in his metaphor of the leader's light or shadow, emphasizes that leaders shape the settings or contexts around them. According to Palmer, leaders are individuals who have "an unusual degree of power to create the conditions under which other people must live and move and have their being, conditions that can either be as illuminating as heaven or as shadowy as hell."[1] In this final section of the text, I'll describe some of the ways to create conditions that illuminate the lives of followers in small group, organizational, and culturally diverse settings. Shedding light means both resisting and exerting influence. We must fend off pressures to engage in unethical behavior while actively seeking to create healthier moral environments.

▣ The Leader and the Small Group

Leaders spend a great deal of their time in small groups, either chairing or participating in meetings. You can expect to devote more of your workday to meetings with every step up the organizational hierarchy. Some top-level executives spend as many as 21 weeks a year working in committees, task forces, and other small group settings.[2]

Groups meet for many purposes—to coordinate activities, to pass along important information, to clarify misunderstandings, and to build relationships. In this chapter, I'll focus on the role of groups in making ethical decisions. Examples of ethical group dilemmas include these:

- A congressional subcommittee debating the morality of the inheritance tax
- Court justices determining if grandparents have visitation rights
- The board of the local United Way responding to a funding request from an abortion clinic
- Foreign aid officials deciding if their agency should send food to a drought-stricken nation ruled by a dictator
- Student officers disciplining a campus organization that has violated university and student government policies
- Corporate executives devising a plan to dispose of toxic waste

Groups have significant advantages over lone decision makers when it comes to solving ethical problems such as those described above. In a group, members can pool their information, divide up assignments, draw from a variety of perspectives, and challenge questionable assumptions. They are more likely to render carefully reasoned, defensible decisions as a result.[3] Of course, groups don't always make good moral choices, as in the case of executives who decide to hide product defects from the public or city officials who bypass regulations to award construction contracts to friends. Our task as leaders is to create the conditions that ensure that teams make the most of the small group advantage. In particular, we must confront the problem of groupthink and engage in productive or "enlightening" communication patterns.

◘ Resisting Groupthink

Social psychologist Irving Janis believed that cohesion is the greatest barrier to groups charged with making effective, ethical decisions. He developed the label *groupthink* to describe groups that put unanimous agreement ahead of reasoned problem solving. Groups suffering from this symptom are both ineffective and unethical.[4] They fail to (a) consider all the alternatives, (b) gather additional information, (c) reexamine a course of action when it's not working, (d) carefully weigh risks, (e) work out contingency plans, or (f) discuss important moral issues. Janis first noted faulty thinking in small groups of ordinary citizens (such as an antismoking support group that decided that quitting was impossible). He captured the attention of fellow scholars and the public, however, through his analysis of major U.S. policy disasters such as the failure to anticipate the attack on Pearl Harbor, the invasion of North Korea, the Bay of Pigs fiasco, and the escalation of the Vietnam War. In each of these incidents, some of the brightest (and presumably most ethically minded) political and military leaders in our nation's history made terrible choices.

Janis identified the following as symptoms of groupthink. The greater the number of these characteristics displayed by a group, the greater is the likelihood that members have made cohesiveness their top priority.

Signs of Overconfidence

1. *Illusion of invulnerability.* Members are overly optimistic and prone to take extraordinary risks.
2. *Belief in the inherent morality of the group.* Participants ignore the ethical consequences of their actions and decisions.

Signs of Closed-Mindedness

3. *Collective rationalization.* Group members invent rationalizations to protect themselves from any feedback that would challenge their operating assumptions.

4. *Stereotypes of outside groups.* Participants underestimate the capabilities of other groups (armies, citizens, teams); they think that people in these groups are weak or stupid.

Signs of Group Pressure

5. *Pressure on dissenters.* Group members coerce dissenters to go along with the prevailing opinion in the group.
6. *Self-censorship.* Individuals keep their doubts about group decisions to themselves.
7. *Illusion of unanimity.* Because members keep quiet, the group mistakenly assumes that everyone agrees on a course of action.
8. *Self-appointed mind guards.* Certain members take it on themselves to protect the leader and others from dissenting opinions that might disrupt the group's consensus.

The danger of falling captive to groupthink increases when teams that are composed of members from similar backgrounds are isolated from contact with other groups. The risks increase still further when group members are under stress (because of recent failure, for instance) and follow a leader who pushes one particular solution.

Resisting groupthink is more important than ever before because more firms are using self-directed work teams (SDWTs). A SDWT is made up of 6 to 10 employees from a variety of departments who manage themselves and their tasks. SDWTs operate much like small businesses within the larger organization, overseeing the development of a service or product from start to finish. SDWTs have been credited with improving everything from attendance and morale to productivity and product quality. Unfortunately, self-directed teams are particularly vulnerable to groupthink. Members, working under strict time limits, are often isolated and undertrained. They may fail at first, and the need to function as a cohesive unit may blind them to ethical dilemmas.[5]

Irving Janis made several suggestions for reducing groupthink. If you're appointed as the group's leader, avoid expressing a preference for a particular solution. Divide regularly into subgroups and then bring the entire group back together to negotiate differences. Bring in outsiders— experts or colleagues—to challenge the group's ideas. Avoid isolation, and keep in contact with other groups. Role-play the reactions of other groups and organizations to reduce the effects of stereotyping and rationalization. Once the decision has been made, give group members one last chance to express any remaining doubts about the decision. Janis points to the ancient Persians as an example of how to revisit decisions. The Persians made every major decision twice—once while sober and again while under the influence of wine!

Interest in the causes and prevention of groupthink remains high.[6] Contemporary researchers have discovered that a group is in greatest danger when the leader actively promotes his or her agenda and when the group doesn't have any procedures in place (such as those described in the last chapter) for solving problems. With this in mind, don't offer your opinions as a leader but solicit ideas from group members instead. Make sure that the group adopts a decision-making format before discussing an ethical problem.

Management professor Charles Manz and his colleagues believe that self-managing work teams should replace groupthink with *teamthink*. In teamthink, groups encourage divergent views, combining the open expression of concerns and doubts with a healthy respect for their limitations. The teamthink process is an extension of *thought self-leadership*.[7] In thought self-leadership, individuals improve their performance (lead themselves) by adopting constructive thought patterns. They visualize a successful performance (mental imagery), eliminate critical and destructive self-talk such as "I can't do it," and challenge unrealistic assumptions. For example, the mental statement "I must succeed at everything or I'm a failure" is irrational because it sets an impossibly high standard. This destructive thought can be restated as, "I can't succeed at everything, but I'm going to try to give my best effort no matter what the task."

Teamthink, like thought self-leadership, is a combination of mental imagery, self-dialogue, and realistic thinking. Members of successful groups use mental imagery to visualize how they will complete a project and jointly establish a common vision ("to provide better housing to the homeless"; "to develop the best new software package for the company"). When talking with each other (self-dialogue), leaders and followers are particularly careful not to put pressure on deviant members, and, at the same time, they encourage divergent views.

Teamthink members challenge three forms of faulty reasoning that are common to small groups. The first is all-or-nothing thinking. If a risk doesn't seem threatening, too many groups dismiss it and proceed without a backup plan. Teamthink groups, in contrast, realistically assess the dangers and anticipate possible setbacks. The second common form of faulty group thinking, described earlier, is the assumption that the team is inherently moral. Groups under the grip of this misconception think that anything they do (including lying and sabotaging the work of other groups) is justified. Ethically insensitive, they don't stop to consider the moral implications of their decisions. Teamthink groups avoid this trap, questioning their motivations and raising ethical issues. The third faulty group assumption is the conviction that the task is too difficult, that the obstacles are too great to overcome. Effective ethical groups instead view obstacles as opportunities and focus their efforts on reaching and implementing the decision.

◻ Enlightening Communication

Communication is the key to both the relationships between group members and the quality of their ethical choices. Shadowy groups are marked by ineffective, destructive communication patterns that generate negative emotions while derailing the moral reasoning process. Healthier groups engage in productive or "enlightened" communication strategies that enable members to establish positive bonds and make wise ethical choices. Enlightening communication skills and tactics include comprehensive, critical listening; supportive communication; productive conflict management; and argumentation.

Comprehensive, Critical Listening

We spend much more time listening than speaking in small groups. If you belong to a team with 10 members, you can expect to devote approximately 10% of your time to talking and 90% to listening to what others have say. All listening involves receiving, paying attention to, interpreting, and then remembering messages. Our motives for listening, however, will vary.[8] *Discriminative listening* processes the verbal and nonverbal components of a message. It serves as the foundation for the other forms of listening because we can't accurately process or interpret messages unless we first understand what is being said and how the message is being delivered. Tom and Ray Magliozzi of National Public Radio's *Car Talk* demonstrate the importance of discriminative listening on their weekly call-in program. They frequently ask callers to repeat the sounds made by their vehicles. A "clunk" sound can signal one type of

Figure 8.1. Dilbert
SOURCE: Dilbert, by Scott Adams, November 23, 1996. Copyright © 1996 United Feature Syndicate, Inc. Reprinted by permission.

engine problem; a "chunk" noise might indicate that something else is wrong.

Comprehensive listening is motivated by the need to understand and to retain messages. We engage in this type of listening when we attend lectures, receive job instructions, attend oral briefings, and watch the evening weather report. *Therapeutic or empathetic listening* is aimed at helping the speaker resolve an issue by encouraging him or her to talk about the problem. Those in helping professions such as social work and psychiatry routinely engage in this listening process. All of us, however, act as empathetic listeners when friends and family come to us for help. *Critical listening* leads to evaluation. Critical listeners pay careful attention to message content, logic, language, and other elements of persuasive attempts so that they can identify strengths and weaknesses and render a judgment. *Appreciative listening* is prompted by the desire for relaxation and entertainment. We act as appreciative listeners when we enjoy a CD, live concert, or play.

Group members engage in all five types of listening during meetings, but comprehensive and critical listening are essential to ethical problem solving. Coming up with a high-quality decision is nearly impossible unless group members first understand and remember what others have said. Participants also have to critically analyze the arguments of other group members to identify errors (see the discussion of conflict and argumentation that follows).

There are several barriers to comprehensive, critical listening in the group context. In one-to-one conversations, we know that we must respond to the speaker, so we tend to pay closer attention. In a group, we don't have to carry as much of the conversational load, so we're tempted to lose focus or to talk to the person sitting next to us. The content of the discussion can also make listening difficult. Ethical issues, because they involve deeply held values and beliefs, can generate strong emotional reactions. The natural tendency is to dismiss the speaker ("What does he know?" "She's got it all wrong!") and become absorbed in our own emotions instead of concentrating on the message.[9] Reaching a agreement then becomes more difficult because we don't understand the other person's position while, at the same time, we're more committed then ever to our point of view.

Listening experts Larry Barker, Patrice Johnson, and Kittie Watson make these suggestions for improving your listening performance in a group setting.[10]

Avoid interruptions. Give the speaker a chance to finish before you respond or ask questions. The speaker may address your concerns before he or she finishes, and you can't properly evaluate a message until you've first understood it.

Seek areas of agreement. Take a positive approach by searching for common ground. What do you and the speaker have in common? Commitment to solving the problem? Similar values and background?

Search for meanings and avoid arguing about specific words. Discussions of terms can keep the group from addressing the real issue. Stay focused on what speakers mean; don't be distracted if they use different terminology than you do.

Ask questions/request clarification. When you don't understand, don't be afraid to ask for clarification. Chances are, others in the group are also confused and will appreciate more information. Asking too many questions, however, can give the impression that you're trying to control the speaker.

Be patient. We can process information faster than speakers can deliver it. Use the extra time to reflect on the message instead of focusing on your own reactions or daydreaming.

Compensate for attitudinal biases. All of us have biases based on such factors as personal appearance, age differences, and irritating mannerisms. Among my pet peeves? Men with Elvis hairdos, grown women with little girl voices, and nearly anyone who clutters his or her speech with "ums" and "uhs." I have to suppress my urge to dismiss these types of speakers and concentrate on listening carefully. (Sadly, I don't always succeed.)

Listen for principles, concepts, and feelings. Try to understand how individual facts fit into the bigger picture. Don't overlook nonverbal cues such as tone of voice and posture that reveal emotions and, at times, can contradict verbal statements. If a speaker's words and nonverbal behaviors don't seem to match (as in expression of support uttered with a sigh of resignation), probe further to make sure you clearly understand the person's position.

Compensate for emotion-arousing words and ideas. Certain words and concepts such as *fascist, euthanasia, gay rights, Bible-thumping,* and *feminist* spark strong emotional responses. We need to overcome our knee-jerk reactions to these labels and strive instead to remain objective.

Be flexible. Acknowledge that other views may have merit even if you may not completely agree with them.

Listen although the message is boring or tough to follow. Not all messages are exciting and simple to digest, but we need to make a concerted effort to understand them anyway. A boring comment made early in a group discussion may later turn out to be critical to the team's success.

Defensive Versus Supportive Communication

Defensiveness is a major threat to accurate listening. When group members feel threatened, they divert their attention from the task to defending themselves. As their anxiety levels increase, they think less about how to solve the problem and more about how they are coming across to others, about winning, and about protecting themselves. Listening suffers because participants distort the messages they receive, misinterpreting the motives, values, and emotions of senders. Supportive messages, on the other hand, increase accuracy because group members devote more energy to interpreting the content and emotional states of sources. These types of messages encourage a cooperative orientation among participants. Psychologist Jack Gibb identified six pairs of behaviors that promote either a defensive or supportive group atmosphere.[11] Our job as team leaders or members is to engage in supportive communication while challenging comments that spark defensive reactions.

Evaluation versus description. Evaluative messages are judgmental. They can be sent through statements ("What a lousy idea!") or through such nonverbal cues as a sarcastic tone of voice or a raised eyebrow. Those being evaluated are likely to respond by placing blame and making judgments of their own ("Your proposal is no better than mine"). Supportive messages ("I think I see where you're coming from," attentive posture, eye contact) create a more positive environment.

Control versus problem orientation. Controlling messages imply that the recipient is inadequate (i.e., uninformed, immature, stubborn, overly emotional) and needs to change. Control, like evaluation, can be communicated through both verbal (issuing orders, threats) and nonverbal (stares, threatening body posture) means. Problem-centered messages reflect a willingness to collaborate, to work together to resolve the issue. Examples of problem-oriented statements include "What do you think we ought to do?" and "I believe we can work this out if we sit down and identify the issues."

Strategy versus spontaneity. Strategic communicators are seen as manipulators who try to hide their true motivations. They say that they want to work with others yet withhold information and appear to be listening when they're not. This "false spontaneity" angers the rest of the group. On the other hand, behavior that is truly spontaneous (unplanned) and honest reduces defensiveness.

Neutrality versus empathy. Neutral messages such as "You'll get over it" and "Don't take it so seriously" imply that the listener doesn't care. Empathetic statements, such as "I can see why you would be depressed" and "I'll be thinking about you when you have that appointment with your boss," communicate reassurance and acceptance. Those who receive them enjoy a boost in self-esteem.

Superiority versus equality. Attempts at one-upmanship generally provoke immediate defensive responses. The comment "I got an A in my ethics class" is likely to be met with this type of reply: "Well, you may have a lot of book learning, but I had to deal with a lot of real-world ethical problems when I worked at the advertising agency." Superiority can be based on a number of factors, including wealth, social class, organizational position, and power. All groups contain members who differ in their social standing and abilities. These differences, however, are less disruptive if participants indicate that they want to work with others on an equal basis.

Certainty versus provisionalism. Dogmatic group members (those who are inflexible and claim to have all the answers) are unwilling to change or consider other points of view. As a consequence, they appear more interested in being right than in solving the problem. Listeners often perceive certainty as a mask for feelings of inferiority. In contrast to dogmatic individuals, provisional discussants signal that they are willing to work with the rest of the team to investigate issues and to come up with a sound ethical decision.

Productive Conflict

In healthy groups, members examine and debate the merits of the proposal before the group, a process that experts call *substantive conflict*.[12] Substantive conflicts produce a number of positive outcomes, including the following:

- Accurate understanding of the arguments and positions of others in the group
- Higher-level moral reasoning
- Thorough problem analysis
- Improved self-understanding and self-improvement
- Stronger, deeper relationships
- Creativity and change
- Greater motivation to solve the problem
- Improved mastery and retention of information
- Deeper commitment to the outcome of the discussion
- Increased group cohesion and cooperation
- Improved ability to deal with future conflicts
- High-quality solutions that integrate the perspective of all members

It is important to differentiate between substantive conflict and *affective conflict* that is centered on the interpersonal relationships between group members. Those caught in personality-based conflicts find themselves either trying to avoid the problem or, when the conflict can't be ignored, escalating hostilities through name-calling, sarcasm, threats, and other means. In this poisoned environment, members aren't as committed to the group process, sacrifice in-depth discussion of the problem to get done as soon as possible, and distance themselves from the decision. The result? A decline in moral reasoning that produces an unpopular, low-quality solution.

As a leader, you can encourage substantive conflict in a number of ways. Begin by paying attention to the membership of the group. Encourage the emergence of minority opinion by forming teams made up of people with significantly different backgrounds. Groups concerned with medical ethics, for example, generally include members from both inside (nurses, surgeons, hospital administrators) and outside (theologians, ethicists, government officials) the medical profession. Individuals and subgroups that disagree with the majority cast doubt on the prevailing opinion and stimulate further thought. In the end, the majority generally comes up with a better solution because members have examined their assumptions and considered more viewpoints and possible solutions.[13]

Next, lay down some procedural ground rules—a conflict covenant—before discussion begins. Come up with a list of conflict guideposts as a group, for example: "Absolutely no name-calling or threats"; "No idea is a dumb idea"; "Direct all critical comments toward the problem, not the person"; "You must repeat the message of the previous speaker—to that person's satisfaction—before you can add your comments." Emphasize that conflict about ideas is an integral part of group discussion and caution against hasty decisions. Encourage individuals to stand firm instead of capitulating. If need be, appoint someone to play the role of devil's advocate with the responsibility to cast doubt on the group's proposals.

During the discussion, make sure that members follow their conflict covenant and don't engage in conflict avoidance or escalation. Stop to revisit the ground rules when needed. Be prepared to support your position. Challenge and analyze the arguments of others as you encourage them to do the same (see the discussion below).

Engaging in Effective Argument

Making arguments is the best way to influence others when the group is faced with a controversial decision. That's why argumentative individuals are more likely to emerge as leaders.[14] An argument is an assertion or claim that is supported by evidence and reasons. In the argumentation process, group members interact with each other using claims, evidence, and reasoning in hopes of reaching the best decision. They avoid personal attacks that characterize affective conflicts.

Argumentation in a small group is not as formal and sophisticated as a legal brief or a debate at a college forensics tournament. In more formal settings, there are strict limits on how long arguers can speak, what evidence they can introduce, how they should address the audience, how the argument should be constructed, and so on. Argumentation in a group is much less structured. No one enforces times limits for individual speakers, and members may interrupt each other and get off track. Nonetheless, when you argue in a group, you'll have to carry out the same basic tasks as the members of a university debate team.[15]

The first task is to identify just what the controversy is about. All too often, teams waste their time debating the wrong issues and end up solving the wrong problem. In Case Study 8.1, the controversy surrounds the actions of the principal and the proper role of religion in this one school district. The conflict is *not* about the truth of the Bible or the role of religion in an administrator's private life. Discussing these issues would defeat the purpose of the school board meeting. Clarify the controversy by putting it in the form of a proposition or proposal. The Carriere school board might debate these proposals: "All religious expression in the Carriere schools should be banned during the school day" or "District principals should be reprimanded for allowing religious meetings to run beyond time limits."

Once the controversy is clearly identified, you need to assemble and present your arguments. Arguments, as I noted above, consist of a claim supported by evidence and reasons. Back your claim with examples, personal experience, testimonials from others, and statistics. Also, supply reasons or logic for your position. The most common patterns of logic include (a) analogical (drawing similarities between one case and another), (b) causal (one event leads to another), (c) inductive (generalizing from one or a few cases to many), and (d) deductive (moving from a larger category or grouping to a smaller one).

You could use all four types of reasoning if you believe that allowing Christians to share their faith in school violates the rights of Jews, Moslems, Buddhists, Hindus, atheists, and other groups. You might appeal to the sympathy of Christian board members by asking them how they would feel if this had been a Fellowship of Hindu Athletes assembly (analogical reasoning). You could argue that Christian expression creates a hostile environment that forces parents of other traditions to place

CASE STUDY 8.1

Religious Revival at Pearl River Central

Time magazine called it "The Day God Took Over." On April 12, 2000, students at Pearl River Central High School in Carriere, Mississippi, were attending a voluntary recruitment assembly for the Fellowship of Christian Athletes. One of the group's skits, a reenactment of the crucifixion, touched off a spontaneous outpouring of religious fervor. Students wept, praised God, and publicly confessed their sins to one another. Principal Lolita Lee explained that administrators couldn't legally join in but did profess that she was a Christian. Her comments let students know that they could participate without fear of reprisal, and at least 450 of the school's 670 students did. The assembly, scheduled to take 90 minutes, ended 5 hours later.

Evangelical Christians and religious broadcasters were thrilled by events at Pearl River Central (the school and principal Lee received thousands of supportive e-mails). Civil libertarians, on the other hand, were upset. They criticized Lee for publicizing the assembly, allowing it to go all day, and participating in it. The New Orleans *Times-Picayune* argued that respect for students' religious expression "doesn't translate into allowing them to take over the rest of the day. And it certainly doesn't mean joining in—an action that seems a lot more like advocating religion than simply allowing students to freely express their beliefs." Lee defended her actions by noting that many of the confessions and apologies didn't mention Christ. "That's why I didn't stop them. It was something that they seemed like they needed to tell each other. It wasn't church. It was just kids." Since that day, school authorities believe that students have been more polite and considerate to each other.

The revival at Pearl River High is part of a renewed controversy involving religion in the public schools. The Supreme Court has affirmed that Christian clubs can meet on school property after classes are over for the day, and such groups have become more assertive. Young Evangelicals have been energized by the deaths of Christian students in the Columbine massacre, and some Evangelical activists believe that the best way to prevent future school shootings is through reinstating teacher-led classroom prayers. Even those opposed to mixing faith and public education acknowledge that there is more conflict ahead. According to one such authority, "There is a huge move toward more religious expression among students during the school day. Schools will have to make policies so that people understand the boundaries."

Imagine that you are a member of the school board in Carriere, Mississippi. You are meeting with the rest of the board to evaluate the actions of principal Lee and to set clearer policies regarding religious activity during class time. You should come out of your discussions with (a) a decision regarding Lee (should she be reprimanded or praised for her handling of the situation?) and (b) a list of guidelines supported by your rationale.

SOURCE: Van Biema, D. (2000, June 5). The day God took over. *Time, 155*, 61.

their children in private schools (causal reasoning). You might suggest that although the district received only a few complaints, these are symptoms of widespread dissatisfaction (inductive reasoning). You could point out that other school districts have been sued for holding similar assemblies and that Carriere could be next (deductive reasoning).

At the same time you formulate your position, you need to identify and attack the weaknesses in the positions of other participants. This process, sometimes called critical thinking, is often neglected in group discussions. Group communication experts Dennis Gouran and Randy Hirokawa found that undetected errors are the primary cause of poor-quality decisions. These errors include using incomplete data, accepting bad information as fact, selecting only that information that supports a flawed choice, rejecting valid evidence, using poor reasoning, and making unreasonable inferences from the facts. Be on the lookout for the common errors in evidence and reasoning found in Box 8.1. According to Gouran and Hirokawa, all groups make mistakes, but members of successful groups catch their errors and get the group back on track through corrective communication called *counteractive influence.*[16] An excellent example of counteractive influence is found in the Leadership Ethics at the Movies case in Box 8.2.

▣ Implications and Applications

- As a leader, much of your work will be done in committees, boards, task forces, and other small groups. Making ethical choices is one of a team's most important responsibilities. Your task is to foster the conditions that promote effective, ethical decisions.

- An overemphasis on group cohesion is the single greatest threat to ethical decision making. Be alert for the symptoms of groupthink. These include (a) signs of overconfidence (illusion of invulnerability, belief in the inherent morality of the group); (b) signs of closed-mindedness (collective rationalization, stereotypes of outside groups); and (c) pressure on dissenters (self-censorship, illusion of unanimity, self-appointed mind guards).

- Adopting teamthink strategies is one way to resist the temptation to put agreement ahead of reasoned problem solving. Encourage your group to visualize successful outcomes, avoid pressure tactics, and challenge faulty assumptions.

BOX 8.1 Common Fallacies

Faulty Evidence

Unreliable and biased sources
Source that lacks proper knowledge and background
Inconsistency (disagrees with other sources, source contradicts him-
  or herself)
Outdated evidence
Evidence that appears to support a claim but does not
Information gathered from secondhand observers
Inaccurate citation of sources
Uncritical acceptance of statistical data

Faulty Reasoning

Comparing two things that are not alike (false analogy)
Drawing conclusions based on too few examples or examples that
  aren't typical of the population as a whole (hasty generalization)
Believing that the event that happens first always causes the event
  that happens second (false cause)
Arguing that complicated problems have only one cause (single
  cause)
Assuming without evidence that one event will inevitably lead to a
  bad result (slippery slope)
Using the argument to support the argument (circular reasoning)
Failing to offer evidence that supports the position (non sequitur)
Attacking the person instead of the argument (ad hominem)
Appealing to the crowd or popular opinion (bandwagon effect)
Resisting change on the basis of past practices (appeal to tradition)
Attacking a weakened version on an opponent's argument (straw
  argument)
Arguing that a claim is right just because it hasn't been demon-
  strated to be wrong (appeal to ignorance)
Reducing choices down to two either-or alternatives (false alterna-
  tives)
Believing that an exception to a rule establishes its truth rather than
  challenging its truth (exception to the rule)

SOURCES: Compiled from Warnick, B., & Inch, E. S. (1994). *Critical thinking and communication: The use of reason in argument.* New York: Macmillan; Conway, D. A., & Munson, R. (1990). *The elements of reasoning.* Belmont, CA: Wadsworth.

BOX 8.2 Leadership Ethics at the Movies: *Twelve Angry Men*

Key cast members: Jack Lemmon, George C. Scott, Ossie Davis,
Tony Danza

Synopsis:

This made-for-television remake of the 1957 film starring Henry Fonda features a more ethnically diverse cast than the original film. Eleven members of a jury deciding the fate of a young Latino murder defendant immediately vote for a conviction. Lemmon convinces the rest of the group to reconsider the evidence, however. Several hours later, they vote to acquit. George C. Scott gives the most compelling performance in the film (one of his last) as the juror who wants to punish the male defendant because he can't punish his own son. This film provides an excellent look at the group process and the ethical issues confronting jurors in capital cases. It is particularly relevant in light of the number of convicted murderers who have been placed on death row only to be freed later.

Rating: Not rated but probably worthy of a PG-13 ranking because of occasional profanity and emotional intensity

Themes: Groupthink, moral courage, group evolution, argumentation, counteractive influence and critical thinking, ethical responsibility, the value of human life, stereotypes, and prejudice

■ If you want a healthy group that makes effective ethical decisions, engage productive or enlightened communication patterns and encourage followers to do the same. Enlightening communication skills and tactics include comprehensive, critical listening; supportive messages; productive conflict management; and effective argumentation.

▣ For Further Exploration, Challenge, and Self-Assessment

1. Interview a leader at your school or in another organization to develop a "meeting profile" for this person. Find out how much time this person spends in meetings during an average week and if this is

typical of other leaders in the same organization. Identify the types of meetings this person attends and her or his role. Determine if ethical issues are part of these discussions. As part of your profile, record your reactions. Are you surprised by your findings? Has this assignment changed your understanding of what leaders do?

2. Have you ever been part of a group that was victimized by groupthink? Which symptoms were present? How did they affect the group's ethical decisions and actions?

3. Evaluate a recent ethical decision made by one of your groups. Was it a high-quality decision? Why or why not? What factors contributed to the group's success or failure? Which keys to effective ethical problem solving were present? Absent? How did the leader (you or someone else) shape the outcome, for better or worse? How would you evaluate your performance as a leader or team member?

4. Identify forms of faulty evidence and reasoning in an argument about an ethical issue. Draw from talk shows, newspaper editorials, speeches, interviews, debates, congressional hearings, and other sources. Possible topics include elimination of the marriage penalty tax, capital punishment, the human genome project, and cloning.

5. With other team members, develop a conflict covenant. Determine how you will enforce this code.

6. Develop a plan for becoming a better listener in a group. Implement your plan and then evaluate your progress.

7. Fishbowl Discussion: In a fishbowl discussion, one group discusses a problem while the rest of the class looks on and then provides feedback. Assign one group to the religious revival incident (Case Study 8.1) or the transplant case at the end of the chapter (Case Study 8.2). Make sure that each discussant has one or more observers who specifically note the discussant's behavior. When the discussion is over, observers should meet with their "fish." Then the class as a whole should give its impressions of the overall performance of the team. Draw on chapter concepts when evaluating the work of individual participants and the group.

CASE STUDY 8.2

Chapter End Case:
A Transplant for Brandy

Millions of Americans can't afford private health insurance, so government agencies pay for their treatment. In the state of Oregon, those without medical coverage are eligible for the Oregon Health Plan, which rations health care on the basis of priority and funding. Highly ranked procedures (such as heart surgery) are always covered. Requests for less important or unproved treatments may be denied when demand for services exceeds the program's budget.

The Oregon Health Plan's rationing system came under attack when 18-year-old Brandy Stroeder sued the state for not paying for a combined lung-liver transplant that could save her life. Stroeder suffers from cystic fibrosis, a disease that fills her lungs with a sticky fluid and makes it hard for her to digest food. Stroeder managed to overcome her illness to graduate from high school but will likely die within 2 years if she doesn't receive the new organs. The Health Services Commission, the group that oversees the Oregon Health Plan, refused to fund the operation on the grounds that it is an experimental procedure and therefore doesn't appear on the priority list. They argued that the $250,000 needed to pay for the transplant would be better spent on proved therapies, such as helping more indigent mothers prevent premature births or providing medication for those who suffer from high blood pressure. The state's governor, an emergency room physician who helped craft the Oregon Health Plan while in the state legislature, supported the commission's decision.

Brandy's case divided editorial writers, talk show hosts, and citizens alike. Some urged the state to hold firm, noting that private insurers wouldn't pay for the operation and that the state has limited funds. Top priority, they claimed, ought to go to existing therapies, and any attempts to increase overall funding for the Oregon Health Plan would mean less money for schools, prisons, and parks. Brandy shouldn't get special treatment just because she captured the public's attention. Others urged health plan officials to dump the rationing system to save the life of this courageous, articulate teen. They asserted that the procedure wasn't experimental, pointing to a few successful double transplant operations carried out in Europe. Critics noted that the plan would cover either a lung transplant or a liver transplant and were puzzled that administrators would not pay for a combined operation.

CASE STUDY 8.2 (Continued)

After further consideration, the Health Plan Commission did allow Brandy to be tested to see if she would be a good candidate for a double transplant in case she won her lawsuit. A wealthy business owner then stepped forward and offered to pay for Brandy's transplant if suitable organs could be found. With funding assured, Brandy is now on a waiting list for a new lung and liver.

Discussion Probes

1. What ethical principles appear to guide the governor, health plan officials, and their supporters? What ethical standards do opponents appear to follow?
2. Did the health plan commission make the right decision in refusing to pay for Brandy's double transplant? Why or why not?
3. Does the generosity of the business owner raise any ethical questions? Did he do the right thing?

Notes

1. Palmer, P. (1996). Leading from within. In L. C. Spears (Ed.), *Insights on leadership: Service, stewardship, spirit, and servant-leadership* (pp. 197-208). New York: John Wiley, p. 200.

2. Rothwell, J. D. (1998). *In mixed company: Small group communication* (3rd ed.). Fort Worth, TX: Harcourt Brace, p. 2.

3. Dukerich, J. M., Nichols, M. L., Elm, D. R., & Vollrath, D. A. (1990). Moral reasoning in groups: Leaders make a difference. *Human Relations, 43*, 473-493; Nichols, M. L., & Day, V. E. (1982). A comparison of moral reasoning of groups and individuals on the "defining issues test." *Academy of Management Journal, 24*, 201-208.

4. Janis, I. (1971, November). Groupthink: the problems of conformity. *Psychology Today*, 271-279; Janis, I. (1982). *Groupthink* (2nd ed.). Boston: Houghton Mifflin; Janis, I. (1989). *Crucial decisions: Leadership in policymaking and crisis management*. New York: Free Press.

5. Moorhead, G., Neck, C. P., & West, M. S. (1998). The tendency toward defective decision making within self-managing teams: The relevance of groupthink for the 21st century. *Organizational Behavior and Human Decision Processes, 73*, 327-351.

6. See, for example,
Chen, A., Lawson, R. B., Gordon, L. R., & McIntosh, B. (1996). Groupthink: Deciding with the leader and the devil. *Psychological Record, 46*, 581-590.
Esser, J. K. (1998). Alive and well after 25 years: A review of groupthink research. *Organizational Behavior and Human Decision Processes, 73*, 116-141.

Flippen, A. R. (1999). Understanding groupthink from a self-regulatory perspective. *Small Group Research, 30,* 139-165.

Street, M. D. (1997). Groupthink: An examination of theoretical issues, implications, and future research suggestions. *Small Group Research, 28,* 72-93.

7. Manz, C. C., & Neck, C. P. (1995). Teamthink: Beyond the groupthink syndrome in self-managing work teams. *Journal of Managerial Psychology, 10,* 7-15; Manz, C. C., & Sims, H. P. (1989). *Superleadership: Leading others to lead themselves.* New York: Prentice Hall.

8. Wolvin, A. D., & Coakley, C. G. (1993). A listening taxonomy. In A. D. Wolvin & C. G. Coakley (Eds.), *Perspectives on listening* (pp. 15-22). Norwood, NJ: Ablex.

9. Johnson, J. (1993). Functions and processes of inner speech in listening. In A. D. Wolvin & C. G. Coakley (Eds.), *Perspectives on listening* (pp. 170-184). Norwood, NJ: Ablex.

10. Barker, L., Johnson, P., & Watson, K. (1991). The role of listening in managing interpersonal and group conflict. In D. Borisoff & M. Purdy (Eds.), *Listening in everyday life: A personal and professional approach* (pp. 139-157). Lanham, MD: University Press of America.

11. Gibb, J. R. (1961). Defensive communication. *Journal of Communication, 11,* 141-148.

12. See, for example,

Bell, M. A. (1974). The effects of substantive and affective conflict in problem-solving groups. *Speech Monographs, 41,* 19-23.

Bell, M. A. (1979). The effects of substantive and affective verbal conflict on the quality of decisions of small problem-solving groups. *Central States Speech Journal, 30,* 75-82.

Johnson, D. W., & Tjosvold, D. (1983). *Productive conflict management.* New York: Irvington.

13. Moscovici, S., Mugny, G., & Van Avermaet, E. (Eds.). (1985). *Perspectives on minority influence.* Cambridge, UK: Cambridge University Press; Maas, A., & Clark, R. D. (1984). Hidden impact of minorities: Fifteen years of minority influence research. *Psychological Bulletin, 95,* 428-450; Nemeth, C., & Chiles, C. (1986). Modeling courage: The role of dissent in fostering independence. *European Journal of Social Psychology, 18,* 275-280.

14. Schultz, B. (1982). Argumentativeness: Its effect in group decision making and its role in leadership perception. *Communication Quarterly, 30,* 368-375.

15. Infante, D., & Rancer, A. (1996). Argumentativeness and verbal aggressiveness: A review of recent theory and research. In B. Burleson (Ed.), *Communication yearbook 19* (pp. 319-351). Thousand Oaks, CA: Sage; Infante, D. (1988). *Arguing constructively.* Prospect Heights, IL: Waveland.

16. Gouran, D. S., Hirokawa, R. Y., Julian, K. M., & Leatham, G. B. (1993). The evolution and current status of the functional perspective on communication in decision-making and problem-solving groups. *Communication Yearbook 16,* 573-600; Gouran, D. S., & Hirokawa, R. Y. (1986). Counteractive functions of communication in effective group decision-making. In R. Y. Hirokawa & M. S. Poole (Eds.), *Communication and group decision-making* (pp. 81-90). Beverly Hills, CA: Sage.

9

Creating an Ethical Organizational Climate

Ethics has everything to do with management. Rarely do the character flaws of a lone actor fully explain corporate misconduct. More typically, unethical business practice involves the tacit, if not explicit, cooperation of others and reflects the values, attitudes, beliefs, language, and behavioral patterns that define an organization's operating culture. Ethics, then, is as much an organizational as a personal issue. Managers who fail to provide proper leadership and to institute systems that facilitate ethical conduct share responsibility with those who conceive, execute, and knowingly benefit from corporate misdeeds.

—Harvard business professor Lynn Sharp Paine

What's Ahead

Organizations cast light when they act with integrity (ethical soundness, wholeness, consistency). This chapter explores the hallmarks of organizational integrity, paying particular attention to shared values, codes of ethics, and continuous ethical improvement.

Organizational Light or Shadow

The distinction between ethical and unethical organizations can be as sharp as the contrast between moral and immoral leaders. Some orga-

---

BOX 9.1 Leadership Ethics at the Movies: *Boiler Room*

Key cast members: Giovanni Ribisi, Nicky Katt, Vin Diesel, Ben Affleck

Synopsis:

This film chronicles the sleazy activities of a securities firm engaged in selling stock in nonexistent companies over the phone (a "boiler room" operation). Brokers drive up the price of the shares, and then their managers sell out, leaving victims with nothing. *Boiler Room* updates the movie *Wall Street*, which also profiled greedy securities dealers, with a hip-hop soundtrack and music-video-like camera work. The orientation and training scenes are particularly memorable. This film will give you a feel for the high-risk, high-stakes atmosphere of Salomon Inc., the legitimate brokerage firm profiled at the end of Chapter 2.

Rating: R, primarily for language

Themes: Greed, dishonesty, creation of an immoral organizational climate, new member socialization, values, conflicting loyalties, sexism, racism, deceit, family loyalty

---

nizations, such as humanitarian relief agencies and socially responsible businesses, shine brightly. Others, such as corrupt police departments and authoritarian political regimes, are cloaked in darkness.

Forming and maintaining a positive ethical climate is one of the most important responsibilities we assume when we take on a leadership role in an organization. All members help shape the collective ethical atmosphere, but leaders exert the most influence. Followers will look to leaders for moral guidance. They'll scrutinize our words and actions for information about mission, values, standards, and organizational priorities. They'll want answers to such questions as these: "What happens to those who break the rules?" "How should I treat suppliers and customers?" "What's most important, making a profit or doing the right thing?" "Am I expected to be an active member of the larger community?"

Don't assume that shaping climate is easy. Leaders are just as likely to be corrupted by the existing moral atmosphere as followers, turning a blind eye to questionable practices because "it's always been done that way." Further, entrenched attitudes and practices are highly resistant to change. Charges of sexual harassment continue to surface in the military, for instance, despite the stiff punishments handed out to prior offenders.

☐ Creating a Climate of Integrity

Ethical climate is best understood as part of an organization's culture. From the cultural vantage point, an organization is a tribe. As tribal members gather, they develop their own language, stories, beliefs, assumptions, ceremonies, and power structures. These elements combine to form a unique perspective on the world, referred to as the organization's culture.[1] How an organization responds to ethical issues is a part of this mix. Every organization will face a unique set of ethical challenges, create its own set of values, develop guidelines for enforcing its ethical standards, honor particular ethical heroes, and so on. Because no two organizations are alike, there is no one-size-fits-all approach to creating an ethical climate. Rather, we as organization leaders need to identify principles and practices that characterize positive ethical climates. Then we need to adapt these elements to our particular organizational setting.

Highly ethical organizations act with integrity (ethical soundness, wholeness, consistency).[2] All units and organizational levels share a commitment to high moral standards, backing up their ethical "talk" with their ethical "walk." According to business ethicist Lynn Sharp Paine, managers who act with integrity see ethics as "a driving force of an enterprise." These leaders recognize that ethical values largely define what an organization is and what it hopes to accomplish. They keep these values in mind when making routine decisions. Their goal? To help constituents learn to govern their own behavior following these same principles. Paine believes that any effort to improve organizational integrity must include the following elements:[3]

Sensible, clearly communicated values and commitments. These values and commitments spell out the organization's obligations to external stakeholders (customers, suppliers, neighbors) while appealing to insiders. In highly ethical organizations, members take shared values seriously and don't hesitate to talk about them.

Company leaders who are committed to and act on the values. Leaders consistently back the values, use them when making choices, and determine priorities when ethical obligations conflict with one another. For example, Southwest Airlines President Herb Kelleher puts a high value both on the needs of his employees and on customer service. It's clear, however, that his workers come first. He doesn't hesitate to take their side when customers unfairly criticize them.

The values are part of the routine decision-making process and are factored into every important organizational activity. Values are integrated into every important decision or action. Ethical considerations shape such activities as planning and goal setting, spending, the gathering and sharing of information, evaluation, and promotion.

Systems and structures support and reinforce organizational commitments. Systems and structures include the organizational chart, how work is processed, performance appraisal, budgeting procedures, and product development. These elements serve the organization's values. If a college puts a high value on creating a sense of community, for instance, it may invite students to sit on university committees and hold activities that involve both staff and students. A company with a stated commitment to the needs of families might start a child care center and let employees take time off for their children's school events.

Leaders throughout the organization have the knowledge and skills they need to make ethical decisions. Organizational leaders make ethical choices every day. To demonstrate integrity, they must have the necessary skills, knowledge, and experience (see the discussion of ethical development in Chapter 2). Ethics education and training must be part of their professional development.

Paine and other observers warn us not to confuse integrity with compliance. Ethical compliance strategies are generally responses to outside pressures such as media scrutiny or the U.S. Sentencing Commission guidelines. Under these federal guidelines, corporate executives can be fined and jailed not only for their ethical misdeeds but also for failing to take reasonable steps to prevent the illegal behavior of employees. Although compliance tactics look good to outsiders, they don't have a lasting impact on ethical climate.[4] Consider, for example, the ethics programs of many *Fortune 1000* companies. Nearly all the nation's largest firms have ethical strategies in place, including formal ethics codes and policies, ethics officers, and systems for registering and dealing with ethical concerns and complaints. Most of these programs, however, have minimal influence on company operations. Many ethics officials devote only a small portion of their time to their ethical duties, and some complaint hotlines are rarely used. CEOs typically discuss ethical topics with their ethics officers once or twice a year, attend no meetings focusing primarily on ethics, and rarely communicate to employees about ethics. Followers generally don't receive more than one ethical message annually, and one fifth to one third of lower-level workers receive no ethics training at all in a given year.[5]

◻ Discovering Core Values

Identifying and applying ethical values is the key to creating a highly moral climate. Leaders undertaking integrity initiatives first define and then focus attention on central ethical values. I noted in Chapter 3 that comparing responses on a standardized values list can be a way to clarify group and organizational priorities. In this section, I will introduce additional strategies specifically designed to reveal shared values, purposes, and assumptions.

Core Ideology

Management educators James Collins and Jerry Porras use the term *core ideology* to refer to the central identity or character of an organization. The character of outstanding companies remains constant even as these firms continually learn and adapt. According to Collins and Porras, "Truly great companies understand the difference between what should never change and what should be open for change, between what is genuinely sacred and what is not."[6]

Core values are the first component of core ideology. Most companies have between three to five such values (see Box 9.2 for some examples). Firms that come up with more than five or six are probably are confusing essential values with business tactics and strategies. One way to determine if a value is sacred to your organization is to ask, "What would happen if we were penalized for holding this standard?" If you can't honestly say that you would keep this value if it cost your group market share or profits, then it shouldn't show up on your final list.

To determine who should be involved in spelling out core values, Collins and Porras recommend the Mars Group technique. In this procedure, managers and others imagine that they have been asked to recreate the best attributes of their organization on another planet. There

---

BOX 9.2 Core Values

Nordstorm

> Service to the customer above all else
> Hard work and individual productivity
> Never be satisfied
> Excellence in reputation; being part of something special

Sony

> Elevation of the Japanese culture and national status
> Being a pioneer—not following others; doing the impossible
> Encouraging individual ability and creativity

Walt Disney

> No cynicism
> Nurturing and promulgation of "wholesome American values"
> Creativity, dreams, and imagination
> Fanatical attention to consistency and detail
> Preservation and control of the Disney magic

SOURCE: Collins, J. C., & Porras, J. I. (1996, September-October). Building your company's vision. *Harvard Business Review, 74*(5), 65-77.

---

are only enough seats on the rocket ship for five to seven people, so they nominate highly credible, competent individuals for the trip. Once identified, these individuals then meet. As a group, they work from personal to organizational values by considering these questions:

> What core values do you personally bring to your work? (values that you would hold regardless of whether or not they were rewarded)
> What values would you tell your children that you hold at work and that you hope they will hold as working adults?
> If you woke up tomorrow morning with enough money to retire, would you continue to live those core vales? Can you envision them being as valid for you 100 years from now as they are today?
> Would you want to hold these core values even if one or more of them became a competitive *dis*advantage?

Figure 9.1. Dilbert
SOURCE: Dilbert, by Scott Adams, July 18, 1997. Copyright © 1997 United Feature Syndicate, Inc.
Reprinted by permission.

If you were to start a new organization in a different line of work, what core values would you build into the new organization regardless of industry?[7]

Core purpose makes up the second part of an organization's ideology. Purpose is the group's reason for being that reflects the ideals of its members. Examples of effective purpose statements include the following:

To strengthen the social fabric by continually democratizing home ownership (Federal National Mortgage or "Fannie Mae")

To solve unsolved problems innovatively (3M)

To give ordinary folk the chance to buy the same things as rich people (Wal-Mart)

To provide a place for people to flourish and to enhance the community (Pacific Theatres)

Asking the "Five Whys" is one way to identify organizational purpose. Start with a description of what your organization does and then ask why that activity is important five times. Each "why" will get you closer to the fundamental mission of your group.

Your organization's purpose statement should inspire members. (Don't make high profits or stock dividends your goal because they don't motivate individuals at every level of the organization.) Your purpose should also serve as an organizational anchor. Every other element of your organization (business plans, expansion efforts, buildings, products) will come and go, but your purposes and values will remain.

Values Adoption Process

Wife-and-husband team Susan and Thomas Kuczmarski believe that everyone in an organization, not just a select group, ought to be involved in the values identification process.[8] Their organizationwide approach is called the values adoption process (VAP). In Stage 1, the CEO or designated facilitator kicks off the process in face-to-face conversations or public meetings. Members record their personal values, ones that they would want to be shared in the workplace. These values are then collected, prioritized, and segmented into department and/or topic groups (manufacturing, research and development, workplace relationships, product quality, innovation). In Stage 2, groups of followers and leaders meet to identify the most important categories and develop a list of specific values for adoption. Roughly 20 values should be identified (10 as "must have" and 10 as "would like to have").

In Stage 3, all members develop a People Values Pledge and an Organization Values Pledge. The People Values Pledge summarizes how each individual should act toward others in the organization (e.g., "have a sense of humor," "set egos aside," "respect diversity"). The Organization Values Pledge reflects the commitment of top leaders to members. For instance, "recognize and reward excellence," "encourage risk taking," and "honor teamwork." Both value statements are distributed to members through cards, plaques, annual reports, newsletters, and other means.

In Stage 4, the organization translates internal values to outside audiences. It surveys customers to determine (a) what values they see the organization conveying through its product, market position, and service; (b) what values they want the organization to communicate; (c) which value should have top priority; and (d) what new value the organization should adopt. This information is then communicated to employees who create a Customer Values Pledge. These values guide the development of new products and services and efforts to market them. For example, Rubbermaid puts a high priority on durability. Everyone from industrial design engineer to salesperson recognizes that any new product must withstand considerable punishment.

Once collective values have been identified, organizations ought to give careful thought to how their values will be translated into action. To this end, the Kuczmarskis encourage individuals and then small groups to identify and to analyze current group norms. Which norms should be dropped? Added? Leaders should make sure that an organization's norms support its values, paying particular attention to these:

- People systems (training, pay, evaluation, promotion)
- Policies and practices (selection and recruiting, management style and decision making, degree of employee participation)
- Physical systems (organization structure, job descriptions, communication and information systems)

▣ Codes of Ethics

Codes of ethics are among the most common ethics tools. Nearly all large corporations have them (see the *Fortune 1000* study cited earlier). The same is true for government departments, professional associations, social service agencies, and schools. Formal ethics statements, however, are as controversial as they are popular. Skeptics make these criticisms:

- Codes are too vague to be useful.
- Most codes are developed as public relations documents designed solely to improve an organization's image.
- Codes don't improve the ethical climate of an organization.
- Codes often become the final word on the subject of ethics.
- Codes are hard to apply across cultures and in different situations.
- Codes frequently lack adequate enforcement provisions.

Defenders of ethical codes point to their potential benefits. One, a code describes an organization's ethical stance both to members and to the outside world. Two, a formal ethics statement can improve the group's image while protecting it from lawsuits and further regulation. Three, referring to a code can encourage followers and leaders to resist unethical group and organizational pressures. Four, a written document can have a direct, positive influence on ethical behavior. Students who sign honors codes, for example, are significantly less likely to plagiarize

CASE STUDY 9.1

Cutting Corners at the University

Academic cheating—claiming someone else's work as your own—has reached epidemic proportions among America's high school and college students. Of top high school students, 80% admit that they cheat to get ahead. Of college students, 87% cheat on papers, and 70% have cheated at least once on a test. Cheating appears to be a means to an end, enabling ambitious high school seniors to get into prestigious universities and helping undergraduates get better jobs and make it into graduate school. Offenders often go unpunished. Those who don't cheat are at a disadvantage and may be seen as naive because they won't manipulate the system.

Many students think of cheating as a personal matter. They don't believe that copying test questions or downloading material from the Internet is a problem for others. Officials at the Educational Testing Service, however, point out that widespread cheating reduces the value of every degree granted by an institution, and dishonest habits established in school can carry over after graduation. There have been reports of police recruits and paramedics using notes and stolen exams to pass CPR and emergency medicine tests. Coast Guard personnel have been charged with cheating on pilot license exams.

Alarmed by the rise in academic dishonesty, your college or university president has created an Integrity Task Force to come up with a plan for reducing cheating among students at your school. The president has asked you to serve as a representative on this panel. What suggestions would you make to the rest of the group?

SOURCES: Universities retreat in war on cheating. (2000, August 25). (www.ncpa.org/pi/edu/jan89o.html)
Cheating is a personal foul. (www.nocheating.org/adcouncil/research/cheatingbackgrounder.html)

and cheat on tests.[9] (See Case Study 9.1 for a closer look at the problem of academic cheating.)

There's no doubt that a code of ethics can be a vague document that has little impact on how members act. A number of organizations use these statements for purposes of image, not integrity. They want to appear concerned about ethical issues while protecting themselves from litigation. Just having a code on file doesn't mean that it will be read or used. Yet creating an ethical statement can be an important first step on the road to organizational integrity. Although a code doesn't guarantee moral improvement, it is hard to imagine an ethical organization without one. Codes can focus attention on important ethical standards, outline expectations, and help individuals act more appropriately. Communication ethicist Richard Johannesen believes that many of the objections to formal codes could be overcome by following these guidelines.[10]

1. Distinguish between ideals and minimum conditions. Identify which parts of the statement are goals to strive for and which are minimal or basic ethical standards.

2. Design the code for ordinary circumstances. Members shouldn't have to demonstrate extraordinary courage or make unusual sacrifices to follow the code. Ensure that average employees can follow its guidelines.

3. Use clear, specific language. Important, abstract terms such as *reasonable, distort,* and *falsify* should be explained and illustrated.

4. Prioritize obligations. Indicate which commitments are most important. To the client? The public? The employer? The profession?

5. Protect the larger community. Don't protect the interests of the organization at the expense of the public. Speak to the needs of outside groups.

6. Focus on issues of particular importance to group members. Every organization and profession will face particular ethical dilemmas and temptations. Lawyers, for example, must balance duties to clients with their responsibilities as officers of the court. Doctors try to provide the best care while HMOs pressure them to keep costs down. The code should address the group's unique moral issues.

7. Stimulate further discussion and modification. Don't file the code away or treat it as the final word on the subject of collective ethics. Use it to spark ethical discussion and modify its provisions when needed.

8. Provide guidance for the entire organization and the profession to which it belongs. Spell out the consequences when the business or nonprofit as a whole acts unethically. Who should respond and how? What role should outside groups (professional associations, accrediting bodies, regulatory agencies) play in responding to the organization's ethical transgressions?

9. Outline the moral principles behind the code. Explain *why* an action is right on the basis of ethical standards (communitarianism, utilitarianism, altruism) such as those described in Chapter 5.

10. Encourage widespread input. Draw on all constituencies, including management, union members, and professionals, when developing the provisions of the code.

BOX 9.3 Ethics Codes: A Sampler

Walter Manley divides the provisions of ethical codes into the following categories. His typology is a good starting point for any group interested in developing its own ethics statement. Your organization may not need to address all these issues, but reading his survey should keep you from overlooking any important areas.

Business dealings and relationships (competition, gifts, lobbying, purchasing)

International business relationships and practices (foreign investment, record keeping)

Management responsibilities (travel, duties to shareholders, member development)

Rights and responsibilities of employers and employees (commitment, rights, privacy)

Fundamental honesty (laws and criminal acts)

Protecting proprietary and confidential information (patents, copyrights, security, espionage, sabotage)

Internal communications

Equal employment (nondiscrimination, equal employment)

Sexual and nonsexual harassment

Substance abuse

Workplace safety, consumer protection, and product quality (employee safety, product safety and quality, testing)

Ethics in marketing and advertising

Compliance with antitrust laws

Managing computer-based information systems (proper use of computers, computer security, use of software)

Ethical duties of accountants

Expense accounts, credit cards, and entertaining

Insider trading and securities laws

Corporate citizenship and responsibility to society (community involvement, charitable activities)

Protecting the environment

BOX 9.3 (Continued)

Sample Provisions

Proper Use of Computer Systems (Aetna)

Management has the responsibility to ensure that computer resources are used to further Aetna's business. You should not allow computers to be used for amusement or other trivial purposes since that is a misuse of a valuable company asset. Private benefit or gain is strictly prohibited. Misappropriation, destruction, misuse, abuse or unauthorized modification of computer resources are offenses for which dismissal will be considered. (pp. 159-160)

Proper Marketing Practices (Lockheed)

All marketing and related practices that infringe on business ethics or could cause embarrassment to Lockheed are strictly forbidden, and violations will not be tolerated. Employees are responsible for adhering to ethical behavior, regardless of any perceived justification for deliberate infractions. (pp. 144-145)

Health and Safety in the Workplace (PPG)

Assuring the health and safety of PPG personnel is a top corporate priority, worldwide.

An important component of this strategy is assuring that both our own personnel and those living near us are clearly informed about the nature of the materials used at our facility.

It is PPG's goal to completely eliminate the incidence of work-related illness or injury. To achieve that goal, the Company has developed a series of emergency response procedures as well as corporate-wide policies related to the safe operation of PPG's equipment, the proper handling of materials, limits on exposure to potentially hazardous substances, and other matters affecting employee health and safety on the job. (pp. 133-134)

11. Back the code with enforcement. Create procedures for interpreting the code and applying sanctions. Ethics offices and officers should set up systems for reporting problems, investigating charges, and reaching conclusions. Possible punishments for ethical transgressions include informal warnings, formal reprimands that are entered into employment files, suspensions without pay, and terminations.

An extensive collection of ethics statements is found in the *Executive's Handbook of Model Business Conduct Codes*.[11] Compiler Walter Manley examined 276 firms and more than 10,000 pages of material. He divides code provisions into the 19 categories found in Box 9.3. If you're interested in developing or refining a code of ethics, you can use these examples as models.

▣ Continuous Ethical Improvement

The Need for Continuing Ethical Learning

Total quality management (TQM) is a buzzword at thousands of firms in Japan, the United States, and other countries. TQM describes a continuous improvement process designed to reduce product defects, improve response times, and eliminate waste. The TQM movement is founded on the belief that organizations, like individuals, learn through experience, observation, training, and other means. Although all organizations learn, some learn faster and more efficiently than others, a characteristic that gives them a competitive edge. Those who learn quickly produce better products in less time while responding to demographic shifts and technological advances. High-tech firms are particularly aware of the importance of rapid learning. They scramble to stay ahead in the development of memory chips, cell phones, software, and other products.

Organizations ought to be as concerned about continuous ethical improvement, what I'll call *total ethical management*, as they are about improving products and services.[12] Three factors should encourage continuing ethical learning: risk, lingering ethical weaknesses, and change. Let's take a closer look at each.

Risk

Serious ethical misbehavior can threaten the survival of an organization. Salomon Inc., profiled in Chapter 2, is one example of a company that nearly collapsed because of ethical lapses. Racial and sexual harassment suits in industry can bring stiff fines and jail sentences; malfeasance in government agencies leads to budget reductions; contributions dry up when the leaders of social service agencies and religious groups live like royalty. Managerial misconduct (whether motivated by poor judgment or criminal intent) is now the leading cause of business crises.[13] No type of organization, be it religious, humanitarian, business, government, or military, is exempt from ethical failure.

On a more positive note, evidence suggests that moral organizations can be extremely effective. The Body Shop, Ben & Jerry's, Tom's of Maine, the Herman Miller Company, and ServiceMaster are highly successful as well as highly ethical. Shared values can increase productivity by focusing the efforts of employees and by encouraging supervisors to empower their subordinates. Having a good reputation attracts customers, clients, and investors and forms the basis for long-term relationships with outside constituencies.[14] (See Case Study 9.2 at the end of the chapter for an example of a successful company that has prospered while helping others.)

Ethical Weakness

Organizations can never claim to have "arrived" when it comes to ethical development. There will always be room for improvement. In addition, the same inconsistencies that plague individual leaders are found in the climate of entire organizations. Starbucks Coffee, for example, has been praised for its commitment to its employees (they make higher than average wages, and part-timers are covered by the company's health insurance plan). Activists complain, however, that the firm doesn't pay coffee growers enough and that valuable rain forest has been destroyed to grow its coffee beans.

Change

Organizational leaders must recognize that they operate in constantly shifting environments. Competitors, suppliers, government regulations, and public tastes are always changing. Each change, in turn, brings new ethical challenges. Take the case of genetically altered foods. Opponents are raising moral objections to these products. They worry about their safety and their impact on the environment. Critics believe that biotechnology companies are putting the health of consumers, as well as the future of native plants and animals, at risk. Leaders of biotech companies must now publicly acknowledge and respond to these arguments.

Like the environments they live in, organizations themselves are in a constant process of transformation. New employees join, divisions reorganize, companies become publicly owned, and products and services are added or dropped. Once again, each change alters the ethical landscape. Consider the impact of a changing workforce, for instance. As more women and minorities join an organization, leaders need to focus more attention on diversity issues. They must consider such questions as these: How do we make diverse individuals feel like valued team members? How do we ensure that everyone has an equal chance of being promoted, regardless of background? How far do we go to meet the needs of subgroups (working mothers, nonnative speakers, religious minorities)?

Enhancing Organizational Ethical Learning

Like other forms of organizational learning, ethical development is more likely under the right conditions. Organization development consultants Anthony DiBella and Edwin Nevis identify 10 practices that enhance organizational learning. Taken together, these elements, called *facilitating factors*, determine the learning potential of an organization.[15] DiBella and Nevis are most interested in the types of learning that improve quality. Nonetheless, the same factors also spur continuous ethical improvement.

1. *Scanning imperative.* Ethical learners look outside the immediate group for information. They continually scan the environment for emerging ethical issues that might affect the organization in the future. They monitor newspapers and trade journals to identify questionable industry practices and consider the ethical impact of entering a new market or introducing a new product (see the earlier discussion of genetically altered foods). In addition, continuous learners take a close look at

how other organizations prevent and manage ethical problems. Organizational learning theorists refer to this process as *benchmarking*. In benchmarking, groups identify outstanding organizations and isolate the practices that make them so effective. They then adapt these practices to their own organizations.[16] Xerox (credited with developing the concept) used benchmarking to improve its manufacturing, billing, and warehousing processes.

Information on effective ethical practices can be found in a variety of sources. You may want to draw on these as you identify ethical benchmarks. Managerial texts and business ethics books include examples of moral and immoral behavior, sample ethics codes, and case studies. There are also two academic journals—the *Journal of Business Ethics* and *Business Ethics Quarterly*—devoted exclusively to ethics in the workplace.

2. *Performance gap.* A performance gap is the distance between where an organization is and where it would like to be. Martin Marietta is one example of an organization that recognized its ethical failings and took steps to correct them. Under investigation for improper travel billings in the mid-1980s, the defense contractor responded by highlighting its code of conduct, starting an ethics training program, developing a system for reporting ethical concerns, and rewarding executives for moral behavior. As a result, the company improved its compliance with federal regulations and reduced the number of ethical complaints filed by employees. The firm also prevented a number of potential crises stemming from bad management, safety problems, and discrimination.

Some organizations turn their moral failures into case studies. At West Point, Army instructors use the massacre at My Lai (profiled in Chapter 4) to teach ethical principles to cadets. Organizations don't have to wait for an ethical disaster to strike to identify performance gaps, of course. Potential problems can be identified through surveys (see below), ethics hotlines, and focus groups.

3. *Concern for measurement.* Organizational priorities are reflected in what leaders pay attention to. For instance, executives at a delivery company that takes pride in its on-time service will reward those who reach delivery targets while disciplining those who don't. In a similar fashion, followers won't take ethics seriously unless leaders measure ethical performance and then use that information to improve ethical climate. Ethics audits (surveys that measure employee perceptions of

values and corporate behavior) and focus groups track the moral climate of the group as a whole. Ethics items on performance appraisal forms provide data on individual performance.

4. *Organizational curiosity.* Learning organizations are populated with individuals who act like experimental scientists or curious children. They tinker with products and systems, continually trying out new ideas. At Wal-Mart, for example, some 250 minor experiments are conducted on any given day. Ethical learning organizations demonstrate the same creative spirit. They don't hesitate to try out new strategies for better identifying and resolving ethical issues. They experiment with better ways to track ethical complaints, to identify ethical problems, and to encourage adherence to federal regulations.

5. *Climate of openness.* Openness refers, first of all, to the free flow of information. In open organizations, leaders make a conscious effort to reduce barriers of all types between individuals and units. In this environment, new ideas are more likely to develop and then to be shared throughout the group as a whole. Learning leaders put few restrictions on what can be shared, rotate individuals between divisions, set up forums for sharing ideas, and form multidepartment task forces. In addition, they create formal (companywide forums, idea fairs) and informal (employee cafeterias, celebrations) settings where members can meet and share information. Furniture manufacturer Herman Miller Company is one organization that values open communication. According to former CEO Max DePree,

> A number of obligations go along with good communication. We must understand that access to pertinent information is essential to getting a job done. The right to know is basic. Moreover, it is better to err on the side of sharing too much information than risk leaving someone in the dark. Information is power, but it is pointless power if hoarded. Power must be shared for an organization or a relationship to work.[17]

Openness also refers to the type of communication that occurs between group members. In learning organizations, individuals recognize that they can glean important information from anyone regardless of their status. When they interact, members treat others as equals and are more interested in understanding than in being understood. They work together to create shared meaning. Philosopher Martin Buber, psychologist Carl Rogers, and others refer to this type of conversation as dia-logue.[18] Dialogue is characterized by

- Asking questions
- Honestly sharing one's own emotions
- Allowing time to think and reflect
- Confirming the right of others to "own" their feelings
- Taking the perspective of the other communicator
- Listening to learn, not to persuade or fix
- Monitoring one's own thinking patterns and motives
- Allowing others the freedom to make their own choices
- Using reasonableness and civility

Dialogue encourages deeper commitment to moral behavior and can be facilitated through designated dialogue sessions. In these gatherings, members meet to engage in open communication about moral questions. Dialogue sessions work best when attendees complete assigned readings in advance, meet in a quiet setting, convene at a round table or in a circle to emphasize equality, and suspend their opinions and judgments.[19]

6. *Continuous education.* Continuous education reflects the organizationwide commitment to the never ending process of learning. Organizations that value learning will make it a priority everywhere, not just in the training department. These groups (a) support on-the-job training (such as when an experienced worker helps a new hire resolve an ethical problem); (b) hold retreats; (c) encourage networking and dialogue; and (d) send individuals to conferences, classes, and workshops to learn more about ethics.

7. *Operational variety.* There is more than one way to reach work goals. By using a variety of strategies, an organization can better adapt to unforeseen problems. At one mutual fund group, managers use three approaches to making investment choices. Employees of Semco, a Brazilian firm, decide if they would rather work for a straight salary, be paid according to incentives, or operate as independent contractors. Innovative organizations also set up entirely new operations to try out alternative procedures. This strategy allows them to test unproved ideas without having to give up their current systems.

Similar tactics can nurture ethical improvement. Organizations may use different types of ethics training or use a variety of media (video, forums, bulletin boards, newsletters) to communicate ethics messages to members. They may also want to conduct an "ethical experiment" in one location before making wholesale changes. For example, a manufacturer might give work teams in one location more freedom to make ethical choices. If these groups adhere to organizational values, the corporation might empower all work teams to enforce moral standards.

8. *Multiple advocates.* New ideas aren't widely adopted unless championed by significant numbers of people throughout an organization. Effective champions are respected individuals who promote an idea at the same time they model its use. The Motorola Corporation identified 300 such individuals and enlisted them as advocates in a quality improvement campaign. Continuous ethical improvement requires the same type of support. Influential leaders of every organizational rank must support ethics initiatives and put them into action.

9. *Involved leadership.* Leaders play a critical role in driving continuous ethical improvement. The key is hands-on involvement. Involved leaders are students. They encourage the learning of others by first learning themselves. If they want to promote diversity, for instance, they are the first to take diversity training. They continue to be involved in the learning process by interacting with followers, visiting job sites, and holding forums on ethical issues.

10. *Systems perspective.* The systems perspective refers to seeing the big picture, recognizing that organizations are highly interdependent. Continuous ethical learners try to anticipate the ethical implications of their decisions for those in other divisions. A big-picture leader may be tempted to "dump" an incompetent employee on another department but recognizes that this strategy benefits her or his unit at the expense of another. The productivity of the organization as a whole suffers because this ineffective individual is still on the payroll. With this in mind, the department head confronts the problem employee immediately.

The open communication climate described earlier facilitates systems thinking. Communicating across boundaries helps members (a) develop a better understanding of the ethical problems faced by other units and (b) learn how their actions may result in moral complications for others.

▣ Implications and Applications

- Creating a positive ethical climate is one of the most important challenges you'll face when you take on a leadership role in an organization.
- Model organizations act with integrity (consistency, wholeness). Integrity develops through clearly communicated values and commitments, leaders who are committed to these values, application of the values to routine decisions, systems and structures that support organizational commitments, and members who are equipped to make wise ethical choices.
- Don't confuse compliance with integrity. Compliance protects an organization from regulation and public criticism but has little impact on day-to-day operations. Integrity is at the center of an organization's activities, influencing every type of decision and activity.
- Shared values are essential to any integrity initiative. Identify these values through the use of task forces, employee meetings, and other means.
- Useful codes of ethics can play an important role in shaping ethical climate. Make sure they define and illustrate important terms and address the problems faced by the members of your particular organization. View ethics statements as discussion starters, not as the final word on topic of organizational morality.
- Risk, lingering ethical weaknesses, and constant change create a demand for continuous organizational ethical development.
- The ethical learning capacity of your organization will be determined by the presence or absence of such factors as ethical benchmarking, measurement, open communication, organizational curiosity, and systems thinking.

▣ For Further Exploration, Challenge, and Self-Assessment

1. Analyze the ethical climate of your organization. Overall, would you characterize the climate as positive or negative? Why? What factors have shaped the moral atmosphere? What role have leaders played in its formation and maintenance? What inconsistencies do you note?
2. Discuss each of the following statements in a group, or, as an alternative, argue for and against each proposition in a formal debate. Your instructor will set the rules and time limits. Refer to the previous chapter for more information on constructing effective arguments.

(text continued on p. 212)

CASE STUDY 9.2

Chapter End Case:
Battling Blindness: Merck Does the Right Thing

River blindness is one of the world's most devastating diseases, affecting approximately 20 million people, mostly in West Africa and South America. The illness is spread by blackflies that breed in fast-moving water. These tiny insects pick up the larvae of a parasite by biting a victim and then leave them behind when they bite someone who is not yet infected. The parasites quickly grow to as long as 2 feet and send out millions of microworms that spread throughout the body. Globs of these worms push through the skin, resulting in loss of pigmentation or "leopard" skin. Left untreated, the worms spread to the eyes, causing blindness, and shorten life expectancy by one third.

For decades, all attempts to wipe out river blindness failed. Pesticides didn't eliminate the flies because they rapidly complete their reproductive cycle in many locations. A few drugs had been developed, but they had serious side effects and could be administered only under close supervision. Unable to defeat the disease, residents of some rural communities fled their traditional homes in the fertile valleys for arid high ground.

In 1978, a research scientist at Merck & Company stumbled across a potential cure for river blindness while developing a treatment for parasitic worms that attack pets and livestock. Realizing that the same microbe would probably eliminate similar parasites in humans, he asked his laboratory director, Dr. Roy Vagelos, for permission to develop the drug for human use. Developing the medication would be expensive, requiring years of laboratory work followed by testing in West Africa. Failure would lower the company's return to stockholders, and nasty side effects could also expose the company to lawsuits. Even if the drug worked, there was little hope that victims could pay for it because most lived in extreme poverty.

Backed by the company's drug development council (the group that made recommendations as to which drugs to support), Vagelos gave his enthusiastic go-ahead. By 1980, the company was field-testing the product called Mectizan in Ghana, Liberia, Mali, and Senegal. The results were nothing short of miraculous. Taken in pill form once a year, the drug killed the microworms and drove the parasites from the skin (preventing flies from spreading them). Side effects were minimal, but relief was immediate and dramatic. The severe itching caused by the microworms eased after just one dose.

Developing the drug was the first step. Next, the company faced the challenge of distributing it. The World Health Organization, the United States Agency for International Development, and other relief groups were skeptical at first and refused to pay for its manufacture and distribution. Finally, in 1987, Vagelos (who had been promoted to CEO 2 years earlier) decided to give the drug away and to ensure its delivery. Later, the same private and public relief organizations that had refused to finance distribution stepped forward to help. In 1995, the World Bank hailed the reduction of river blindness as "one of the most remarkable achievements in the history of development assistance."

Children no longer faced the prospect of early death and blindness; communities returned to the riverbanks. The cost to Merck was high, however. Lost income from the drug totaled more than $200 million.

Merck has a long tradition of "doing well by doing good." Following World War II, the company donated streptomycin to combat an outbreak of tuberculosis in Japan. It produces a variety of lifesaving drugs such as penicillin, streptomycin, and Mevacor, a cholesterol-lowering drug that greatly reduces the risks of heart attack. Company values clearly state that improving the health of customers and patients takes priority over the needs of stockholders. According to George Merck, son of the company founder,

> We try never to forget that medicine is for the people. It is not for the profits. The profits follow, and if we have remembered that, they have never failed to appear. The better we have remembered it, the larger they have been. (p. 29)

Even with the support of the organization's culture, the ultimate fate of Mectizan rested on the shoulders of Vagelos. Senior vice presidents were deadlocked on the issue, fearing that free distribution would undercut sales of other products in developing countries. Vagelos ended the debate, declaring later that "I thought the company couldn't have done otherwise." He didn't even tell his board of directors what he was going to do before his public announcement. Not a single shareholder complained about the company's decision, however.

In the end, Vagelos reminded the corporation of its ultimate purpose—to reduce the suffering of humanity. The company's example encouraged other firms to follow suit. Glaxo gave away a new antimalarial drug. DuPont now donates nylon to filter guinea worm parasites out of drinking water, while American Cyanimid provides a larvacide to kill them.

Roy Vagelos admits that his decision boosted Merck's reputation and made it easier to recruit talented researchers. But he declares that he would have made the same choice even without side benefits. Combating river blindness was the culmination of a life that he had dedicated, first as a professor of medicine and then as a pharmaceutical executive, to meeting the needs of others.

Discussion Probes

1. Would Vagelos have been criticized had he decided not to develop and distribute the Mectizan?
2. What other firms "do well by doing good"? How can we encourage more firms to do the same?
3. What elements of a climate of integrity were present at Merck?
4. Professor-writer Michael Useem, who profiles both the Merck and Salomon cases, refers to critical decisions as "leadership moments." Leaders must make the right moves at these points, or the group or organization will suffer. What leadership moments (decisions) have you faced? What ethical implications did they have?
5. What leadership lessons do you draw from this case?

SOURCE: Useem, M. (1998). *The leadership moment: Nine stories of triumph and disaster and their lessons for us all.* New York: Times Books.

Pro or con: Formal codes of ethics do more harm than good.

Pro or con: Ethical businesses are more profitable over the long term.

Pro or con: Organizational values can't be developed; they must be uncovered or discovered instead.

Pro or con: An organization's purpose has to be inspirational.

Pro or con: An organization can change everything except its core values and purpose.

3. Compare and contrast an organization with a climate of integrity with one that pursues ethical compliance.

4. Develop a shared set of values for your class using strategies presented in the chapter.

5. Evaluate an ethical code on the basis of chapter guidelines. What are its strengths and weaknesses? How useful would it be to members of the organization? How could the code be improved? What can we learn from this statement?

6. Design a total ethics management program for your organization that incorporates the 10 facilitating factors that make up ethical learning potential.

Notes

1. Pacanowsky, M. E., & O'Donnell-Trujillo, N. (1983). Organizational communication as cultural performance. *Communication Monographs, 50,* 126-147.

2. A number of authors use the term *integrity* to describe ideal managers and organizations. See, for example,

Pearson, G. (1995). *Integrity in organizations: An alternative business ethic.* London: McGraw-Hill.

Petrick, J. A. (1998). Building organizational integrity and quality with the four Ps: Perspectives, paradigms, processes, and principles. In M. Schminke (Ed.), *Managerial ethics: Moral management of people and processes* (pp. 115-131). Mahwah, NJ: Lawrence Erlbaum.

Solomon, R. C. (1992). *Ethics and excellence: Cooperation and integrity in business.* New York: Oxford University Press.

Srivastva, S. (Ed.). (1988). *Executive integrity.* San Francisco: Jossey-Bass.

3. Paine, L. S. (1994, March-April). Managing for organizational integrity. *Harvard Business Review, 72*(2), 106-117.

4. Weaver, G. R., Trevino, K. L., & Cochran, P. L. (1999). Integrated and decoupled corporate social performance: Management commitments, external pressures, and corporate ethics practices. *Academy of Management Journal, 42,* 539-552.

5. Weaver, G. R., Trevino, K. L., & Cochran, P. L. (1999). Corporate ethics practices in the mid-1990s: An empirical study of the *Fortune 1000. Journal of Business Ethics, 18,* 283-294.

6. Collins, J. C., & Porras, J. I. (1996, September-October). Building your company's vision. *Harvard Business Review, 74*(5), 65-77, p. 66.

7. Collins & Porras (1996), "Building your company's vision," p. 68.

8. Kuczmarski, S. S., & Kuczmarski, T. D. (1995). *Values-based leadership.* Englewood Cliffs, NJ: Prentice Hall.

9. McCabe, D., & Trevino, K. L. (1993). Academic dishonesty: Honor codes and other contextual influences. *Journal of Higher Education, 64,* 522-569.

10. Johannesen, R. L. (1996). *Ethics in human communication* (4th ed.). Prospect Heights, IL: Waveland, Ch. 10.

11. Manley, W. W., II. (1991). *Executive's handbook of model business conduct codes.* Englewood Cliffs, NJ: Prentice Hall.

12. For more information on the link between learning and organizational integrity, see

Kolb, D. A. (1988). Integrity, advanced professional development, and learning. In S. Srivastva (Ed.), *Executive integrity: The search for high human values in organizational life.* San Francisco: Jossey-Bass.

13. Millar, D. P., & Irvine, R. B. (1996, November). *Exposing the errors: An examination of the nature of organizational crises.* Paper presented at the National Communication Association conference, San Diego, CA.

14. Paine, L. S. (1997). *Cases in leadership, ethics, and organizational integrity: A strategic perspective.* Boston: Irwin McGraw-Hill, Part I.

15. DiBella, A., & Nevis, E. C. (1998). *How organizations learn: An integrated strategy for building learning capability.* San Francisco: Jossey-Bass; DiBella, A. J., Nevis, E. C., & Gould, J. M. (1996). Organizational learning as a core capability. In B. Moingeon & A. Edmondson (Eds.), *Organizational learning and competitive advantage* (pp. 38-55). London: Sage.

16. Camp, R. C. (1989). *Benchmarking: The search for industry best practices that lead to superior performance.* Milwaukee, WI: Quality Press.

17. DePree, M. (1989). *Leadership is an art.* New York: Doubleday, p. 92.

18. See, for example,

Anderson, R., & Cissna, K. N. (1997). *The Martin Buber-Carl Rogers dialogue.* Albany: State University of New York Press.

Buber, M. (1965). *The knowledge of man.* New York: Harper & Row.

Waters, J. A. (1988). Integrity management: Learning and implementing ethical principles in the workplace. In S. Srivastva (Ed.), *Executive integrity: The search for high human values in organizational life* (pp. 172-196). San Francisco: Jossey-Bass.

19. Brown, J. (1995). Dialogue: Capacities and stories. In S. Chawla & J. Renesch (Eds.), *Learning organizations: Developing cultures for tomorrow's workplace.* Portland, OR: Productivity Press.

10

▣ Meeting the
▣ Ethical Challenges
▣ of Cultural Diversity

Human beings draw close to one another by their common nature, but habits and customs keep them apart.

—Confucian saying

▣ What's Ahead

This chapter examines the problems and opportunities posed by cultural differences. To master the challenges of ethical diversity, leaders must overcome ethnocentrism and prejudice, understand the relationship between cultural values and ethical choices, seek synergistic solutions, and find ethical common ground.

▣ Leadership and Ethical Diversity

Globalization may be the most important trend of the 21st century. We now live in a global economy shaped by multinational corporations, international travel, immigration, and satellite communication systems.

Increased cross-cultural contact means that leaders must be prepared to make moral choices in diverse settings. Cultural diversity makes the difficult process of ethical decision making even harder. Every ethnic group, nation, and religion approaches ethical dilemmas from a different perspective. What is perfectly acceptable to members of one group may raise serious ethical concerns for another. Consider, for example, the differing responses to these common ethical problems.[1]

> *Bribery.* Spurred by reports that Exxon Oil had paid $59 million to Italian politicians to do business in that country, Congress passed the Foreign Corrupt Practices Act of 1977, which forbids U.S. corporations from exchanging money or goods for something in return. Those guilty of bribery can be fined and sent to prison. Malaysia has even stricter bribery statutes, executing corporate officers who offer and accept bribes. On the other hand, bribery is a common, acceptable practice in many countries in Africa, Asia, and the Middle East. In recognition of this fact, small payments to facilitate travel and business in less developed nations are permitted under the Corrupt Practices Act.

> *False information.* Mexico and the United States might be geographical neighbors, but citizens of these countries react differently to deception. In one encounter, American businessmen were offended when their Mexican counterparts promised to complete a project by an impossible deadline. The Mexicans, on the other hand, viewed their deception as a way to smooth relations between the two sides while protecting their interests.

> *Intellectual property rights.* Copyright laws are rigorously enforced in many Western nations but are less binding in many Asian countries. Piracy is legal in Thailand, Indonesia, and Malaysia.

> *Gender equality.* Treatment of women varies widely. Denmark and Sweden have done the most to promote gender equality, whereas Japan and Saudi Arabia offer some of the stiffest resistance to women's rights. In Japan, women are expected to care for the home and are excluded from leadership positions in government and business. In Saudi Arabia, women (who must wear traditional garb) aren't allowed to drive or form relationships with non-Moslem men.

Cultural differences can cause leaders to cast some serious shadows. Ethnocentric leaders often impose their cultural values on followers, either consciously or unconsciously. *Ethnocentrism* is the tendency to see the world from our cultural group's point of view. From this vantage point, our customs and values then become the standard by which the rest of the world is judged. Our cultural ways seem natural; those of other groups fall short. According to cross-cultural communication experts William Gudykunst and Young Yun Kim, a certain degree of ethnocentrism is inevitable.[2] Ethnocentrism can help a group band together and survive in the face of outside threats. Ethnocentrism, however, is a significant barrier to cross-cultural communication and problem solving. High levels of ethnocentrism can lead to

- Inaccurate attributions about the behavior of strangers (we interpret their behavior from our point of view, not theirs)
- Expressions of disparagement or animosity (ethnic slurs, belittling nicknames)
- Reduced contact with outsiders
- Indifference and insensitivity to the perspectives of strangers
- Pressure on other groups to conform to our cultural standards
- Justification for war and violence as a means of expressing cultural dominance

Examples of ethnocentrism abound. For many years, the U.S. Bureau of Indian Affairs made assimilation its official policy, forcing Native Americans to send their children to reservation schools where they were punished for speaking their tribal languages. Government officials in Australia kidnapped aboriginal children and placed them with white families. In other cases, well-meaning individuals assume that their values and practices are the only "right" ones. Many early missionaries equated Christianity with Western lifestyles and required converts to dress, live, think, and worship like Europeans or North Americans.

Prejudice is the prejudgment of out-group members on the basis of prior experiences and beliefs. Prejudice, like ethnocentrism, is universal (most of us prefer to socialize with those of our own age and ethnic group, for example). The degree of prejudice, however, will vary from person to person, ranging from slight bias to extreme prejudice such as that displayed by racist skinheads. Negative prejudgments can be dangerous because they produce discriminatory behavior. For instance, police in many urban areas believe that African Americans are more likely to commit crimes. As a consequence, officers are more likely to stop and question black citizens, particularly young males, and to use force if they show the slightest sign of resistance.[3]

The challenges posed by cultural variables can discourage leaders from making reasoned moral choices. They may decide to cling to their old ways of thinking or blindly follow local customs. Cultural relativism ("when in Rome, do as the Romans do") is an attractive option for many. Nevertheless, being in a new culture or working with a diverse group of followers doesn't excuse leaders from engaging in careful ethical deliberation. Just because a culture has adopted a practice doesn't make it right. Female circumcision may still be carried out in parts of Africa, but the vast majority of Americans are appalled by this custom.

Fortunately, we can expand our capacity to act ethically in multicultural situations and, in so doing, brighten the lives of diverse groups of followers. To do so, we first need to come to grips with our ethnocentrism and prejudice. Next, we need to deepen our understanding of the relationship between cultural differences and ethical values. Third, we should strive for cultural-ethical synergy when interacting with individuals of different cultural backgrounds. Finally, we need to reject cultural relativism and search instead for moral common ground.

▣ Overcoming Ethnocentrism and Prejudice

As I noted earlier, ethnocentric tendencies and negative prejudices are the cause of a great number of moral abuses. Confronting these tendencies can go a long way toward improving the ethical atmosphere of multicultural groups. (For examples of ethnocentrism and prejudice in action, see Leadership Ethics at the Movies in Box 10.1.)

According to Gudykunst and Kim, we can reduce our levels of ethnocentrism and negative prejudice by committing ourselves to the following:

1. *Mindfulness.* In most routine encounters, we tend to operate on autopilot and perform our roles mechanically, without much reflection. When we're engaged in such mindless interaction, we're not likely to challenge the ethnocentric assumption that ours is the only way to solve problems. Mindfulness is the opposite of mindlessness. When we're mindful, we pay close attention to our attitudes and behaviors. Three psychological processes take place.[4]

   The first is *openness to new categories.* Being mindful makes us more sensitive to differences. Instead of lumping people into broad catego-

---

BOX 10.1 Leadership Ethics at the Movies: *Paradise Road*

Key cast members: Glenn Close, Pauline Collins, Cate Blanchett,
Frances McDormand

Synopsis:

In this Australian-made film, a group of women held captive in a
Japanese POW camp overcome their cultural differences to form a
symphonic chorus. The English, Dutch, United States, and Australian
prisoners, led by Close, use music to bond together, to maintain their
dignity, and to cope with inhumane conditions. The group continues
until half of its members die and the remaining vocalists are too weak
to continue. The film is based on real-life events.

Rating: R for violence and brief nudity.

Themes: Ethnocentrism, overcoming cultural differences, courage, compassion, the power of music and the arts, hope, forgiveness

---

ries based on age, race, gender, or role, we make finer distinctions
within these classifications. We discover that not all student government officers, retirees, professors, Japanese exchange students, or professors are alike.

The second psychological process involves *openness to new information.* Mindless communication closes us off to new data, and we fail to
note the types of cultural differences I described earlier. We assume
that others hold the same ethical values. In mindful communication,
we pick up new information as we closely monitor our behavior along
with the behavior of others.

The third psychological process is *recognizing the existence of more
than one perspective.* Mindlessness results in tunnel vision that ignores
potential solutions. Mindfulness, on the other hand, opens our eyes to
other possibilities. As the later discussion of cultural-ethical synergy
shows, there can be more than one way to make and implement ethical
choices.

2. *Dignity and integrity.* Dignity and integrity ought to characterize all
   our interactions with people of other cultures. We maintain our own dignity by confronting others who engage in prejudicial comments or
   actions; we maintain the dignity of others by respecting their views.

Respect doesn't mean that we have to agree with another's moral stance. But when we disagree, we need to respond in a civil, sensitive manner.

3. *Moral inclusion.* As Chapter 4 showed, widespread evil occurs when groups have been devalued or dehumanized. This sanctioning process is referred to as *moral exclusion.*[5] Exclusionary tactics include biased evaluation of women and minorities, hostility, contempt, condescension, and double standards (one for insiders, another for outsiders). Moral inclusiveness rejects exclusionary tactics of all types. If we're dedicated to inclusiveness, we'll apply the same rules, values, and standards to strangers as well as to neighbors.

By committing ourselves as leaders to mindful communication, the dignity of others, and moral inclusion, we can reduce ethnocentrism and prejudice in the group as a whole. Using morally inclusive language and disputing prejudiced statements, for instance, improves ethical climate because followers will be less likely to attack other groups in our presence. If we don't speak out when followers disparage members of outgroups, however, the practice will continue. We'll share some of the responsibility for creating a hostile atmosphere such as the one described in Case Study 10.1.

▣ Cultural Differences and Ethical Values

Defining Culture

The same factors that make up an organization's culture—language, rituals, stories, buildings, beliefs, assumptions, power structures—also form the cultures of communities, ethnic groups, and nations. Cultures are comprehensive, incorporating both the visible (architecture, physical objects, nonverbal behavior) and the invisible (thoughts, attitudes, values). In sum, a culture is "the total way of life of a people, composed of their learned and shared behavior patterns, values, norms, and material objects."[6]

Several features of cultures are worth noting in more detail. Cultures are

- *Created.* Ethnocentrism would have us believe that ours is the only way to solve problems, but there are countless ways to deal with the environment, manage interpersonal relationships, produce food, and cope with

CASE STUDY 10.1

Sexual Intimidation at Mitsubishi

Japanese automakers have become a major force in the U.S. market by producing high-quality products and marketing them through a series of savvy ad campaigns. These manufacturers have demonstrated that they can adapt to American customs, laws, and tastes. In light of this success, it is hard to understand how one major Japanese car company—Mitsubishi—did nearly everything wrong when confronted with charges of sexual harassment.

In 1992, four women from Mitsubishi's Normal, Illinois, plant filed a lawsuit alleging sexual harassment with the Equal Employment Opportunity Commission (EEOC). Four years later, after an extensive investigation, the EEOC filed charges against the company, alleging a widespread pattern of discrimination. The commission estimated that 400 male employees participated in sexual intimidation. Among the charges were these:

- Women were called "inferior" at new employee orientation.
- Managers sent to training in Japan attended sex bars where they and their Japanese hosts had sex with prostitutes on stage.
- Sexual graffiti (sexual comments, gestures, organs) were affixed to cars as they moved down the assembly line at the Normal plant.
- Women were referred to as "whores" and "bitches," and some men exposed themselves to their female coworkers.
- Male employees and managers brought and displayed pornographic pictures.
- Females were attacked physically and verbally through threatening phone calls, assaults in cars, and unwanted touching and rubbing.
- Local sex parties were organized by plant managers on company time.
- Complaints had to be made first to immediate supervisors (often those doing the harassing).
- Only three male employees had been fired for their sexual behavior; most were given only the mildest of rebukes.

When the EEOC suit became public, Mitsubishi began a counterattack. Top officials denied all allegations, calling them "outrageous," and employees were urged to use any means possible (phone calls, the Internet, petitions) to influence public opinion. In its most dramatic act of defiance, the company paid 3,000 workers to demonstrate in front of the EEOC's Chicago offices.

Soon, the National Organization of Women announced plans to picket dealerships, and the Reverend Jesse Jackson called for a boycott of Mitsubishi products. The company then softened its position, hiring an outside consultant (former Secretary of Labor

CASE STUDY 10.1 (Continued)

Lynn Martin) to help it improve working conditions for women. A few months later, the Mitsubishi Motor Company's board of directors replaced the firm's chairman. Nearly 2 years after the EEOC filed its case, the company agreed to pay $34 million in damages and to allow the agency to monitor working conditions for 3 years. In addition, the firm instituted "zero tolerance" policies and improved complaint procedures.

Cultural differences clearly contributed to the problems at Mitsubishi. After-hour sex parties are much more common in Japan. Women who work play a subservient role as "office ladies" and are expected to quit after they marry. Yet other Japanese firms have been careful to comply with U.S. regulations, and Mitsubishi never once raised a moral objection to equal opportunity laws. Instead, the firm denied that problems existed. Ultimately, the failure was an ethical one. Company executives denied the humanity and dignity of their female workers.

Not all the blame can be placed on Japanese ownership. There were only 70 Japanese managers at the Normal plant, and they were in upper-management positions. Middle managers and employees were U.S. residents. Hundreds of U.S. men participated in and condoned the intimidating behavior. Said one EEOC attorney, "I've been doing sexual harassment litigation for years and I don't think any culture's got a lock on it."

Discussion Probes

1. Who deserves most of the blame for what happened at the Normal plant? Top executives in Japan? The Japanese managers working at the plant? Male American managers and employees?
2. Why do you think Mitsubishi made so many mistakes?
3. What steps can leaders and organizations take to prevent sexual discrimination and intimidation in the workplace?
4. What leadership lessons can we draw from Mitsubishi's ethical miscues?

SOURCE: Paul, E. F. (1999). Strangers in a strange land: The Mitsubishi sexual harassment case. In T. T. Machan (Ed.), *Business ethics in the global market* (pp. 87-136). Stanford, CA: Stanford University Press.

death. Each cultural group devises its own way of responding to circumstances.

- *Learned.* Elements of culture are passed on from generation to generation and from person to person. Cultural conditioning is both a formal and an informal process that takes place in every context, including homes, schools, playgrounds, camps, and games. The most crucial aspects of a culture, such as loyalty to country, are constantly reinforced. Patriotism in the United States is promoted through high school civics classes, the singing of the national anthem at sporting events, flag-raising ceremonies, and Fourth of July and Memorial Day programs.

■ *Shared.* The shared nature of culture becomes apparent when we break the rules that are set and enforced by the group. There are negative consequences for violating cultural norms of all types. Punishments vary, depending on the severity of the offense. You might receive a cold stare from your professor, for example, when your cell phone goes off in class. You may face jail time, however, if you break drug laws.

■ *Dynamic.* Cultures aren't static but evolve. Through time, the changes can be dramatic. Compare the cultural values of the *Leave It to Beaver* television show with those found in modern situation comedies. The world of the Cleavers (a wholesome, two-parent family with a well-dressed, stay-at-home mom) has been replaced by portrayals of unmarried friends, single parents, blended families, and gay partners.

Cultural Values Orientations

Ethical decisions and practices are shaped by widely held cultural values. Although each culture has its own set of ethical priorities, researchers have discovered that ethnic groups and nations hold values in common. As a result, cultures can be grouped according to their values orientations. These orientations help explain ethical differences and enable leaders to predict how members of other cultural groups will respond to moral dilemmas. In this section of the chapter, I'll describe two widely used cultural classification systems. First, however, keep in mind four cautions. One, all categories are gross overgeneralizations. They describe what most people in that culture value. Not all U.S. residents are individualistic, for example, and not all Japanese citizens are collectivists. *In general,* however, more Americans put the individual first, whereas more Japanese emphasize group relations. Two, scholars may categorize the same nation differently and have not studied some regions of the world (such as Africa) as intensively as others (Europe, Asia, the United States). Three, political and cultural boundaries are not always identical. The Basque people, for instance, live in both France and Spain. Four, as I noted earlier, cultures are dynamic, so values change. A society may change its ethical priorities, making older values rankings obsolete.

Programmed Values Patterns

Geert Hofstede of the Netherlands conducted a very extensive investigation of cultural value patterns, surveying more than 100,000 IBM employees in 50 countries and three multicountry regions to uncover these value dimensions.[7] He then checked his findings against those of other researchers who studied the same countries. Four value orientations (which Hofstede believes are programmed into members of every culture) emerged.

Power Distance. The first category describes the relative importance of power differences. Status differences are universal, but cultures treat them differently. In high-power-distance cultures, inequality is accepted as part of the natural order. Leaders enjoy special privileges and make no attempt to reduce power differentials; they are expected, however, to care for the less fortunate. The wealthy landowner in the Philippines must respond to the neighboring peasant who comes to him or her for help. Low-power-distance cultures, in contrast, are uneasy with large gaps in wealth, power, privilege, and status. Superiors tend to downplay these differences and strive for a greater degree of equality.

High Power Distance	Low Power Distance
Philippines	Ireland
Mexico	New Zealand
Venezuela	Denmark
India	Israel
Singapore	Austria

Individualism-Collectivism. Hofstede's second values category divides cultures according to their preference for either the individual or the group. Individualistic cultures put the needs and goals of the person and her or his immediate family first. Members of these cultures see themselves as independent actors. In contrast, collectivist cultures give top priority to the desires of the larger group (extended family, tribe, community). Members of these societies stress connection instead of separateness, putting a high value on their place in the collective. Think back to your decision to attend your current college or university. As a resident of Canada or the United States, you probably asked friends, high school counselors, and family members for advice, but in the end, you made the choice. In a collectivist society, your family or village might well make this decision for you. There's no guarantee that you would have even gone to college. Families with limited resources can afford to send only one child to school. You might have been expected to go to work to help pay for the education of a brother or sister.

High Individualism	Low Individualism
United States	Taiwan
Australia	Peru
Great Britain	Pakistan
Canada	Colombia
Netherlands	Venezuela

Masculinity-Femininity. The third dimension reflects attitudes toward the roles of men and women. Highly masculine cultures maintain clearly defined sex roles. Men are expected to be decisive, assertive, dominant, ambitious, and materialistic. Women are encouraged to serve. They are to care for the family, interpersonal relationships, and the weaker members of society. In feminine cultures, the differences between sexes are blurred. Both men and women can be competitive and caring, assertive and nurturing. These cultures are more likely to stress interdependence, intuition, and concern for others.

Masculine	Feminine
Japan	Finland
Austria	Denmark
Venezuela	Netherlands
Italy	Norway
Switzerland	Sweden

Uncertainty Avoidance. This dimension describes the way that cultures respond to uncertainty. Three indicators measure this orientation: (1) anxiety level, (2) widely held attitudes about rules, and (3) employment stability. Members of high-uncertainty-avoidance societies feel anxious about uncertainty and view it as a threat. They believe in written rules and regulations, engage in more rituals, and accept directives from those in authority. In addition, they are less likely to change jobs and view long-term employment as a right. People who live in low-uncertainty-avoidance cultures are more comfortable with uncertainty, viewing ambiguity as a fact of life. They experience lower stress and are more likely to take risks such as starting a new company or accepting a new job in another part of the country. These individuals are less reliant on written regulations and rituals and are more likely to trust their own judgments instead of obeying authority figures.

High Uncertainty Avoidance	Low Uncertainty Avoidance
Greece	Ireland
Portugal	Hong Kong
Belgium	Sweden
Japan	Denmark
Peru	Singapore

Of the four value patterns, individualism-collectivism has attracted the most attention. Scholars have used this dimension to explain a variety of cultural differences, including variations in ethical behavior. Management professors Stephen Carroll and Martin Gannon report that individualistic countries prefer universal ethical standards such as Kant's categorical imperative.[8] Collectivistic societies take a more utilitarian approach, seeking to generate the greatest good for in-group members. Citizens of these nations are more sensitive to elements of the situation. To see how these orientations affect ethical decisions, let's return to the four dilemmas I introduced at the beginning of the chapter.

Bribery. Payoffs tend to be more common in collectivist nations and may be a way to meet obligations to the community. In some cases, there are laws against the practice, but they take a back seat to history and custom. Individualistic nations view bribery as a form of corruption; payoffs destroy trust and benefit some companies and people at the expense of others.

False Information. Individualists are more likely to lie to protect their privacy; collectivists are more likely to lie to protect the group or family.

This accounts for the conflict between the Mexican and U.S. business-persons described earlier. Mexicans, who tend to have a collectivist orientation, promise what they can't deliver to reduce tensions between their in-group and outsiders. Americans (among the world's most individualistic peoples) condemn this practice as deceptive and therefore unethical. Individualists and collectivists also express disagreement differently. Germans and Americans, for instance, don't hesitate to say "no" directly to another party. Japanese may answer by saying "that will be difficult" rather than by offering an out-and-out refusal. This indirect strategy is designed to save the "face" or image of the receiver.

Intellectual Property Rights. Although individuals own the rights to their creative ideas in individualist societies, they are expected to share their knowledge in collectivist nations. Copyright laws are a Western invention based on the belief that individuals should be rewarded for their efforts.

Gender Equality. Resistance to gender equality is strongest in collectivist nations such as Saudi Arabia and Japan. Women are seen as an out-group in these societies. Many men fear that granting women more status (better jobs, leadership positions) would threaten group stability. Individualist nations are more likely to have laws that promote equal opportunity, although in many of these countries (such as the United States), women hold fewer leadership positions than men and continue to earn less.

Seven Cultures of Capitalism

Charles Hampden-Turner and Alfons Trompenaars call the creation of wealth "a moral act." To flourish, capitalism must be supported by cultural values that (a) support the production and sale of products and (b) encourage people to work together to create these goods. Corporations also make a series of value judgments as they conduct business. The authors surveyed 15,000 managers and discovered that leaders of capitalist organizations must balance seven sets of contrasting values. Hampden-Turner and Trompenaars focus their attention on corporations, but leaders of governments and nonprofits must also weigh the importance of these competing values.[9]

1. Universalism Versus Particularism. Universalist societies emphasize standards and obedience to the rules. There is strong resistance to creating exceptions to established guidelines from fear that the system will collapse. Particularist nations focus on the present circumstances, opting to break the rules based on friendship, family connections, and other factors. Universalists don't think they can trust particularists who put their friends ahead of the rules; particularists don't trust universalists who won't help a friend in need. The following moral dilemma illustrates the difference between these two perspectives.

> You are riding in a car driven by a close friend. He hits a pedestrian. You know he was going at least 35 miles per hour in an area of the city where the maximum allowed speed is 20 miles per hour. There are no witnesses. His lawyer says that if you testify under oath that he was driving only 20 miles per hour, it may save him from serious consequences.
> What right has your friend to expect you to protect him?

More than 90% of respondents from Canada, the United States, Australia, and northern Europe would refuse to lie in this situation. Respondents from South Korea, Venezuela, and Russia, on the other hand, are much more likely to lie on the stand. The greater the consequences of the incident, the more the two groups diverge. Universalists believe that the more serious the accident, the more important it is to obey the law, to uphold principles. Particularists are convinced that the friend deserves even more help when the pedestrian's injuries are severe. After all, he could lose his license, be fined, or serve jail time.

2. Individualism Versus Communitarianism. This dimension appears to be identical to individualism-collectivism. Canadian, American, and Norwegian managers are most individualistic; Nepalese, Kuwaitis, and Egyptians are most communitarian.

3. Analyzing Versus Integrating. Members of analytical cultures (United States, Canada, Belgium) prefer to break products and operations down to identify and correct defects. They focus on tasks, numbers, facts, and units. Members of integrative cultures (Japan, France, Singapore) look for the whole pattern and emphasize relationships.

4. Inner-Directed Versus Outer-Directed Orientation. Inner-directed leaders are guided by their own judgments and commitments and expect their followers to be self-directed as well. Outer-directed leaders are more interested in responding to the environment. They're sensitive to business and cultural trends and adjust to these changes. The United States, Germany, Canada, and Austria tend to be inner-directed cultures, whereas Belgium, Sweden, Singapore, and Japan are more outer directed.

5. Achieved Status Versus Ascribed Status. Status can be granted on the basis of individual achievement or bestowed (ascribed) to organizational members on the basis of some other characteristic such as age, seniority, gender, or education. Business leaders from the United States, Austria, and Canada are more likely to emphasize achievement. Their counterparts from Singapore, Japan, and Korea give more weight to ascribed status.

6. Time as Sequence Versus Time as Synchronization. Sequential individuals view time as a linear process. They try to complete their tasks quickly and efficiently by following a series of steps. To them, time is a precious commodity that is carefully measured and managed. Sequential thinkers have a short-term perspective and tend to be future oriented. Synchronizing people, on the other hand, see time more as a cycle than as a straight line. To them, time is a friend, one that will come again. Synchronic thinkers have a long-term perspective and are more likely to honor the past and present. Less concerned about punctuality, they try to coordinate several tasks at once (e.g., talking on the phone and checking on stock quotes while conducting an interview). The United States, Great Britain, and the Netherlands are sequential societies, whereas many Latin American, African, and Middle Eastern cultures are synchronic.

7. Equality Versus Hierarchy. Followers can be given a great deal of freedom to make their own decisions (equality), or they may be required to carry out the wishes of their bosses (hierarchy). West Germany, the United States, and the Netherlands are most equalitarian; Pakistan, Venezuela, and China are the most hierarchical.

No organization or society can adhere to one value to the exclusion of its contrasting value. For example, a business couldn't function without at least some common standards and procedures (universalism). Yet no set of guidelines can cover every contingency, so the corporation must learn to deal with exceptional situations (particularism). Leaders must acknowledge *both* values in each set if they and the groups they lead are to prosper in a multicultural world. Further, there is more than one way to succeed. Instead of one capitalist culture (United States), there are many (French, British, Japanese, Dutch). We can learn from the choices of other cultures. In the words of Hampden-Turner and Trompenaars,

> You can combine the traditions of excellence from many nations, provided you can manage cultural diversity and not allow it to descend into a Tower of Babel. In the same way you can also learn, and make your own, the strategies and thought processes behind these traditions of excellence.[10]

Our cultural values may not generate the best response to a particular ethical dilemma. Analysis can be counterproductive in cultural settings that stress connection and relationships. Sequential thinking is not always the most efficient approach; sometimes juggling several tasks at once can be more productive. Honoring achievement may work well in the United States but backfire in status-conscious societies.

▣ Cultural-Ethical Synergy

The belief that leaders and followers can learn from the insights of other cultural groups is the foundation of *cultural-ethical synergy*. Synergy refers to creating an end product that is greater than the sum of its parts. In cultural-ethical synergy, diverse decision makers come up with a better-than-anticipated solution to a moral dilemma by drawing on the perspectives of a variety of cultures. They combine their insights to generate highly ethical, creative solutions.

According to cross-cultural management expert Nancy Adler, culturally synergistic problem solving is a four-step process.[11] The first step, *situation description*, is to identify the problem facing a dyad or group. This is far from easy. Because of differing cultural perspectives, one party may not realize that there is a problem. As we saw earlier, lying to maintain harmony seems normal for many members of collectivist societies but is perceived as unethical by many individualists. Bribery is a criminal offense in some cultures but an accepted way of life in others. Even when parties acknowledge that a problem exists, they may define it differently. For example, negotiations between a Canadian and an Egyptian executive broke off when the Canadian insisted on meeting the next day with lawyers to finalize contract details. When the Egyptian party never showed up, the Canadian wondered if his counterpart was expecting a counteroffer or couldn't locate attorneys. In reality, the Egyptian was offended by the presence of lawyers. Lawyers marked the end of successful negotiations for the Canadian (a universalist), but they symbolized distrust to the Egyptian (a particularist) who had given his binding verbal commitment.

The second step, *cultural interpretation,* is to determine why people of other cultures think and act as they do. This step is based on the assumption that people act rationally from their culture's point of view but that we misinterpret their logic on the basis of our cultural biases. Accurate interpretation depends on identifying similarities and differences while taking multiple perspectives. Cultural classification systems help in this process. If you can determine a culture's value orientations (individualist or collectivist, for example), you'll have a much better chance of predicting how members of that group will respond to ethical problems.

The third step, *cultural creativity,* is driven by the question, "What can people of one culture contribute to people of another culture?" In this stage, problem solvers generate alternatives and then come up with a novel solution, one that incorporates the cultural perspectives of all group members but transcends them.

The fourth step, *implementation,* puts the solution into effect. Whenever possible, give the other parties as much leeway as possible in implementing decisions. As a leader of a transnational organization, empower local personnel to implement changes, distribute awards, and punish ethical misbehavior.

The process of cultural-ethical synergy is demonstrated in the following case. An international relief agency appointed a new program director in a Latin American country who, after assuming his position, discovered that his treasurer had stolen $50,000 from the organization. He reported the theft to his supervisor, the vice president of program development at the organization's U.S. headquarters. The vice president wanted to fire the embezzler immediately and to bring charges against him. The national director advised otherwise. There was no chance of recovering the money, he argued, and the country's labor laws made it extremely difficult to fire the thief. Government authorities were likely to side with the treasurer, and pressing charges would make the new director's job harder. Needy citizens might suffer if the agency's relationships with the government and local communities deteriorated. In the end, the director went to the thief in private, confronted him with his crime, and then negotiated a settlement. This solution acknowledged the perspectives of both cultures while combining elements of each. The embezzler was fired for his crime (the goal of the individualistically oriented vice president) but in a manner that was suitable to the host country's collectivist culture. The national director preserved harmony, avoided a protracted legal battle, and was free to concentrate on his new responsibilities. (To try your hand at creating a culturally synergistic solution to an ethical problem, read and respond to Case Study 10.2 at the end of the chapter.)

◻ Standing on Moral Common Ground

Confronted with a wide range of ethical values and standards, a number of philosophers, business leaders, anthropologists, and others opt for ethical relativism. In ethical relativism, there are no universal moral codes or standards. Each group or society is unique. Therefore, members of one culture can't pass moral judgment on members of another group.

I'll admit that at first glance, ethical relativism is appealing. It avoids the problem of ethnocentrism while simplifying the decision-making process. We can concentrate on fitting in with the prevailing culture and never have to pass judgment. On closer examination, however, the difficulties of ethical relativism become all too apparent. Without shared standards, there's little hope that the peoples of the world can work together to address global problems. There may be no basis on which to condemn the evil of notorious leaders who are popular in their own countries. Further, the standard of cultural relativism obligates us to follow (or at least not to protest against) abhorrent local practices such as female circumcision or the killing of brides by their in-laws in the rural villages of Pakistan. Without universal rights and wrongs, we have no basis on which to protest such practices.

I believe that there is ethical common ground. The existence of universal standards has enabled members of the world community to punish crimes against humanity and to create the United Nations and its Declaration of Human Rights. Responsible multinational corporations such as Merck, the Body Shop, and Levi-Strauss adhere to widely held moral principles as they conduct business in a variety of cultural settings. In this final section, I'll describe several approaches to universal ethics, any one of which could serve as a worldwide standard. As you read each description, look for commonalties. Then decide for yourself which approach or combinations of approaches best capture the foundational values of humankind (see exercise 6 in the section "For Further Exploration, Challenge, and Self-Assessment").

A Global Ethic

Many of the world's conflicts center on religious differences: Hindu versus Moslem, Protestant versus Catholic, Moslem versus Jew. These hostilities, however, did not prevent 6,500 representatives from a wide range of religious faiths from reaching agreement on a global ethic.[12] A council of former heads of state and prime ministers then ratified this statement. Delegates of both groups agreed on two universal principles. First, every person must be treated humanely regardless of language, skin color, mental ability, political beliefs, and national or social origin. Second, every person and group, no matter how powerful, must respect the dignity of others. These two foundational principles, in turn, led to these ethical directives or imperatives:

- Commitment to a culture of nonviolence and respect for all life
- Commitment to a culture of solidarity and a just economic order (do not steal, deal fairly and honestly with others)
- Commitment to a culture of tolerance and truthfulness
- Commitment to a culture of equal rights and partnership between men and women (avoid immorality; respect and love members of both genders)

The Platinum Rule

A number of ethicists believe that the Golden Rule ("Do unto others as you would have others do unto you") can serve as a universal ethical standard. Mass communication professor Milton Bennett disagrees. He argues that the Golden Rule is based on the mistaken assumption that all people are essentially alike and therefore want the same things we do. This presumption of similarity encourages ethnocentric thinking. In Bennett's words,

> Treating other people the way we would like to be treated assumes one very important thing—that the other person wants to be treated in the same way as we would like. And under this assumption lies another, more pernicious belief: that all people are basically the same, and thus they really do want the same treatment (whether they admit it or not).[13]

Bennett argues that cross-cultural communicators must recognize both the essential differences between individuals of various cultures and the presence of multiple realities. In place of the Golden Rule, we need to follow the "Platinum Rule." The Platinum Rule is "Do unto others as they themselves would have done to them." To follow this standard, we need to replace sympathy with empathy. Feeling sympathetic means placing ourselves in the position of the other person and imagining how *we* would respond in this situation. Feeling empathetic, in contrast, means putting ourselves in the position of another individual and trying to understand what *they* are thinking and feeling. Sympathy originates from our perspective, but empathy comes from what we imagine to be the perspective of the other person.

The Golden Rule calls for sympathy because it is based on the assumption that people are basically identical. The Platinum Rule requires empathy because it assumes differences and requires us to see the world from another's point of view. To establish empathy, we need to start with a solid sense of who we are and then set this identity aside to imagine how the other person might respond. Empathetic experiences are always temporary. We reestablish our personal identities after we've made empathetic connection.

Eight Global Values

Ethicist Rushworth Kidder and his colleagues at the Institute for Global Ethics identify eight core values that appear to be shared the world over. They isolated these values after conducting interviews with 24 international "ethical thought leaders."[14] Kidder's sample included United Nations officials, heads of states, university presidents, writers, and religious figures drawn from such nations as the United States,

Vietnam, Mozambique, New Zealand, Bangladesh, Britain, China, Sri Lanka, Costa Rica, and Lebanon. Each interview ran from 1 to 3 hours and began with this question: "If you could help create a global code of ethics, what would be on it?" These global standards emerged:

1. *Love:* spontaneous concern for others; compassion that transcends political and ethnic differences
2. *Truthfulness:* achieving goals through honest means; keeping promises; being worthy of the trust of others
3. *Fairness (justice):* fair play, evenhandedness, equality
4. *Freedom:* the pursuit of liberty; right of free expression and action and accountability
5. *Unity:* seeking the common good; cooperation, community, solidarity
6. *Tolerance:* respect for others and their ideas; empathy; appreciation for variety
7. *Responsibility:* care for self, the sick, and needy, the community, and future generations; responsible use of force
8. *Respect for life:* reluctance to kill through war and other means

Kidder and his fellow researchers don't claim to have discovered the one and only set of universal values, but they do believe that they have established ethical common ground. Kidder admits that the eight values are ordinary rather than unique. Yet that the list contains few surprises is evidence these standards are widely shared.

The Peace Ethic

Communication professor David Kale argues that peace ought to be the ultimate goal of all intercultural contact because living in peace protects the worth and dignity of the human spirit.[15] Conflicts are inevitable. Nevertheless, with the help of those in leadership roles, peoples and nations can learn to value the goals of other parties even in the midst of their differences. The four principles of the Peace Ethic are as follows:

Principle 1: Ethical communicators address people of other cultures with the same respect they desire themselves. Verbal and psychological violence, like physical violence, damages the human spirit. Demeaning or belittling others makes it hard for individuals to live at peace with themselves or their cultural heritage.

Principle 2: Ethical communicators describe the world as they see it as accurately as possible. Perceptions of what is truth vary from culture from culture, but all individuals, regardless of their cultural background, should be true to the truth as they perceive it. Lying undermines trust that lays the foundation for peace.

Principle 3: Ethical communicators encourage people of other cultures to express their cultural uniqueness. Individuals and nations have the right to hold and to express different values and beliefs, a principle enshrined in the United Nations Universal Declaration of Human Rights. As leaders, we shouldn't force others to adopt our standards before allowing them to engage in dialogue.

Principle 4: Ethical communicators strive for identification with people of other cultures. Whenever possible, we should seek mutual understanding and common ethical ground. Incidents of racial harassment at colleges and universities are unethical, according to this principle, because they lead to division, rather than peace.

International Rights

Philosopher Thomas Donaldson believes that multinational corporations should recognize that citizens of every culture have the 10 fundamental rights listed below.[16] Each of these rights protects something of great value that can be taken away from individuals.

1. The right to freedom of physical movement
2. The right to ownership of property
3. The right to freedom from torture
4. The right to a fair trial
5. The right to nondiscriminatory treatment (freedom from discrimination on the basis of race or sex or other characteristics)
6. The right to physical security
7. The right to freedom of speech and association
8. The right to minimal education
9. The right to political participation
10. The right to subsistence

Honoring these 10 rights imposes certain duties or responsibilities. At the least, business leaders have a responsibility to do no harm. They shouldn't enslave or deliberately injure workers. Leaders of corporations and other international organizations may need to take a more active stance, however, by actively protecting fundamental rights. This might mean

- Establishing nondiscriminatory policies in cultures that discriminate according to caste, sex, age, or some other factor
- Maintaining the highest safety standards for all employees in every nation
- Refusing to hire children if this prevents them from learning how to read or write
- Paying a decent wage even if not required by a country's laws
- Protesting government attempts to take away the rights of free speech and association

▣ Implications and Applications

- Cultural differences make ethical decisions more difficult. Resist the temptation, however, to revert to your old ways of thinking or to blindly follow local customs. Try instead to expand your capacity to act ethically in multicultural situations.
- Ethnocentrism and prejudice lead to a great many moral abuses. You can avoid casting cross-cultural shadows if you commit yourself to mindfulness, human dignity, and moral inclusiveness.
- Understanding the relationship between cultural differences and ethical values can help you predict how members of that group will respond to moral questions. Two popular cultural values classification systems are (a) programmed values (power distance, individualism-collectivism, masculinity-femininity, uncertainty avoidance) and (b) capitalistic values (universalism vs. particularism, individualism vs. communitarianism, analyzing vs. integrating, inner-directed vs. outer-directed, achieved vs. ascribed status, time as sequence vs. time as synchronization, equality vs. hierarchy).
- No culture has a monopoly on the truth. In your role as a leader, you can learn from the strengths of other cultures and help others do the same.
- Strive for cultural-ethical synergy, combining insights from a variety of cultures to create better than expected ethical solutions.
- Universal standards can help you establish common ground with diverse followers. These shared standards can take the form religious commitments, empathy, global values, a commitment to peace, or international rights.

CASE STUDY 10.2

Chapter End Case:
Industrial Disaster and International Justice

Around midnight on December 2, 1984, a massive chemical leak at Union Carbide's Bhopal, India, pesticide plant resulted in the world's most devastating industrial accident. As many as 13,000 area residents died from inhaling the toxic fumes, and another 200,000 were injured.

Immediately following the accident, Union Carbide CEO Warren Anderson traveled to India to offer assistance and was promptly jailed by the Indian government. At the urging of U.S. embassy officials, he was freed and returned home. In 1989 (the year Anderson retired), the company settled a civil case brought by the Indian government for $470 million. Victims were to receive approximately $600 for injuries or $3,000 for the death of a family member. Nearly half of the money is still to be distributed.

The terms of the settlement did not satisfy victims and their supporters. They launched a civil suit against Union Carbide and Anderson in 1999, claiming that the company and its chief officer had violated international law and human rights. At the same time, the Indian government issued a criminal warrant for Anderson's arrest, charging him with manslaughter because many of the safety devices found at the company's U.S. plants weren't installed in India. Warning sirens were also turned off. The former CEO could not be found, however, and company officials refused at first to accept the court summons on his behalf. They claimed that the earlier settlement shielded the company and its officers (including Anderson) from all further litigation. They argued that the leak had been caused by sabotage and offered dramatically lower estimates of the number of dead and injured. In their view, the 78-year-old Anderson should be left in peace to enjoy his retirement.

▣ For Further Exploration, Challenge, and Self-Assessment

1. Brainstorm a list of the advantages and disadvantages of ethical diversity. What conclusions do you draw from your list?
2. Using the Internet, compare press coverage of an international ethical issue from a variety of countries. How does the coverage differ and why?
3. Rate yourself on one or both of the cultural classification systems described in the chapter. Create a values profile of your community, organization, or university. How well do you fit in?

CASE STUDY 10.2 (Continued)

Frustrated in their attempts to locate Anderson, the Indian government contacted Interpol, the international police force, to help them locate the fugitive. Union Carbide finally accepted the summons on his behalf to avoid further negative publicity. The two sides remain far apart as the legal process continues. According to a Carbide spokesman, the firm "fulfilled our moral responsibility" to the victims. Not so claims a plaintiff: "They [Carbide officials] have to accept and take care of people. They can't just write it off like a balance sheet."

Discussion Probes

1. If you were an executive at Union Carbide, would you have accepted the summons for Anderson? Why or why not?
2. Was the company justified in following lower safety standards in India than in the United States?
3. Has Union Carbide fulfilled its "moral responsibility" to the victims of the disaster? What more could the company do? On the basis of universal values, how would you evaluate the company's actions?
4. Describe the cultural values of both sides. How have differences in perspectives contributed to this conflict?
5. Is there any way that this legal standoff could have been avoided?

SOURCES: Union Carbide, ex-chief to face trial in U.S. (2000, June 5). *The Hindu* (India).
Turning on the heat. (2000, June 16). *The Statesman.*
Chrzan, A. (2000, March 26). Bhopal disaster survivors seek Vero Beach man. *Vero Beach (FL) Press Journal,* p. A1.
Hedges, C. (2000, March 5). A key figure proves elusive in a U.S. suit over Bhopal. *New York Times,* p. A4.
Hennessy-Fiske, M. (2000, March 28). Bhopal disaster catches up with ex-Union Carbide CEO. *Palm Beach (FL) Post,* p. 1B.

4. Describe an encounter with a stranger(s) that involved ethical differences. Describe your perspective and that of the other person. What cultural values, beliefs, and assumptions guided each of you? What was the outcome of the situation? How would you evaluate your actions? What would you do differently next time? What principles can you apply to future cross-cultural encounters?
5. Create a synergistic solution for the Bhopal case at the end of the chapter or for another cross-cultural ethical dilemma of your choice. Record your findings.
6. Is there a common morality that peoples of all nations can share? Which of the global codes described in the chapter best reflects these

shared standards and values? If you were to create your own declaration of global ethics, what would you put on it?

Notes

1. Carroll, S. J., & Gannon, M. J. (1997). *Ethical dimensions of management*. Thousand Oaks, CA: Sage.

2. Gudykunst, W. B., & Kim, Y. Y. (1997). *Communicating with strangers: An approach to intercultural communication* (3rd ed.). New York: McGraw-Hill; Gudykunst, W. B., Ting-Toomey, S., Suydweeks, S., & Stewart, L. P. (1995). *Building bridges: Interpersonal skills for a changing world*. Boston: Houghton Mifflin.

3. Drummond, T. (2000, April 3). Coping with cops. *Time, 155,* 72-73.

4. Langer, E. J. (1989). *Mindfulness*. Reading, MA: Addison-Wesley.

5. Opotow, S. (1990). Moral exclusion and injustice: An introduction. *Journal of Social Issues, 46,* 1-20. Opotow provides an extensive list of what she calls direct and indirect exclusionary tactics.

6. Rogers, E. M., & Steinfatt, T. M. (1999). *Intercultural communication*. Prospect Heights, IL: Waveland, p. 79.

7. Hofstede, G. (1984). *Culture's consequences*. Beverly Hills, CA: Sage; Hofstede, G. (1991). *Cultures and organizations: Software of the mind*. London: McGraw-Hill. An expanded survey using data from 116,000 employees in 72 countries is presented in Hofstede, G. *Culture's Consequences: Comparing Values, Behaviors, Institutions, and Organizations Across Cultures* (2nd ed., 2001). Thousand Oaks, CA: Sage.

8. Carroll & Gannon (1997), *Ethical dimensions of management*.

9. Hampden-Turner, C., & Trompenaars, A. (1993). *The seven cultures of capitalism*. New York: Currency/Doubleday; Trompenaars, F. (1993). *Riding the waves of culture: Understanding diversity in global business*. Burr Ridge, IL: Irwin.

10. Hampden-Turner & Trompenaars (1993), *Seven cultures of capitalism*, p. 17.

11. Adler, N. J. (1991). *International dimensions of organizational behavior* (2nd ed.). Belmont, CA: Wadsworth. See also Moran, R. T, & Harris, P. R. (1982). *Managing cultural synergy*. Houston, TX: Gulf Publishing.

12. Kung, H. (1998). *A global ethic for global politics and economics*. New York: Oxford University Press; Kung, H. (1999). A global ethic in an age of globalization. In G. Enderle (Ed.), *International business ethics: Challenges and approaches* (pp. 109-127). Notre Dame, IN: University of Notre Dame Press.

13. Bennett, M. J. (1979). Overcoming the Golden Rule: Sympathy and empathy. In D. Nimmo (Ed.), *Communication yearbook 3* (pp. 407-422). New Brunswick, NJ: Transaction Books, p. 407.

14. Kidder, R. M. (1994). *Shared values for a troubled world: Conversations with men and women of conscience*. San Francisco: Jossey-Bass.

15. Kale, D. W. (1994). Peace as an ethic for intercultural communication. In L. A. Samovar & R. E. Porter (Eds.), *Intercultural communication: A reader* (7th ed., pp. 435-440). Belmont, CA: Wadsworth.

16. Donaldson, T. (1989). *The ethics of international business*. New York: Oxford University Press.

Epilogue

It's only fair to tell you fellows now that we're not likely to come out of this.

—Captain Joshua James, speaking to his crew
during the hurricane of 1888

Captain Joshua James (1826-1902) is the "patron saint" of the search and rescue unit of the U.S. Coast Guard. James led rescue efforts to save sailors who crashed off the shores of Massachusetts. When word came of shipwreck, James and his volunteer crew would launch a large rowboat into heavy seas. James would keep an eye out for the stricken vessel as his men rowed, steering with a large wooden rudder. During his career, he never lost a crewman or a shipwrecked person who had been alive when picked up. The captain's finest hour came during a tremendous storm in late November 1888. During a 24-hour period, James (who was 62 years old at the time) and his men rescued 29 sailors from five ships.

Philip Hallie, who writes about James in his book *Tales of Good and Evil, Help and Harm*, argues that we can understand James's courageous leadership only as an extension of his larger community. James lived in the town of Hull, a tiny, impoverished community on the Massachusetts coast. Most coastal villages of the time profited from shipwrecks. Beachcombers would scavenge everything from the cargo to the sunken ship's timbers and anchors. Unscrupulous individuals called "mooncussers" would lure boats aground. On dark, moonless nights, they would hang a lantern from a donkey and trick sea captains into sailing into the rocks.

Unlike their neighbors up and down the coast, the people of Hull tried to stop the carnage. They built shelters for those who washed ashore, cared for the sick and injured, protested against shipping companies and insurers who sent inexperienced captains and crews into danger, and had their lifeboat always at the ready. During the storm of 1888, citizens burned their fences to light the way for Captain James, his crew, and victims alike. According to Hallie,

> Many of the other people of Hull tore up some picket fences near the crest of the hill and built a big fire that lit up the wreck and helped the lifesavers to avoid the flopping, slashing debris around the boat. The loose and broken spars of a ruined ship were one of the main dangers lifesavers had to face. But the sailors on the wrecked ship needed the firelight too. It showed them what the lifesavers were doing, and what they could do to help them. And it gave them hope: It showed them that they were not alone.[1]

The story of Captain James and his neighbors is a fitting end to this text. In their actions, they embodied many of the themes introduced earlier: character, values, good versus evil, altruism, transformational and servant leadership, and purpose. The captain, who lost his mother and baby sister in a shipwreck, had one mission in life—saving lives at sea. Following his lead, residents took on nearly insurmountable challenges at great personal cost. They recognized that "helpers often need help." By burning their fences, these followers (living in extremely modest conditions) cast a light that literally made the difference between life and death. But like other groups of leaders and followers, they were far from perfect. In the winter hurricane season, the village did its best to save lives. In the summer, pickpockets (helped by a corrupt police force) preyed on those who visited the town's resorts. The dark side of Hull, however, shouldn't diminish the astonishing feats of Captain James and his neighbors. Hallie calls what James did during the storm of 1888 an example of "moral beauty."

And moral beauty happens when someone carves out a place for compassion in a largely ruthless universe. It happened in the French village of Le Chambon during the war, and it happened in and near the American village of Hull during the long lifetime of Joshua James.

It happens, and it fails to happen, in almost every event of people's lives together—in streets, in kitchens, in bedrooms, in workplaces, in wars. But sometimes it happens in a way that engrosses the mind and captivates memory. Sometimes it happens in such a way that the people who make it happen seem to unify the universe around themselves like powerful magnets. Somehow they seem to redeem us all from deathlike indifference. They carve a place for caring in the very middle of the quiet and loud storms of uncaring that surround—and eventually kill—us all.[2]

Notes

1. Hallie, P. (1997). *Tales of good and evil, help and harm.* New York: HarperCollins, p. 146.
2. Hallie (1997), *Tales,* p. 173.

Index

Leadership development programs, 27-28, 37-43
Leadership ethics in movies. *See* Movies, leadership ethics in
Leading from within, 9-10
Leading versus following, 6
Learned elements of culture, 222-223
Learning:
  enhancing organizational ethical, 204-208
  ethical, 204-205
  need for continuing ethical, 202-204
Learning capacity of organization, 209
Lee, Lolita, 180
Legacy, honoring your, 64
Legitimate power, 11
Levels of response to ethical problems, 155-156
Lewinsky, Monica, 16, 24
Lewis, C. S., 78
Liar's Poker, 45
Life story, writing your, 64
Lifelong process of ethical development, 43
Light and shadow metaphor, 9, 22, 167-168, 189-191
Light casting, 40, 168
Lincoln, Abraham, 58
Lisman, C. David, 57-58
Listening, 61-62, 135, 172-175
Literature, ethical models in, 57-58
Looking for a third way, 147
Loss, 59, 68
Loyalty:
  conflicts in, 146-147, 150
  guideposts for decision making about, 24-25
  misplaced/broken, 19-21
  self-, 24
  to organizations, 35
  versus truth telling, 145, 146
Luther, Martin, 89
Lying, 16, 36
Lying: Moral Choice in Public and Private Life (Bok), 16-17

Machiavelli, Niccolo, 4
Making a decision, 147-148

Management, of inner fears/insecurities, 68
Management-by-exception, 123-124
Management of insecurity, 68
Managerial misconduct, 203
Manley, Walter, 200-201
Manz, Charles, 171-172
Mars Group technique, 193-194
Martin, Lynn, 222
Martin Marietta, 205
Masculinity-femininity dimension of cultural values, 225
MASH, 102
McCoy, Bowen, 115-118
Measurement, concern for, 205-206
Media Ethics: Cases and Moral Reasoning (Christians, Rotzoll, & Fackler), 152
Meditation, 88-89
Meetings, types of listening in, 173
Memos, credo, 64-65
Mendonca, Manuel, 112
Mental imagery, 171
Mentoring, 91
Mercer, Lucy, 51
Merck & Company, 210-211
Mercy, 81, 84, 146
Mergers and acquisitions, 17, 20
Meriwether, John, 44
Messages sent in group listening situations, types of, 175-177
Messick, David, 30, 32, 33
Metaphors:
  emotional bank account, 61-62
  leading from within, 9-10
  light and shadow, 9
Micromanagement, 141
Midlife, 86-87
Milestones of increasing ethical competency, 41-42
Military images of leadership, 29
Mill, John Stuart, 100
Mindfulness/mindlessness, 218-219
Mind guards, 170
Misconceptions, about forgiveness, 82
Misconduct, managerial, 203
Misplaced loyalties, 19-21, 137
Mission statements, 62-64, 69
  See also Purpose statements
Mistakes, in business, 59
Misunderstanding of actions, 151

About the Author

Craig E. Johnson is Professor of Communication and Chair of the Department of Communication Arts at George Fox University, Newberg, Oregon. He also serves as faculty director of the university's interdisciplinary leadership studies minor. He teaches courses in leadership, communication theory, organizational communication, interpersonal communication, and public relations. In 1994, he received a faculty achievement award for teaching. He is coauthor (with Michael Z. Hackman) of *Leadership: A Communication Perspective*. His research interests include leadership ethics, leadership education, cross-cultural communication, and language behaviors. His findings have been published in the *Journal of Leadership Studies*, *Communication Quarterly*, *Communication Reports*, *Journal of the International Listening Association*, and *Communication Education*. In addition, he is a member of the editorial review board of the *Journal of Leadership Studies* and *Communication Teacher*.